MENTOR

LIFE AND LEGACY OF JOE ROSENFIELD

NOTES ON GEORGE DRAKE'S BIOGRAPHY OF JOE ROSENFIELD

November 2, 2018

This is a readable, often absorbing biography of a big man from a small college. The College is Grinnell, in central Iowa. The man, Joseph Rosenfield. The author draws us ineluctably into his story as we grasp the setting of a private liberal arts college, originally religious based or "sectarian", as were so many of its peers, from Harvard and Yale to Oberlin, Carleton, Pomona and others. The college and its ethic of service had a profound impact on Joseph Rosenfield, perhaps because he was raised to appreciate commitment to community and the public. He was the product of four Jewish merchant families who arrived in the state in the 19th century. Those families began a culture of integrity in their business lives and of service to their communities in smaller Iowa cities and then Des Moines.

Rosenfield's years at Grinnell in the 1920s led to a life-long love affair with the college. He was there at a time when Grinnell produced a gold-winning Olympic athlete, an internationally celebrated men's glee club, and was an epicenter for the "Social Gospel Movement" which produced Harry Hopkins who went on to be Franklin Roosevelt's alter ego in the New Deal and World War II.

But after he went on to law practice, the College's fortunes were not inevitably bright. Unlike his beloved Chicago Cubs, whose comeback he did not live to witness, Joe did see and was instrumental in Grinnell's move away from financial peril and uncertainty about its future.

It was Rosenfield's role to become the force to build Grinnell into one of the most successful of America's liberal arts colleges. Joe had the gift of humor; he had the gift of extraordinary prowess at investing. He had a gift of friendship. He had a gift of listening, particularly understanding students as mores changed over the 59 years he served as a Grinnell Trustee.

And he gave. Often writing checks to balance the books of the college at the end of a fiscal year, he drew others in on his almost pure fun of working to make Grinnell, as he put it, "financially impregnable."

Money Magazine, in a cover story about Joe termed him "the most successful investor you've never heard of." This was one reason he and nearby Omaha-dwelling Warren Buffett came together. Buffett heard of Joe. They formed a remarkable team to help the college which Buffett would spend time almost every week to help even though he had no connection to it other than his growing esteem for, and keen pleasure of conspiring with Rosenfield. Together, they would make highly unusual, often highly risky, investments for the college. They would commit that if the investment went sour, the loss was on them. If successful, it would redound entirely to the college's endowment.

This is then a story about a college which inspired love in a man, who inspired affection and respect in others. It is not a universal tale. Rather, it is very much about one midwestern man and his college and his co-conspirators to make that college able to carry on into the indefinite future, giving the gift to others which he knew had been his to treasure.

John Price

Mentor: Life and Legacy of Joe Rosenfield is published by Business Publications Corporation Inc., an Iowa corporation.

Copyright 2019 by George Drake.

Reproduction or other use, in whole or in part, of the contents without permission of the publisher and author is strictly prohibited.

ISBN-978-0-9986528-4-9
Library of Congress Control Number: 2019935006
Business Publications Corporation Inc., Des Moines, IA

Business Publications Corporation Inc.
The Depot at Fourth
100 4th Street
Des Moines, IA 50309
515-288-3336

MENTOR

LIFE AND LEGACY OF JOE ROSENFIELD

GEORGE DRAKE

DEDICATION

I dedicate this biography of Joe Rosenfield to two people who knew him well: my wife, Sue, who cared deeply about the telling of Joe's story; and Jim Cownie, who created this project out of a powerful sense of unfulfilled gratitude.

CONTENTS

Foreword	xi
Author's Foreword	xiii
Acknowledgements	xv
Introduction	xix
PART ONE Joe Rosenfield and Grinnell College	1
PART TWO Joe Rosenfield's Family	41
PART THREE Joe Rosenfield, Community Catalyst	107
PART FOUR Joe Rosenfield, Trustee	153
Epilogue & Obituary	241
Appendix	251
A Note on Sources	253
Notes	259
Index	285

FOREWORD

Many years ago a reporter from *The Des Moines Register* interviewed me for a story about Joe Rosenfield. I told him I loved Joe and could talk almost endlessly about why that was so.

The reporter smiled and said my reaction was exactly what he was receiving from all he had contacted—young and old, female and male, CEOs and household help, you name it. What he had been struck by in particular was how frequently the word "love" was used in describing Joe.

If true wealth is measured by how many people love you—which is not a bad yardstick—Joe would have ranked number one on the *Forbes* 400 list.

Joe was wise, humorous, generous, friendly, public-spirited—possessing all of these qualities to an extraordinary degree. But, most of all, he was interested in *you*. Whether a presidential hopeful planning campaign strategies or a confused student contemplating his or her future, the person seeking Joe's wisdom received his full attention.

And what wisdom that inquiring person would receive! Joe's knowledge covered all bases, but his truly invaluable insights centered on his understanding of human behavior. I could spend an hour describing some seemingly intractable problem I was encountering with a difficult person or business situation. Then—presto!—Joe would deliver a sentence or two that provided a simple and effective solution to my problem.

Joe never asked for anything in return. He was not a fellow who kept score; the great friends never do. I knew, however, that there was one act of mine that would delight him: He wanted very much for me to become involved with Grinnell and focus on its finances.

And, of course, I wanted equally as much to please Joe. I would never be able to balance the books in terms of what we did for each other. But I *could* at least try. So I joined the Board simply because Joe loved the school and I loved Joe.

Joe sponsored my appointment to the Finance Committee at the college and thus began many years of fun. At 86, I can't recall any committee assignments in my lifetime in which I experienced such pleasure. When Joe would call me at night to discuss some action that would swell Grinnell's coffers, his enthusiasm was that of a kid in a candy shop. I couldn't help but share it.

So we conspired to have the college buy convertible debentures in a start-up (Intel); shorted securities in a "can't-lose" arbitrage (AT&T); made a leveraged buyout of a network television station (WDTN in Dayton); and the list goes on. The more outrageous the act might seem for a college endowment, the better Joe and I liked it. Every investment move was always entertaining for us and always (well, almost always) profitable. In fact, we truly had more fun making money for the college than we did in making investments for ourselves.

All of this took place because Joe loved the Grinnell students as he loved the members of his own family. They were his flock. And his interest did not diminish in any way after their graduation. He regularly filled me in on what the graduates were accomplishing, describing them with the words and tones of a proud grandfather.

You will read in this book the story of an important institution that has helped many thousands of young men and women proceed to a better life than they thought possible. You will read of the school's journey from survival to excellence. It is a story that could not have been written without a lifetime love affair between Joe Rosenfield and Grinnell College.

Warren E. Buffett
February 2017, Omaha, Nebraska

AUTHOR'S FOREWORD

On November 2, 2016, the Chicago Cubs defeated the Cleveland Indians 8-7, winning game seven of the World Series, making the Cubs "World Champions" for the first time since 1908. The win ended a 108-year championship drought—the longest in the history of US major league sports. I have been a longsuffering Cubs fan since 1947, and I was exhilarated that night, but the first thing I thought was, "I hope wherever he is, Joe Rosenfield knows his unrequited love affair with the Chicago Cubs is finally consummated."

Joe was the chief minority stockholder of the Cubs during the long Phil Wrigley ownership, and in his later years, he watched almost daily from his apartment on Grand Avenue as the Cubs lost almost every game. In 1998, two years before he died, Joe said, not for the first time, that he was determined to live long enough to see the Cubs win the World Series. He missed that moment by sixteen years, but his seemingly unconditional love of the Chicago Cubs was one of the many endearing qualities of Joseph Frankel Rosenfield, a man revered and beloved by legions in central Iowa and beyond.

In 2014, Beth Halloran, Vice President for Development and Alumni Relations at Grinnell College, asked me if I would be willing to undertake a biography of Joe Rosenfield. Jim Cownie, a Des Moines developer and civic leader, had coordinated with Beth to find someone to write the Rosenfield biography, and Beth thought of me. I had worked with Joe for nine years as a Grinnell College Trustee and then for another 12 years as the College's president; I knew Joe better than most others did. It took me less than a day to commit, saying, as Warren Buffet and so many others before me, "I could not refuse to do anything for Joe." I was and continue to be honored and excited by this opportunity, though, as is usually the case, it has taken longer to accomplish than I hoped.

Jim Cownie feels that he owes much of the success of his business career to Joe, who at crucial moments made investment decisions that first launched and later saved Heritage Communications, the American cable network Jim and his partner, Jim Hoak, built into the ninth largest in the nation. In a business career punctuated by reaching out to promising young talent, Joe identified the two Jims, both in their late 20s, as well as Robert Noyce, co-inventor of the integrated circuit on a chip and the founder of Intel.

I am deeply grateful to Jim Cownie for the financial support that has made this biography possible, and I can only hope the final product is worthy of his trust.

George Drake

ACKNOWLEDGEMENTS

Every writer is heavily dependent on the help of many talented people both for the production of the book and to provide sources that form the skeleton of the story. Almost four years ago, I was approached by Beth Halloran, Vice President for Development and Alumni Relations at Grinnell College asking, "Would you be interested in writing a biography of Joe Rosenfield?" It took me less than a day to accept this challenge, telling Beth as so many before me had averred, "I could not refuse to do anything for Joe." In fact, it was a privilege to be chosen to tell Joe's story.

The inspiration for Beth's request was Des Moines developer Jim Cownie, who is convinced that Joe was essential to his very successful business career. Jim feels a very deep debt to Joe and this biography is at least a partial repayment. Jim has underwritten the direct costs of researching this book and he also is a significant source for Joe's life.

Judy Hunter, retired Director of the Grinnell College Writing Lab edited all of the manuscript as did Kathrin Herr, editor for Business Publications Corp. Their contributions were essential and any errors and infelicities remaining are entirely mine. Grinnell College Technical Support Assistant De Dudley transcribed over thirty personal, telephone and video interviews. Chris Jones, Grinnell Colleges Archivist and his Assistant. Allison Haack were unfailing guides to the collections of the Iowa Room at Burling Library. A similar essential service was performed by Ellen Bridenstine, an Archivist at the State Historical Society of Iowa. Sandi Yoder and Sarah Carlson at the Iowa Jewish

Museum Historical Archives were extraordinarily helpful as well.

The Grinnell Development and Alumni Office as one of the sponsors of this book provided assistance successively from Shelby Carroll, Mary Stahl and Adam Laug. Connie Wimer, the CEO of Business Publications Inc. and a Grinnell College Trustee deserves special thanks for publishing this book and underwriting part of the cost as her contribution to Grinnell College. She also is an important source for Joe's story. Ashley Bohnenkamp was the production manager for the book and I am very deeply in her debt.

Interviews were essential sources for Joe's life and work and before undertaking the project I had almost no experience with oral history. Therefore, I turned to my Grinnell faculty colleague, Karla Erickson (Sociology) who is a veteran interviewer. Though I had to learn "on the fly," Karla's initial guidance provided the template for my interviews. All of the interviews contributed substantially to the story, but a few were particularly valuable. Who else but Warren Buffett deserves pride of place not only for his invaluable insights into Joe's mind and character, but also because he graciously agreed to write the Foreword to Joe's biography. Fred Little, who for all practical purposes was Joe's Godson, provided me with two days of insightful conversation in his San Francisco apartment. Jill June, retired CEO of Planned Parenthood of the Heartland knew Joe better than almost anyone, spending countless hours with him in frank and personal discussion. Michael Gartner who has had too many roles to list is an invaluable source for the history and character of Des Moines as well as Joe's importance to the city. Jim Cownie and his former partner Jim Hoak provided essential insights into Joe's business and investment acumen as well as his success as a mentor. Bill Knapp knew Joe in so many ways from business to mentoring to politics and he generously shared his insights. Bill Friedman, former Younkers President was a valuable source both for the corporation and Joe's leadership of Younkers. Bill also provided an essential catalog of the Younker's Archives at the State Historical Society of Iowa.

Jon Batesol and Stan Richards gave insights into Joe and General Growth as did Kay Bucksbaum and her son, John. David Clay, Tom Marshall, Bob Musser and Waldo Walker were essential to the story of Joe's trusteeship and investments for Grinnell College. Bob Burnett, retired Meredith CEO and former chair of the Grinnell Board of Trustees was essential for the Grinnell story as well as Joe's business career in Des Moines. Connie Wimer was especially helpful regarding Joe as a mentor and Chris Green knew Joe as a lawyer while also sharing insights into the Gamble law firm. Tom Harkin, Tom Miller and John Culver generously shared their knowledge of Joe's remarkable support of a generation of very successful Iowa Democratic politicians.

Fred Hubbell worked with Joe in support of Planned Parenthood and he also had insights into the history of Younkers. Ellain Steinger was invaluable as a witness to Joe's interactions with the Des Moines Jewish community. Stacey Henderson brokered some of Joe's investments. Pat Gessman, who was the General Growth Administrative Assistant who worked closely with Joe in his last twenty years, was most generous in sharing not only her insights, but also a file of information about Joe that she had maintained for many years. That file now resides in the Grinnell College Archives.

Videographer, David Buck, produced two interviews with Joe; one ten years before his death and the other just two years before Joe died. Those interviews provide essential parts of Joe's story.

I am deeply grateful to three authors: Joe's sister Louise Noun and her autobiography, *Journey to Autonomy*, William B. Fridricks, who wrote excellent biographies of Bill Knapp and John Ruan, both of whom were a part of Joe's life; and finally, Vicki Ingham for her recently published short history of Younkers.

My wife Sue has endured countless conversations about Joe and has read the manuscript as it scrolled from my computer. It is to her that I dedicate this book

INTRODUCTION

The year is 1968, in the heart of the student revolution of the '60s and '70s. Picture a tense meeting of the Grinnell College Board of Trustees. The College administration, after several years of student pressure, finally brought a recommendation to the Board that coed dormitories be established in the next academic year. The debate was intense, pitting those Trustees who either were tired of the battle or who genuinely believed colleges should not be "in loco parentis" against those who believed strongly that colleges in general should uphold societal norms and that highly residential, small liberal arts colleges like Grinnell had a special obligation to shield young students from their worst proclivities. The debate was extended and intense, and it eventually dissolved, as often was the case without Joe Rosenfield intervening. The Trustees were exhausted when Joe finally spoke up.

"Well," he said, "I am for coed dorms if they make them retroactive."[1] The meeting dissolved in spontaneous laughter as Joe, a 1925 Grinnell graduate, immediately settled the issue with incisive humor; the Board voted unanimously to approve coed dormitories.

This story shows two important things about Joe: One is the extraordinary influence Joe asserted during his fifty-nine-year tenure as a Grinnell Trustee—usually while employing only a few words. Second is his wit as a man who was known as "Line a Day Rosenfield" during his student days at Grinnell (1921–1925). The best way to make Joe's acquaintance is to meet him first as the witty college student in 1921. This is where our story begins.

PART ONE
JOE ROSENFIELD & GRINNELL COLLEGE

JOE ROSENFIELD AT GRINNELL: 1921-1925

September 21, 1921, freshman move-in day on the Grinnell College Campus, marked the beginning of a love affair with Grinnell College that would last until Joe Rosenfield's death in the year 2000. Though the College Archives offer little direct evidence of the precise reasons for his affection, there are abundant tracks for us to follow Joe's life at Grinnell. The life and character of the College shine out in the twice-weekly newspaper, the *Scarlet and Black* (*S&B*), in the college annual, *The Cyclone*, in the *Malteaser* (the humor magazine Joe joined his freshman year), and the school catalog, the *Bulletin*. Such publications suggest Grinnell was a good and dynamic college in the early 1920s when Joe entered the scene, and those same publications would bear his mark throughout his time on campus.

In an interview with Joseph Wall, Professor of History and me, on November 26, 1990, Joe said,

> "Well, I'm not sure I picked [Grinnell College]. I guess I probably did in the end . . . getting out of high school I really didn't know where I wanted to go to college. I was pretty immature. I know I didn't want to go East, I know that. I gave a little thought to the University of Iowa and some thought to Grinnell. And I think that my mother knew I was going to Grinnell. And, probably my father too. Maybe I did too. But I passed on the University of Iowa, which I'm glad I did, although I went there later and took law. [I] entered Grinnell in the fall of 1921, not knowing exactly what I'd find down there, but after I'd been there about three weeks I'd fallen in love with the place and you couldn't have driven me out of there with a team of horses.*

> *I just took to Grinnell right away. Whether Grinnell took to me, I don't know.*

When Professor Wall asked what it was about Grinnell that so attracted him, Joe responded, "Oh, the whole spirit of the institution; partially the quality of the instruction, but the dormitory system, the lack of fraternities and sororities, the kind of people you found there and the rather liberal atmosphere. The whole thing, some of [it] quite tangible, but I just liked it."

In a 1998 interview for the Des Moines History Project, Joe said,
> *"I entered the school when I was seventeen. I just fell in love with the school almost immediately and stayed that way for 73 years. . . I went down there, I didn't know a thing about—I didn't know where I wanted to go to college. I was kind of scared of college. And then I think it was my mother more than anything else probably, although I'm not sure—decided that Grinnell would be a good place for me. Very liberal you know. So, my father took me down there to look it over and signed me up; and [I] came home and packed up and went down there. Within three weeks I was happy as a lark. So, I've been that way for 75 years now.*

Assessing the quality of the college he attended compared to 1980s Grinnell, Joe said:
> *"It was a good school, but they had no money to go out and hire faculty . . . They could teach, most of them had been there, for quite awhile . . .they didn't expect a raise from year to year because the College didn't have any money . . . We could not have been considered one of the best liberal arts schools in the country in 1921. Today we are. That's the difference. But it was a good school. It was the best school in Iowa and it had a good reputation.*

On May 14, 1998, two years before Joe died, Fred Little, Joe's closest friend and fellow Trustee, asked Joe why he chose a liberal arts college:
> *"I suppose number one, my family. It was just assumed that in our family we would go to a liberal arts college . . . and I am very glad that I did. It broadened my horizon and I would be very disappointed in myself today and what I try*

to do with my life if I hadn't gone on to Grinnell and then later on to law school . . . [even though] I think probably I had no idea what I was going to do until I was in the middle of Law School and I found that I liked the law very much. I did well in Law School and by the time I got through. . . there was no question in my mind or my family's mind that that's where I should be . . . I went to work for a law firm in Des Moines.

Joe's life at Grinnell revolved around college publications. He joined the business staff of the *Malteaser* early in his first semester and became a reporter for the *S&B* in the second semester of his sophomore year. Beginning as a sophomore and continuing until graduation, Joe was the Business Manager of the *Malteaser*, also serving as Managing Editor for several issues late in his junior year and early in his senior year. His work with the *S&B* continued throughout his Grinnell career, capped by a humor column entitled, "DORIC: A Column of Pure Beauty," written with his close friend, Bob Fell, throughout their senior year. Joe was also the Business Manager for the 1925 *Cyclone*, which, according to Grinnell custom, was produced during his junior year. The dereliction of and consequent last minute resignation of the Editor propelled Joe into the editorship under pressure to produce the volume within just a couple of weeks.

Joe was quite forthcoming when Professor Wall, in the 1990 interview, asked about his most engaging activities at Grinnell:

Well, all kinds of newspaper and magazine work. I worked on the Scarlet & Black *for three or four years. I guess I was a reporter. [I] tried out for the editorship my last year, but didn't make it. The first woman editor of the Scarlet & Black was chosen ahead of me, which was okay. I then reverted to writing a column with my roommate called 'DORIC . . . A Column of Pure Beauty', which was a type of scandalous thing, which was supposed to be humorous. And it was really the feature part of the* Scarlet & Black *. . . Then there was the* Malteaser, *which was a humorous magazine [where] I was Business Manager for three years. I guess Harold Swanson, who was one of our distinguished alumni, was the editor my first year and Bob Fell, a close* *friend of mine, I think, was editor one year. And I also was Business Manager of the school annual [*The Cyclone*] and finally had to take over the editorship when we found that the editor had not been doing his work; and I had to take the thing over. [I] remember that I had to go down to Iowa City and spend a whole week with the printer down there ... that's where* The Cyclone *was published. This printer spent from 8:00 in the morning to 11:00 at night with me getting the thing out.*

In March of 1923, in recognition of his many journalistic contributions, Joe was elected to the Grinnell chapter of Sigma Delta Chi, the national collegiate journalism society. Much later, when I asked Joe about his years at Grinnell, he always mentioned his journalism, especially the *Malteaser* and very little else, except, importantly, that he was drawn to Grinnell because it did not have fraternities and sororities. That fact must have been exceptionally important to a Jewish student in the 1920s, an era of unabashed anti-Semitism. Joe's friend and fellow Trustee Kay Bucksbaum, who graduated from Grinnell in 1951, said when she came to Grinnell as a young Jewish woman, she, for the first time in her life, "did not feel different from anybody else." She speculated that Joe must have had the same experience.

Joe lived in Langan Hall throughout his four years at Grinnell. Both the men's residence halls and women's cottages were relatively small dormitories, housing only forty to fifty students. The men remained in the same hall throughout their time in college, whereas the women changed cottages from year-to-year. Constructed early in the second decade of the twentieth century, some of the dorms and cottages, such as Langan, were named, while some still bore numbers (e.g., Building II and Building III). In his sophomore year, Joe lived across the hall from Frank (Gary) Cooper. Cooper adopted his middle name when he moved to Hollywood before graduating from Grinnell.

Joe was a Political Science major with a minor in History. Graduation requirements included six credits of English, six credits of math, Latin, or Greek, six credits of hygiene for men, six credits of laboratory science, six credits of history/social science, six credits of philosophy/psychology, 12 credits of foreign language, 24 credits for the major, and 16 for the minor. With a total of 120 credits required for graduation, the remainder were filled with electives.[4]

History, Joe's minor, was a larger department than was the department of his major, Political Science. Paul Peck, Charles Payne, and Cecil Lovell were History mainstays, with John Ganaway and Geddes Rutherford teaching most of the Political Science courses. The latter featured such subjects as Comparative Free Government, Municipal Functions and Problems, Political Philosophy, Constitutional Law, Self-Governing Systems, Contemporary Political Problems, State Administration, National Administration, and International Law and Relations; History courses focused on US and European history, with one course on the Orient and some historiography.[5]

In the November 1990 interview, Joe commented briefly on the faculty:

I think Eleanor Lowden was my English teacher. I think I put her probably number one on my list. Paul Peck in History, I thought was a very good teacher. John Ryan was a colorful teacher in speech. There was some hot air connected with him, but he was a very popular teacher. We enjoyed his classes. In Political Science for one year, or two years, they had a man named Rutherford there who really was a pretty good teacher, the only one in the department who really was good.

Because he was so immersed in college publications, there is more evidence of Joe's life at Grinnell[6] than there is for the majority of students. He was not a prominent student body leader, though he was Treasurer of the Senior Class of 1925 and was elected to the most prestigious and ancient of the four Men's Literary Societies in his freshman year, Chrestomathia—founded in 1852 before the College had moved from Davenport to Grinnell. His early election to the most prestigious of these exclusive societies is highly significant. There were no more than six Jewish students at Grinnell, and these Societies were the closest thing to a fraternity that Grinnell officially sponsored. The societies were self-selecting and, as we will see later in this chapter, very much under attack for their exclusivity. The fact that a Jew could be selected to the top society, especially as a freshman, speaks volumes about the relative absence of anti-Semitism at Grinnell in age of virulent anti-Semitism on most college campuses. I have long felt that a key to Joe's love for Grinnell may have been that it was one of the few colleges or universities in the 1920s where a Jewish student could feel full acceptance and comfort. His election to Chrestomathia in his freshman year is the clearest evidence of Joe's acceptance. Many years after he was elected to Chrestomathia, fellow Trustee Bob Musser heard Joe say he thought he was one of the first Jews to attend Grinnell "and that's why he has a love for Grinnell he can't get over."[7]

In the interview with Fred Little, Joe's closest friend and fellow Trustee, conducted two years before Joe's death, Fred asked Joe about his fondest memory of Grinnell:

My fondest memory of Grinnell? Probably the people that I met down there. The faculty, students, others connected to the College. All of them became friends of mine, all very liberal in their thinking. The kind of people that I liked. That, I think is the first remembrance I have. The atmosphere of the College, clearly the College respected the student body. I was very happy there for four years."

IN JOE'S COLLEGE DAYS

By today's standards, Grinnell was a small college in Joe's time. It was largest in his first year, 1921–1922, when there were 776 in the College and a total of 880 including the students at the School of Music.[8] Harkening back to the days when women were thought not to have appropriate minds for the liberal arts, Grinnell long featured a School of Music shaped especially for women. The total enrollment had dropped to 755 by Joe's senior year, 1924–1925. Joe's freshman class was quite large at 408 students, but it had dwindled sharply to 136 by the time he graduated in 1925.

Prior to the GI Bill days, following World War II, university and college enrollments were much smaller. In the 1920s, the University of Iowa had only a few more than 5,000 students, and when Grinnell began to grow beyond 1,000 following World War II, the Trustees asked for assurances from the administration that the College would "return to normal" when the glut of veterans expired.[9]

Yearly tuition in 1921, Joe's first year, was $160, with board and room set at $425 and $7.50 in fees, for a comprehensive fee of $592.50. In the following year, tuition was raised to $200, or $100 per semester, but the other charges remained stable.[10] Lest we chuckle at what seem to us to be ridiculously low numbers, bear in mind what a former Grinnell President and expert in economics of Higher Education, Howard Bowen, repeated on several occasions: Over the years, college tuition has pretty reliably tracked the cost of a mid-sized car.[11]

An *S&B* editorial, published on April 4, 1923, claimed Grinnell was "the Scholastic Cream of the West." In those days, Grinnell was classified as a western college, as were all institutions west of the Mississippi. Some likened it to Harvard; indeed, Grinnell was one of the few colleges to be part of an annual Harvard faculty exchange. A deeper look at the Harvard comparison reveals the connection had more to do with athletics than academics, since both Harvard and Grinnell were athletic powerhouses in the late-nineteenth and early-twentieth centuries.

Though it was no Harvard, Grinnell was an extremely good liberal arts college in the 1920s. The faculty was well qualified, many holding doctorates from major universities. Louis V. Phelps, the longtime Treasurer of the College, gave a set of statistics to the *S&B* for the fall of 1922, Joe's sophomore year. The proportion of faculty to administrators was much more favorable to the faculty than it is today. According to Phelps, the instructional staff in the College numbered 60, with 18 in the School of Music; the administration stood at 12, with an additional six full-time and three part-time staff in the library.

Grinnell was sufficiently prestigious to be included in a study of thirteen outstanding colleges conducted by the Commonwealth Fund.[12] President John Hanson Thomas Main was elected to the Carnegie Foundation Board in April of 1924, joining, among others, Presidents Aydelotte of Swarthmore and Lowell of Harvard. That election was an important recognition of Grinnell's quality as well as Main's stature.

Women consistently outperformed men in the classroom, and among athletes, track and field surpassed both basketball and football.[13] The temper of the faculty is evident in a poll of their favorite literary masterpieces, published by the *S&B* on April 21, 1923. Shakespeare led with 17, followed by the Bible with 16, H.G. Wells' *Outline of History* at five, *The Dialogues of Plato* with four, Faust with three, *Divine Comedy* at three, and *The Iliad* and *Odyssey*, *Outline of Science* and Browning's Poems with three votes each.

The College was not unusual in the way it functioned without an admissions office. When such an operation was established in the 1940s, it was under the heading "Public Relations." The majority of students came from Iowa, and the best recruitment tools were the churches, especially the Congregational, whose ancestors had founded Grinnell in 1846 as Iowa College in Davenport (it moved to Grinnell in 1858). During the annual spring theological Gates Lectures, all of the Congregational ministers in Iowa were invited to campus, and scores came. The recruiting impact of this connection is evident in the 1922–1923 count of the religious affiliation of Grinnell Students: There were 297 Congregational, with the Methodists 100 behind at 197. The list continued: 89 Presbyterians; 28 Baptists; 29 Disciples of Christ; 23 Episcopalians; 10 Christian Science; 7 Catholics; 6 United Presbyterian; 6 Lutherans; 6 Jewish; 3 Reformed; and 50 claiming no religious affiliation.[14] This count from 1922 is in stark contrast with the Grinnell of today, with present day enrollment at only two or three percent Congregational (UCC) and Catholics being the largest Christian group. Contemporary Grinnell features significant percentages of Jews, Muslims, and Hindus. The other major student recruitment force was the many Grinnell graduates teaching in the public schools of Iowa and neighboring states. Together with the churches, they provided the main portal to Grinnell—which is, again, in stark contrast with the College today, since few Grinnell graduates teach in the public schools and religious affiliation is a negligible factor. Cultural life at Grinnell College in the 1920s was surprisingly rich. While Joe was a student, both the St. Louis and Minneapolis Symphonies played at Herrick Chapel, as did Cellist Pablo Casals and Hungarian violinist Emil Telman.[15] The *S&B* ran frequent features on contemporary events. Charles Payne, Professor of European History, displayed his wide knowledge in frequent articles on the background of current European events. The *S&B* editor during Joe's senior year was Hilda Mauch, the first woman ever to edit the college newspaper.

Women had won the vote with the Nineteenth Amendment, ratified in 1920, and Mauch frequently urged the women to become better informed in order to exercise responsibly their newly won franchise. She advised the cottages to subscribe to regional and national newspapers, suggesting the women read them regularly. These were the Harding and Coolidge years. In fact, an election eve *S&B* student straw poll showed Coolidge beating Davies and LaFollet in 1924.[16]

Grinnell graduate and novelist James Norman Hall visited campus twice in Joe's time. On the second visit he gave an interview to an enterprising *S&B* reporter, and classmate of Joe, James Work, in the penultimate *S&B* of 1924–1925 (published June 6, 1925). It ran with the headline "Found: A Grinnell alumnus who hates western civilization, abominates evangelical missionaries and detests radio." Speaking about radio, Hall, then living in Tahiti, said, "I wouldn't own one of them if they were perfect. I hate them! Just another mark of western industrial, machine-made soulless civilization." Regarding missionaries, he added:

"They've all done nothing but harm. The natives would be a thousand times better off had they had never come . . . they [were] living simply and naturally when the missionaries came . . . But the missionaries told them it was wicked for a woman to have more than one husband; monogamy was instituted; there was a preponderance of unmarried men, and the inevitable results followed. The missionaries may have done some good in putting down cannibalism, but they have done immeasurable harm."

Hall's condemnation was sweeping: "Before the appearance of westerners, disease was unknown in the islands. Now, with the inroads of western civilization, western society and western morality, disease and sickness has wiped out the main portion of the natives, and the few that are left are sickly and disease ridden."

Hall ended his interview in the *S&B* with common sense advice: "Why do we have to think that what's good for us is good for everybody else too? . . . How would we like it if the Buddhist and Confucionists, the Mahometans and the rest of the Orientals would come over here trying to force their religion and customs and civilization on us? They have as much right to do that as we have to go over there, yet we'd make a mighty big fuss were they to try it."

Hallie Flanagan, future Director of Franklin Roosevelt's Federal Theatre Project, was another famous Grinnell alumna who happened to be teaching English and theatre while Joe Rosenfield was a student. Her production of *Romeo and Juliet* in Joe's senior year was regarded as one of the most exceptional Grinnell theatre experiences in years, and there was a plethora of productions each year. Flanagan's reputation drew an appointment to the Vassar theatre department in 1925, which was delayed when she won a Guggenheim Fellowship for 1925–1926. She was recommended for the Guggenheim by the President of the Carnegie Corporation, who had been on campus for the *Romeo and Juliet* production.[17]

Perhaps the most noteworthy campus organization in the 1920s was the Men's Glee Club. In the spring of 1924, it attracted national attention when it won the Western Glee Club competition at a sold-out Orchestra Hall in Chicago, defeating the University of Michigan and twelve other universities and colleges. As the winner in the West, Grinnell was invited to participate in the Eastern competition in New York City, essentially turning that event into a national contest. Judged by Walter Demerosch, among others, it was called "the best singing in years." Yale won overall, but Grinnell defeated the bulk of the eastern schools, tying with Penn State for fourth, only eleven points behind Yale on a 300 point scale. Grinnell's strong showing insured that no western school would be invited east in subsequent years.[18]

In the fall of 1924, Oxford University debaters—featuring Malcom MacDonald, son of the British Prime Minister Ramsey MacDonald— visited Grinnell to debate "the Principle of Prohibition." A supposedly "unbiased" student vote gave the victory to Grinnell.[19] The following year, Cambridge came to campus to debate Grinnell.

Yes, Grinnell College exhibited a remarkably vital culture in the early 1920s, including the strength of the Grinnell-in-China Program, frequent, non-compulsory, twenty-minute chapel talks each week, and the annual Gates Lectures, which featured the famous liberal preacher, Harry Emerson Fosdick, who ignited the campus in Joe's senior year. A new college literary magazine, *Junto*, first was published in Joe's senior year and, as we shall see, was quickly suppressed. With culture and connection coming out of every vein, the College was anything but lost in the cornfields of Iowa.

In addition to Joe Rosenfield, Grinnell had some interesting faculty, staff, and students. Among them was President John Hanson Thomas Main. Most excellent colleges can point to a long-term presidency in the early twentieth century that was both innovative and stable. Main's was such a presidency, lasting from 1906 until his death in office in 1931. As was classicist, he had been Dean of the College before presiding. He was an imposing figure, standing at more than six feet, four inches. I recall meeting some alumni from the late '20s who, upon learning that I was the president of Grinnell, let me know by their facial expressions and body language that there was no way a "kid" like me could fill the illustrious shoes of John Hanson Thomas Main.

Main's vision for two sets of residence halls, evoking Oxford and Cambridge quadrangles, established both the visual and social flavor of Grinnell College. He recruited and sustained a strong faculty, and his lean administration governed effectively. He was directly responsible for recruiting the most prolific professor in the College's history, Edward Steiner. Main met Steiner when he was Dean, and Steiner at that time was a Congregational pastor in Sandusky, Ohio. They met on an ocean liner bound for Europe. Based on that acquaintance and study of his publications, Main later offered Steiner the Chair in Applied Christianity—a position whose only previous occupant had been the notorious George Herron, who had toured the country preaching against property in the name of a Social Gospel that eschewed private property.

Steiner was a brilliant appointment.

At the age of nineteen, Steiner emmigrated to the United States from Slovenia. He spoke no English when he arrived in New York, though he had mastered several European languages. Completely on his own, he gradually made his way across the country from an inaugural job at the bottom of the New York garment industry, through Pennsylvania, where he worked in a steel mill, to Chicago and Minnesota, working on Midwestern farms. While accompanying cattle on a train passing through Ohio, he was thrown off by a mugger. He quite literally landed in Oxford, Ohio, which he called Bethlehem in his autobiography, *From Alien to Citizen*. His English was good enough by this time that he was able to land a job as a clerk in a local shop. He soon met and, for a time, lived with a Congregational minister and his wife. He converted from

Judaism to Christianity and enrolled in Oberlin Seminary. He held three pastorates before Sandusky, using his spare time to research and write a biography of Tolstoy, whom he had traveled on foot to meet at his Russian estate shorty before coming to America.

Steiner's research and writing focused on the immigrant experience, and he based his writing on field experience. In the summers, he would journey back and forth to Europe, often in steerage, where he would interview both those coming to America and those returning to Europe after sampling immigration. He wrote a shelf-full of books (26 to be exact) after mastering English narrative prose. Few authors did more to interpret the immigrant experience to a national audience in the first half of the twentieth century than Edward Steiner of Grinnell College. He was so in demand as a lecturer throughout the US that he was frequently away from campus for weeks and even semesters. His broadest influence on the students of Joe Rosenfield's era was through chapel talks and articles in the *S&B*.

Steiner's name sounded German, and he suffered virulent anti-German prejudice after the US entered World War I. His house was painted yellow, and he was verbally attacked by super-patriot Professor of Speech John Ryan. This same John Ryan greatly influenced generations of Grinnell students who, decades later, vividly recalled his introductory speech course. In fact, alumni of the '20s and '30s spoke of Ryan with fondness unequalled for any other faculty member in their memory. Joe remembered him. Those who graduated during the Depression credited him with teaching the communication skills that led to unanticipated professional and personal success.

Graduates from the Depression era also spoke with extravagant respect for Louis Phelps, who served the College as Business Manager from 1916 to 1948—an exceptional tenure. Phelps was also Secretary of the Board of Trustees and was in charge of the Buildings and Grounds. For many years, his only staff member was a secretary. It is a wonder that he was able to accomplish so much without any other help. What alums from that time remembered was that Phelps made it possible for them to attend and stay at Grinnell. He somehow found employment for students and often made favorable payment arrangements so that, even in the depths of the Depression, they could afford to graduate from Grinnell. Finances were not an issue for Joe

Rosenfield and many of the students in the early 1920s, but even so, Phelps was a major part of their college experience as well.

Two superb athletes overlapped with Joe's student years: Leonard Paulu graduated in 1922 and Morgan Taylor, who lived across the hall from Joe, in 1926. Both were track athletes at a time when Grinnell was known as the "greatest little track school in the West."[20] Doc Huff, who left for the University of Kansas after the 1925 season, coached both Paulu and Taylor. Huff was noted as a sprints coach; Paulu was a two-time national collegiate 100-yard and 220-yard champion, and Taylor won the 400-meter hurdles in the 1924 Olympics.

Leonard Paulu, a Phi Beta Kappa chemistry graduate, returned to Grinnell as a wounded World War I veteran. Shrapnel had damaged his right leg and taken his right eye. Even with a shortened right leg and a glass eye that sometimes dropped out during races, he nevertheless managed 9.8 seconds in the 100-yard dash. His exploits made him the cover story in the national *Interscholastic Magazine*, but he lost to Charlie Paddock in the 1924 Olympic Trials.

Morgan Taylor had been a consistent winner in the 120-yard high and 220 low hurdles in the Missouri Valley Conference and in the all-Iowa University meets. Grinnell was in the Missouri Valley Conference in the 1920s, joining the University of Kansas, Kansas State, Missouri, Iowa State (then called "Ames"), Nebraska, Oklahoma, Drake, and Washington University. Grinnell was not particularly competitive in football and basketball, but it usually placed among the top three in track and field.

Morgan Taylor would have been a marvelous decathlete as he usually competed and placed or won both hurdles, the 440-yard run, and the high jump and long jump; in addition, he usually anchored the mile relay. He had never run the 400-meter hurdles when he competed in the preliminary Olympic Trials in Iowa City on May 3, 1924. He placed second to Coulter of Iowa, which was good enough to qualify for the finals in Boston, where both runners broke the world record—finishing at 53.2 and 53.3 seconds. Taylor won with that new world record time, defeating Brookings and Coulter, and he went on to win at the Paris Olympics—the first American to win at the Twenty-Fourth Olympiad.

Taylor returned to Grinnell for his senior year, playing as an end on the football team and continuing to establish track records. His forty-yard catch in the Iowa State game was the crucial play in a 14-13 victory. By the time he graduated in 1926, he held five world records: 45-yard, 70-yard, and 80-yard high hurdles (all indoor) and the 400-meter and 440-yard hurdles outdoors. He went on to place third in the 400-meter hurdles in both the 1928 and 1932 Olympics, carrying the US flag at the latter. At the time, he was the only American to ever medal in the same event in three successive Olympics.

Taylor entered Grinnell with Joe Rosenfield, but he took part of another year to graduate. As the national interscholastic low and high hurdle champion at Sioux City, coached by Grinnellian, Chuck Hoyt, he already had a national reputation when he came to the College. His accomplishments were not limited to the track, as he was a tenor in the Western Champion Men's Glee Club (fourth nationally), active on the stage crew in theatre productions, and elected chairman of his residence hall his senior year.[21]

Joe was intensely interested in both Paulu and Taylor. He said in his November, 1990 interview, "I was a great spectator . . . don't think that I ever missed a sporting event. I was no athlete at all, but I don't think that I missed a football game or a basketball game or a track meet. I would go out and watch football practice and basketball practice. [I] got a big kick out of it although Grinnell was not doing an awful lot of winning." Joe's spectatorship even extended to out of town football games; several of his friends from Langan went to Columbia, Missouri for the Grinnell/Missouri football game in 1922.[22] Joe continued to love sports after graduation, most famously becoming the chief minority stockholder and super fan of the Chicago Cubs.

By far the most famous person to attend Grinnell in the early 1920s was the Academy Award Winning actor Gary Cooper—two-time winner of the Academy award for leading male actor: *Sargeant York* (1941) and *High Noon* (1953). Known as Frank in his college days, he lived across the hall from Joe in Langan Hall. Though he received a bid for the Debating Union, there is no record that he was active in debate and, more significantly, no record that he ever participated in a theatre production.[23] He was elected to the 1926 *Cyclone* Board but did not assume his duties because he had left for Hollywood. Legend has it he was in pursuit of a girlfriend who was trying the Hollywood scene. Frank Cooper was well thought of on campus; he was one of the nominees for the Men's Senate. His one recorded utterance was a thoughtful response to the question: "Do you think Grinnell women in general come up to the University type?" Frank Cooper responded: "I believe they do. As a rule they are much more democratic. In bearing and poise and general attributes, the Grinnell women are superior. Sorority life is a cramp on individuality, while quad life broadens them much more."[24] Joe Rosenfield relayed vivid memories of Gary Cooper:

"Yes, he was there for two years while I was there. He came to Grinnell [as] a freshman while I was a sophomore, but he was older; he had been out of school several years. [He] came to Grinnell from Montana because another fellow from Montana kind of brought him there who was already in school. Gary's father was a justice of the Montana Supreme Court. He wasn't known as Gary Cooper then; he was Frank Cooper, but called Cowboy Cooper. And the first year he was there he lived across the hall from me, so I got to know him reasonably well. He was really kind of a recluse. He didn't circulate around too much. He did a lot of drawing and I think he went to California. . . to become a commercial artist, but somehow or other he got a shot at film . . . and you know he made quite a success of it . . . You didn't see a lot of him. He spent a lot of time in his room. He didn't have, as I determined, a lot of close friends and I had kind of gathered that he didn't care an awful lot about the place. But curiously enough about six or seven years ago, I was at a birthday party in New York for Warren Buffet's 50th Birthday and they called on me for a few remarks and I put in a few plugs for Grinnell. And after dinner a young woman, I don't know how young she was (forty or fifty or something) came up and introduced herself. She was Gary Cooper's daughter and she told me how much her father had liked Grinnell; and her house was stacked full of memorabilia and pictures and the whole business about Grinnell College, and it was one of the loves of his life, which was quite a surprise to me."

Another sign of the College's high scholastic standing at the time was Joe's classmate Neil Crone, the sixth Rhodes Scholar elected from Grinnell, a total that led the entire state of Iowa at that time.

Also, two women in the class of 1925 stand out: Hilda Mauch was the first woman to edit the *S&B*, and she did so with great distinction. Her editorial insights and campaigns over various major issues at Grinnell during Joe's student years were prominent influences on the entire campus. It also is worth noting that she was the editor who gave Joe and his good friend, Bob Fell, license for their humor column, DORIC in the 1924–1925 *S&B*.

Another 1925 woman of note was Phi Beta Kappa graduate Marguerite Merryman, who became notorious for the "Blairsburg Sketches," published in the College's new literary magazine, *Junto*, in February, 1925. James Kissane, Professor of English, published an account of this infamous incident in October, 1977 Grinnell Magazine, "Blairsburg Sketches, Grinnell's Other *Cyclone*." Merryman was a student leader and brilliant English major. As a class exercise, she wrote sketches of personalities in her hometown of Blairsburg, Iowa. Her professor, Joseph Walleser (Grinnell class of 1903 and Rhodes Scholar) printed the sketches in the third issue of *Junto* without inquiring about or changing the names of the sketch subjects. It turned out that Margurite had used actual names, except for the sketch about her own family. A storm was unleashed when a copy of *Junto* inevitably found its way to Blairsburg. The carnage led to Waleser's forced resignation from the Grinnell faculty and a lawsuit against the College, which was dropped in the following year. The plaintiff was Mrs. Genevieve B. Coble, the Blairsburg High School Principal, who was satirized in the Blairsburg Sketches as "Genevieve Bendorf Cable:"

> *"It was you who of all the teachers in Hamilton County ranked highest in the intelligence test—you the principal of Blairsburg high school—the one who did more in one hour than other teachers did in three—efficient, enterprising, alert. It was you who talked to the high school girls about rolled hose.*
>
> *At Christmas time you sent out announcements of your marriage to Harry Cable—the drafted ex-hero who was waiting for his bonus. And you bought yourself a wedding ring and went on teaching while the students gambled as to whether it would be a boy or girl.*
>
> *Harry, Junior, was born the week after commencement*

and the next week you bought a cream station for Harry and you worked down there.

Five months and this time it was the farmers who were gambling as to whether it would be a boy or a girl. They had every day of four months to gamble, because you were much around town. You were writing items for the Webster City Daily News, so you met all the trains.

But you had told the girls not to roll their hose and you had passed a high intelligence test."

There were eight other sketches, some even more "scandalous," which prompted Margurite's parents to suggest she not return home for spring break. The College decided to cancel the senior class play, Sheridan's *The School for Scandal*, substituting Shaw's *Arms and the Man*, and Marguite Merryman, lying low, managed to graduate in June and launch a successful teaching career of her own.

The Blairsburg Sketches were grist for Rosenfield humor in DORIC. Periodically, DORIC provided spoof "Who's Who in Grinnell" vignettes, and Marguerite Merryman merited an entry in the March 11, 1925 *S&B*:

Name: Marguerite Merryman
Hometown: Blairsburg
Hobby: Sketches
Favorite Song: "There'll Be a Hot Time in the Old Town Tonight"
Favorite Breakfast Food: Wild Oats
Favorite Magazine: JUNTO
Clubs: Sketch Club, Blairsburg Chapter P.Y.A.
Degree: Third

The *Malteaser*, not to be outdone by DORIC, in its spring 1925 Number, published a parody titled, "Green River Pathology." It presented seven profiles a la Blairsburg Sketches, two of which follow:

HELEN HELLIN
I was a college widdow,
And a gay time I had too!
First there was Tom, back in '14
Then came Joe and Harry,
Two good scouts
Then came Henry Henrikson—

God, but I fell for him
Proper.
One night he said he loved me
So, I said:
'How many other girls have you told that?'
He choked me in less than ten minutes;
What was it angered him?
PROF. NUMBLESON
Fresh from college
I came to Green River;
Imagined that I was all-smart
And that I would create a sensation
In the local high school.
I did; I took one of the teachers
To a road-house one night
And the next day they canned me
And since then I have found
That all towns under ten thousand
Are dear old Green River
With another name.

The Blairsburg Sketches scandal was tailor-made for DORIC and *Malteaser*. Joe and Fell often similarly seized on other 1924–1925 events for DORIC, especially in the town of Grinnell. For example, in the fall of 1924, Merchants National Bank, which was housed in the famous Louis Sullivan designed building, collapsed—declaring bankruptcy. Its collapse affected student depositors, and the ongoing reorganization efforts were closely followed in the *S&B* throughout the spring of 1925. DORIC first commented on November 12, 1924, "On the Banks of Old Grinnell: Aristotle, our demon reporter brings news that Merchants National Bank opened yesterday. . . to let three Directors out the back door." After a second Grinnell bank, the Grinnell Savings Bank, failed in January 1925, DORIC published, "Notice: There will be a meeting of all the students who did not lose money in either the Merchants or Savings Bank; said meeting to be held in the Southeast corner of the reading room in A.R.H."

Another town crisis that deeply affected the College was the diminishing water supply, causing officials to frequently shut the water off after 10:30 p.m.[25] Officials considered supplementing with water from Arbor Lake (which was rejected) or extending the deep wells (which was not undertaken while Joe was a student). This crisis provided delicious material for DORIC: "The management of Arbor Lake wishes to announce that from now on a charge of fifty cents will be levied for each mud bath taken."[26] A month before graduation, DORIC announced: "The Superintendent of Buildings and Grounds wished to announce that the all-college swimming pool is at last completed and will be ready for occupation about June first. He advised students as well as faculty to pray for rain as last Saturday the city reservoir was drained."[27]

JOE AS A STUDENT

Joe Rosenfield never described himself as a strong student at Grinnell, but we can understand his grades when we consider his intense participation in campus publications. In interview after interview, we heard,

"Joe was very smart." That was certainly my experience working with Joe. If we take into account the *Malteaser*, *Cyclone* and, above all, the *S&B*, particularly DORIC, one wonders how Joe found time to participate in all of the publications, attend all the games and many team practices, and also do any amount of studying. Composing DORIC during all of his senior year would have been extraordinarily time consuming, as the long humor column appeared virtually every week. This offers a goldmine of material either directly authored by Joe or given his editorial imprimatur. In later life, Joe was known for his humor and ability to defuse tension with quick wit (e.g., during a heated Trustee debate in the late 1960s considering whether to approve coed dormitories, story in the Author's Foreword). Joe was known for his "one-liners" when he was a student, and humor was so essential to his nature throughout his life that it is worth looking at DORIC in some depth. Though he was a radical feminist later in life, DORIC humor was moderately misogynist, particularly with a running gag: "The Girl in my English Class." There were at least six in the series and a few illustrate the flavor. During the presidential election of 1924, he wrote, "The Girl in my English Class says that she is glad Grinnell isn't mixed up in politics the way that horrid old Electoral College is."[28] Later, "The Girl in my English Class says that she reads in the paper that it took 34,000 muskrats to make all the Hudson Seal coats worn last year and she thinks it's just wonderful how those dear little animals can be taught to do such work."[29] And, "The Girl in my English Class says she is SO interested in the foreign exchange and that she got so excited when the Mark and the Frank went down and she wishes she could find the exchange rate on the Latin Quarter."[30]

Much of the moderate misogyny was concentrated into the earlier columns in the fall of 1924. Eventually, Joe and Bob Fell let women do one column on December 10. This bit of humor introduced the idea:

"Yesterday some bobbed-haired-Betty asked why the Column seemed to ignore the inmates of the Quadrangle. We lifted our collective hat (see 'Etiquette of Gentlemen and College Students pp. 437–437 inc.') and answered, "If that is so we are sorry. But not so sorry that our minds' eye is obscured by tears. To be frank, you women are more interesting objectively than otherwise. You are like the moon that is most beautiful and alluring when it is near the horizon and slightly obscured by bending poplars and scudding clouds. It loses much of its mystery and charm when it aspires to the void of mid-heaven. So should you stay by the poplars of enchanting silence and avoid the cold void of the printed word.

"However if any [of] the Quad feels that she (or her) has anything of worth, she should submit her brainchild to us secure in the knowledge that we will treat it as our own. The above proposal is subject to veto by Plato the linotype operator."[31]

Misogyny did creep into some of the spring semester columns: "ARISTOTLE, our demon press-feeder says women are like second-hand clothes. They're always hanging around."[32] Or, the ultimate insult: "If Noah had realized that he was saving a race that in future years would produce that which is known by the name of co-ed, he would have scuttled the [ark]."[33] Finally, "We always thought that coeds, as a class, were barnacles on the Ship of Progress until last week when one of them tried to play footy-footy with us at the library."[34]

Joe could flirt in DORIC: "Official Notice: Messrs Rosenfield, Pierce and Norris wish to announce to the Quadrangle that they will be out of town on Saturday."[35] And nothing was sacred to DORIC, not even its harboring newspaper: "SEGREGATION OF CRIME NEWS: DORIC wishes to compliment *The Des Moines Register* for its laudable stand in regard to separating crime news. We would also suggest that the *S&B* adopt the same policy, leaving the front page blank."[36]

There was a series of DORIC jokes about a College's Endowment Campaign intending to raise $650,000. The campaign was announced in the October 22, 1924 issue of *S&B*. This issue is of particular interest because of Joe's later success in building Grinnell's endowment: "A Few Suggestions: Plans now underway to raise six hundred and fifty thousand dollars for the Grinnell Endowment. Here are a few suggestions as to how to raise the money: 1) Get one man to give it all; 2) Get six hundred and fifty thousand alums to give one dollar apiece; 3) Burn the Science Building—if it is insured; 4) Sell sandwiches; 5) Do away with professors' salaries for a period of three years; 6) Sell the Chapel."[37] A week after this advice, they offered another suggestion: "Bull College: It cost Mr. Duke, the tobacco king, about six million to get a school named after him. It will cost Mr. Durham just $650,000 to change the name of this school, and that is no Bull."[38]

Joe and Bob Fell persisted on the Endowment Campaign in April 1925:

"Endowment Coming in Fine: Can Hear Every Dollar Clink: The following letter received from a former student in regard to the endowment campaign.

> *'Dear Mr. Phelps: Would like to know if you are accepting soap wrappers and United Cigar coupons as contributions to the campaign fund? Have saved enough to win a Buster Brown flash. . . but would be glad to sacrifice for old Grinnell. Let me know.*
> *ALUMNUS'*
>
> *Dear ALUMNUS:*
> *Yes we will accept them.*
> *Yours thriftily, L.V. Phelps."*[39]

Not content to lampoon the Endowment Campaign, Rosenfield and Fell took on the college budget with an analysis of how much the College saved on the annual Flunk (Skip) Day:

> *"Flunk Day to Replenish College Exchequer: The College statistician, H.W. Matlack, after laboring with a blue pencil for 37 hours has doped out that the all-college Flunk Day will net the College an enormous sum. Here is his reasoning:*
>
> *"First there will be great saving on meals with 800 students out of town, missing 3 meals each, making a grand total of 2400 meals (if everyone had gotten up for breakfast). It will mean a saving of $12.08, less pie which has already been purchased by Marty Ward.*
>
> *"Secondly, there will be no hot water which will net the College $0.08. No books will be stolen as the Libe will be closed that day, adding another $0.65 to the total."*[40]

The reference to stolen library books is another example of DORIC missing no opportunity to pillory an *S&B* campaign; one of Hilda Mauch's editorial crusades was to stop library pilfering. One can certainly recognize the future businessman and investor both in the tenor of Joe's humor and his various business manager roles.

The omnipresent Louis Phelps was the subject of one of the final DORIC columns under the headline: "Check and Balance: L.V. Phelps, Chancellor of the Exchequer, Treasurer, Keeper of the Funds, Holder of Mortgages, Shepherd of a Flock of Bills, and Avenger of the College Seal, has been granted a year or more of leave of absence in order that he may teach Applied Christianity throughout the Country. You can bank on that, but don't write any checks."[41] The reference to teaching Applied Christianity throughout the country, of course, is a jab at Professor of Applied Christianity Edward Steiner, who often was away from campus for extended lecture tours.

DORIC, true to the last, spoofed its own demise:

> *The Crumbling Column: As we sit here in our room watching the last sanguine glow of the setting sun with all the mysteries of crepuscular shadows about us, we are sad, discouraged. Despondent? Just a little Depressed? A trifle. This is the last DORIC, our last line. Born of*

good intentions and expiring as a broken body. Our best intentions have been misconstrued. At every turn we have been called malicious. Like a bowl of soup we came in hot and were carried out cold.[42]

Of course, they were not finished. The next week came,

We Appear Again: The cold soup has been taken to the kitchen and warmed over. Our thousands of friends have beseeched us to continue DORIC, and we have heeded, yes, but with a distinct change of policy. From now on we slander no one, we cast aspersions upon nobody's character, we do not direct our efforts toward personalities. From now on DORIC will assume a new standard of gentility.[43]

Naturally, these promises were unfulfilled in the year's final columns.

The swan songs of Joe and Bob Fell as departing seniors, were both funny and touching:

"With the awaking of Spring, the profs followed suit and reports have been assigned in everything from sewage disposal to the Kingdom of God. Now for the old determination on the last home stretch...get a compass[sic] and determine the exact location of the chapel; find out what your major is; start another endowment; solve the Grinnell-in-China mystery; abate the smoke evil of the quadrangle; rid the campus of dandelions."[44]

And then, the following week, ran the honest to goodness last words of Joe Rosenfield and Bob Fell:

The Last Line; It's really harder to write than the first, especially when it's the grande finale. For four years we've watched the general, the watermelon feed, the chapel dates; for four years we've heard the M&St.L, [railway] the chapel bell, the lecture room talks. We'll miss Doctor Stoops, the college truck ribroast and Johnson's sarcastic grin. We've made real friends and some damn fine enemies. More dirty socks have been directed our way than a laundry ever thought of receiving and we still enjoy the fray and pray for more of it.[45]

As time consuming and important as DORIC was to Joe the student, he most often mentioned the *Malteaser* when asked later in life to comment on his activities as a Grinnell student. His contributions to this college humor magazine with a wide circulation beyond campus was clearly his proudest accomplishment. Though he served as Business Manager for his last three years, after joining the business staff as a freshman, Joe certainly contributed to the humor. His work on DORIC leads to this conclusion, which is verified by a notice in the October 8, 1924 issue of the *S&B* encouraging freshmen to pick up a copy of the *Malteaser* to enjoy "the combined wit of Fell and Rosenfield [who have] succeeded in making the *Malteaser* run true to form, a laugh from Kivah to Kivah."

The *Malteaser* was the 1919 creation of the Grinnell chapter of the journalistic fraternity, Sigma Delta Chi. By the time Joe joined the staff in 1921, the *Malteaser* (a play on words for the Maltese Cross, the Grinnell athletic logo) had matured, settling into six issues per year. In the fall of 1923, it was recognized in a New York theatre program, and it had the best sale of any college or university publication in the state of Iowa, with good sales in surrounding states as well. The New York periodical *The American Student* congratulated the *Malteaser* as a "corking publication."[46] Each issue featured book reviews, called "Cabbages and King" as well as jokes, humorous vignettes, and cartoons. Issues bore snappy titles: "Crime and Scandal Number"; "Raspberry Number"; "Travesty Annual"; "Midwest Number"; "Fireside Number"; "Voodvill Number"; "Valentine Number"; "Wrong Number"; "Jesse James Number"; "Back Again Number"; and "Greenwich Village Number." The advertisements, Joe's bailiwick, were numerous and slick, with General Electric and Arrow Shirts frequently on full color pages. Joe was able to solicit his family department store, Frankel's, but never for a full page or even half page like those purchased by their other store, Harris/Emery. There were never fewer than three and often up to five pages of ads in each issue.

Each spring, the "Malteaser Follies" were sponsored by the magazine. The skit by Joe and Bob Fell in their senior year received a grudging review from James Work in the May 23, 1925 *S&B*. After mentioning the packed house in A.R.H. Auditorium and the "atrocious lighting," Work praises the musical numbers while criticizing the skits on both inherent merit and execution. He then launched into

"Skeletons of Yesterday," Joe's and Fell's skit:

> *"Skeletons of Yesterday" by Fell and Rosenfield, a sketch of ribald horse play at the expense of the faculty, which had somehow managed to pass the Board of Censors, scored a distinct hit with the audience. In common with two other original skits, it reflected the attitude of the smart child who "shows off" his acquired profanity, sophistication, and voice before company secure in the knowledge that mother cannot spank."*

The *Malteaser* book reviews were serious, as was the *Malteaser* Class Fund sponsored by the Class of 1925. Since Joe was treasurer of the class and a key *Malteaser* staff member, I suspect he played an important role in this initiative. It is the kind of initiative he sponsored throughout his adult life. According to the *S&B*, May 2, 1925, the class had established a loan fund for students. The class was willing to raise $12,000, with every member to pledge $100. D.W. Norris of Marshalltown—father of John Norris, who was a member of the class and later fellow Trustee and Iowa Business Hall of Fame inductee with Joe—pledged to add $10,000 and the money would form an endowment, with the income to be lent to students. The Loan Committee would be composed of the College Treasurer Louis Phelps, the Dean of Women, and Dean of Men, together with a male student and a female student. The conditions were that the receiving student must have completed one year, plan to graduate, have financial need, and have a good record and character. With this initiative, Joe Rosenfield had certainly begun to serve his College's future.

If we assume that one of the principal reasons for Joe's love of Grinnell was the College's lack of anti-Semitism, one aspect of the *Malteaser* is troubling. In 1922–23, Joe's sophomore year and his first as Business Manager, the publication featured two anti-Semitic cartoons. One was a cartoon where one man addresses another: "I hear that the Jewish golf players don't call 'Fore' before a shot any more." "Why not?" asks the other man. "They've made it '3.98'," responds the first. Across the page from that cartoon is a one-line joke: "Jewish national flower: the mint."

There was clearly some anti-Semitism at Grinnell, and Joe was just as clearly willing to tolerate it. He probably did not have the editorial input as a sophomore that he acquired in his junior and senior years, but, still, the presence of this cartoon and joke in a publication that had his name on the masthead is as troubling to us as it must have been to him.

Despite this incident, the *Malteaser* was Joe's pride and joy as a student and that feeling lingered throughout his life.

He was also proud of having rescued the *Cyclone* (college annual) from oblivion in 1924, late in his junior year. The juniors produced the *Cyclone*, which was confusingly titled by their graduation year: that is, the 1925 *Cyclone* records the 1923–1924 academic year. Contrasting the spoof biography of J. Frankel Rosenfield in the 1923–1924 *Malteaser* is the straightforeword biography of Joseph F. Rosenfield in the 1925 *Cyclone*. Along with a photo, Joe, the Business Manager (and later editor), is described as being from Des Moines, a Political Science major with a History minor, a member of Chrestomathia, Business Manager of the *Malteaser* as a sophomore and junior, on the staff of the *Scarlet and Black*, and Sigma Delta Chi secretary his junior year. His humor is recognized with the closing "inventor of the 'Line-a-Day.'" The latter is the best evidence we have for Joe's reputation for quick wit, which so many enjoyed in later years.

Unique among the *Cyclones* for these years is 1925's section on the history of *Cyclones*. The *Cyclone* began in 1889 and was continuous from that time, though for three years after 1895 it was variously known as *Hornets*, *Bluebook*, and *The Imp*.

I have already told the story of Joe's last minute promotion to Editor and his rescue of the 1925 *Cyclone*. This was one of the few specific incidents of his undergraduate years that Joe later talked about; it left an indelible imprint on his memory, as well it should. His rescue of the *Cyclone* has to be one of his most enduring contributions to his generation of students and to the records of the College.

Ever the humorist, Joe added an addendum to the joke and cartoon section that closed each issue of the *Cyclone* in the 1920s. Typical of Joe's interest in business, he included a faux balance sheet with staff perks astronomical and production costs miniscule:

FINANCIAL STATEMENT 1925 CYCLONE LIABILITIES
Set of mahogany office furniture. . . $450.00
Butlers, office boys and stenographers . . . $1,122.00
Hush money for janitors . . . $3.75

Valet for Editor-in-Chief . . . $17.50
Private secretary for Business Manager . . . $25.50
Public secretary for Editor-in-Chief . . . $24.50
"Refreshments" for Art Editor . . . $798.25
Stationary for staff members . . . $264.00
Manicures . . . $38.00
Bail for staff men after Drake game . . . $200.00
Tobacco, cigars, and cigarettes . . . $24.00
Taxicabs . . . $.05
Life and Accident Policy for Humor Editor . . . $375.00
Staff banquets and parties . . . $2,645.12
Car fare for staff on day of issue . . . $9,237.71
Endowment fund and pensions . . . $16,522.89
Engraving for Cyclone . . . $26.50
Printing of Cyclone . . . $13.75
Binding of Cyclone . . . $9.18
Surplus undivided salaries and profits . . . ????.??
ASSETS
Received for printing photos . . . $8,329.81
Received for not printing photos . . . $19,257.26
Subscriptions . . . $26.50
Advertising . . . $13.75
Spare time work for staff . . . $273.37

Joe did reform, since he did not approve of such accounting during his fifty-nine-year Trusteeship of Grinnell College.

Generally, Joe's wit was incisive as well as sardonic, but as he recounted in a compendium of alumni memories of their undergraduate days in a 1990s college publication, "What We Remember," Joe revealed that his humor could, on occasion, be blunt and disruptive:

"I remember once we sneaked into the chapel. We knew that the president of the College was going to conduct chapel the next morning, and he was pretty deaf . . . So, we set an alarm clock for 10 minutes after 10. The next morning in chapel the alarm clock went off. The president didn't hear it. He kept on talking and talking. My roommate and I were in chapel that day. The dean of men called us in and said, 'You were the guys, probably that did that.' And I said, 'Why are you accusing us?' He said, 'Because you were in chapel today.'"

The 1926 *Cyclone*, published in Joe's senior year, had a farewell to the Class of 1925: "What will you do without us? How the ranks of the Drama Club will be depleted! To say nothing of the Glee Club and orchestra, football, track and basketball. We've a Rhodes Scholar and an Olympic Champion to our credit. We've started a lot of things and finished them creditably. What will you do without us? We're leaving it to you."

The May 27, 1925 issue of the *S&B* described the class of 1925 as having 136 graduates, claiming it was the largest west of the Ohio, with students from North Dakota, Nebraska, Montana, Minnesota, Illinois, Wyoming, California, Pennsylvania, Missouri, Ohio, South Dakota, and, of course, Iowa. This was a pretty good spread for a small Midwestern College. Commencement was to be held on June 9th, with Samuel Straus L.L.D as speaker.

A less sanguine note appeared in the *Malteaser*, featuring a hobo over the caption:

"MOST ANY MEMBER OF THE CLASS OF '25 ANY TIME AFTER JUNE 15." It contrasted with a S&B survey of Grinnell College women taken in the spring of 1923, "What sort of men do you wish for your husband?" The results reveal a lot about the youthful coed desires of the time. Eighteen preferred dark men, while only seven opted for light men. Tall men were preferred by a whopping total of thirty-three, with blue eyes winning fifteen votes and brown sixteen. Nine women preferred wealth, while twenty-one said it was not necessary. Twenty-one wanted a college-educated husband and twenty insisted on a sense of humor. Eighteen wanted a home lover and fifteen needed a good talker who could dance. Athletic inclination was necessary for fifteen, and it was important for twenty of the coeds to have an experienced lover. Only fourteen thought it was essential he be a man of his word, but twenty-two desired an ambitious and energetic husband. Interestingly, only six women thought it was important to have a striking personality, but twenty-one desired a cave man. Nineteen thought that being jealous of his wife was important for a husband, but only nine elevated the

> *trait of being kind and thoughtful. Six wanted a lover of children; eight saw being optimistic as essential. Sixteen were for chivalry, but only six thought it was essential to be neat. Being a sweetheart husband garnered twenty-four votes, but only three women thought good-nature essential. Near the bottom were being well built (three), intellectual (five), faithful (10), generous (six), and having high ideals (three). Finally, eight women wanted a smoker and fourteen thought non-smoking was important.[47]*

This, after all, was the age of the "flapper." In contrast, an *S&B* survey in May 1923, tallied "What do Grinnell Grads do?"

> *Fifteen percent enter University teaching and 10 percent do other educational work. Nine percent enter medicine or surgery, 9 percent are in banking while 7 percent are ministers. Journalism attracts 5 percent and 5 percent also pursue social and public service. Graduate study has 5 percent, and 4 percent are in manufacturing with 4 percent in agriculture. Finally, 3 percent are engineers.[48] Both of these snapshot surveys help us to understand the milieu in which Joe Rosenfield matured. Significantly, there is no category in either survey for "savior of a college."*

IMPORTANT COLLEGE ISSUES, 1921-1925

It is important to understanding Joe's love of the school and how Joe was formed at Grinnell to discuss some of the challenging issues the College faced during Joe Rosenfield's student days. They are significant because they suggest how Joe achieved the deep understanding of the College and its students, which he displayed during his long tenure as a Trustee. This was most notable during the agonizing student revolution of the '60s and '70s when Joe was a consistent voice of understanding for both what the College faced and for why the students behaved as they did. Joe's empathy with the students and the character of the Grinnell College community proved indispensable to his Trustee colleagues and to the College's administration and faculty. His education in college issues as an undergraduate contributed significantly to his later leadership. Each of the salient issues in Joe's student days had to do with the self-proclaimed democratic ethos of Grinnell, an ethos that has persisted to this day. Both *S&B* "editorials" and "letters to the editor" are replete with assertions of the democratic ethos of Grinnell and the way this ethos was undercut by secret fraternities, a vigilante, Ku-Klux-Klan-like organization, Literary Societies, and putative, ineffective student government.

A SECRET FRATERNITY

The absence of fraternities and sororities at Grinnell was important both to Joe's decision to attend and to his subsequent experience at the College. However, Grinnell was forced to confront the issue of fraternities in the spring of Joe's freshman year when the *S&B* exposed a secret fraternity that had existed on campus for many years. The opening shot appeared on April 19, 1922, when the editorial admitted many Grinnell men wanted fraternities because their friends at universities had them. However, opined the Editor, fraternities would "undercut Grinnell democracy" by establishing social hierarchies; the Editor claimed that Grinnell men were currently on equal footing to prove themselves. In addition, the editorial continued, personal jealousies would emerge.

One of the Grinnell community newspapers, *The Grinnell Register*, picked up the story, adding that the presence of fraternities affected the College's athletic teams, with votes for captaincy of football and basketball aligning along fraternity and non-fraternity lines. It had been rumored that fraternity football men went so far as to fail to block for a non-fraternity back.[49] On the 29th of April, the *S&B* claimed there were three sororities and one fraternity hiding on the Grinnell campus. The fraternity was thought to have a membership of seventeen or eighteen, ten of whom were members of Honor G (athletic lettermen). The *S&B* echoed the *Register*, maintaining one football back had no blockers and adding that the team "quit" against both Drake and Washington University. Fortunately, the

S&B added, the track and field athletes had refused to join the fraternity. An editorial in the same *S&B* said the secret fraternity had existed for twenty-three years and the only time Grinnell football had won more than it lost was in 1915, 1916, and 1917, when then coach McAlman "had waged a continuous war against the fraternity."

To supplement its coverage of the issue, the *S&B* ran articles about schools that did not have fraternities, such as Oberlin.[50] In the same issue, the fraternity was named: Delta Phi Rho. A satire on the fraternity was also published in the same issue of the *S&B*, the writer claiming to have infiltrated a secret fraternity meeting in the basement of a local business. A sign reading, "To Hell with the Public. Alexander Hamilton." hung over the entrance and a single, 15-watt bulb "casts its flickering, lurid glow upon the eighteen noble Greeks therein assembled, draped over and upon sugar sacks, cracker boxes, flour barrels and other sumptuous Pan-Hellenic furniture." Mounted on a crate of pork and beans, the Keeper of the Cellar Key addresses the brethren, saying these are parlous times and Grinnell democracy is under threat. The glory and greatness of the College depends on us, he says. The brethren "grunt hoarsely in agreement." The Lord Guardian of the Spirit "rises from his divan of potato sacks, saying 'This has went far enough.'" The brothers chant the 1st, 2nd, and 4th verses of the latest Greek epic. They plot how to restore the old Grinnell spirit for a "bigger, better, more democratic Grinnell." They bewail the loss of student fraternal spirit "wondering why, perhaps, why the student body didn't go wild over the basketball team, or why it should care if a couple of good backfield men were 'frozen out' last fall."

In contrast, a letter to the editor in the same issue pointed out:
> *Grinnell today is proud that she is a democratic school. Our ideal is that everyone is on a par with everyone else. But when any group of men and women band together and have to do it secretly, they cannot but work against the best interests of the college. It is not in accord with the Grinnell of yesterday, the Grinnell of today and what we earnestly hope the Grinnell of tomorrow will be.[51]*

In the previous April, an editorial had aptly pointed out that the college dormitory system had been designed thoughtfully for small groups to live together closely, obviating the need for fraternities and sororities. President Main's vision of Oxbridge-style small dorms established small-group living that has persisted today as a foundation against the threat of fraternities and sororities.[52]

The *S&B* of April 13th indicated the secret fraternity had temporarily disbanded, but it still met with the support of town men, alumni, and friends whom the *S&B* identified as the nucleus "of the trouble." The persistence of this "trouble" led to a dramatic *S&B* attack on the administration. An editorial published on May 17 challenged President Main and the administration to do something about the secret fraternity, hinting that the frat men might have the support of the administration. The Editor claimed the public was aware of the fraternity, and if the administration did not act, it would be seen as "weak," and such an assessment would be correct. Furthermore, if nothing were done, Grinnell would be in danger of losing students over the issue. The *S&B* had been accused of bringing "bad advertisement" to the College and, "Yes," replied the Editor, the College fully deserved it. In fact, the May 24th *S&B* carried a letter to the editor, commenting that "the Midwest smiles" when Grinnell claims to have no fraternities.

The 1923 *Cyclone* (published by the Class of 1923 in the spring of 1922) carried an epitaph to the secret fraternity and sororities. "We dedicate this page to the unpleasant memory of Delta Phi Rho and the three Greek Letter Sororities at the Quadrangle. 'May they die so completely and may they be so extinct that they may never again come to life upon the campus of Grinnell College. Peace to their ashes.'"[53]

There, the issue rested for 1921–1922. One is keen to see if it lingered into the next academic year and the answer is "no," so far as the *S&B* was concerned. The only hint is President Main's annual opening Convocation talk: "Park Your Grouch Outside." The title suggests that negativism is destructive both to society and personal character. The *S&B*'s early fall editorials focused on pep rallies and support of the football team. It seems likely that President Main took the *S&B* editorial staff to task late in the spring or during the summer, chastising their negativism; the lack of coverage suggests they had listened.

THE ORACLE

Having abandoned the secret fraternity issue, the focus of the spring 1923 *S&B* was the "Oracle," yet another threat to Grinnell democracy. The "Oracle" was accused of being a Ku-Klux-Klan-like secret society that handed out punishments for sundry offences "in the dark of the night." The Ku-Klux-Klan accusation was a dramatic one, as the '20s were the apogee of the Klan.[54] Once again, as with the secret fraternity, it seems some of the prominent athletes were members. Richard Steiner, '24, the son of prominent faculty member, Edward Steiner, sent a letter to the editor on February 7, 1923 saying he had been before the Oracle and the experience was not a "square deal." Its methods were inconsistent and arbitrary; altogether a bad experience. He added that there is contempt for this court at Grinnell. In fact, the editorial in the same issue of the *S&B* claimed "the Oracle is no more" and, as stated in the Homecoming edition of the *S&B*, that was true.[55]

LITERARY SOCIETIES

The exposé of the secret fraternity in Joe's freshman year and a concerted attack on Literary Societies in his senior year were bookends of the effort to make Grinnell as democratic as contemporary students thought it should be. The attack on the Literary Societies was the work of the relentless Hilda Mauch '25, who raised the issue in the fall of 1924 in an editorial attacking them as "anything but literary, with only a "thimblefull" of social training. She charged them with being "antiquated, rusty, outgrown . . . undemocratic anachronisms" whose "day has come and gone."[56] She was back at it in the next issue of the *S&B*, focusing on the women's societies, predicting that the cottages would fill the void if the societies were to disappear. She added that the Literary Societies meant more to those who were left out than to those who were included. Finally, if Grinnell is supposed to be a democratic school, she asked, how does this depiction align with Literary Societies?[57] In the very next issue, Hilda counsels "striking while the iron is hot" to eliminate the societies, since, she claims, they exist only for themselves and "people know that."[58]

The *Malteaser*, true to form, satirized the *S&B* campaign against Women's Literary Societies in its fall 1924 issue;

> *"The management of the* Malteaser *feels that it is its duty to discuss college problems in its editorial pages, so we now introduce a new subject, one which we are sure has never been discussed; that of the Literary Society. We believe that the Society has too long been a power on campus, and that the time has come to dethrone the dangerous monster. No one can doubt for an instant that the Literary Society is not only in danger of wrecking the entire morale of college life, but also that it may sweep further and scourge the entire country."*[59]

The relentless drumbeat continued in the November *S&B* when the editorial labeled Literary Societies "ghosts of the past."[60] The *S&B* campaign met with success as the banner headline in the November 5th *S&B* proclaimed: "WOMEN'S SOCIETIES VOTED OUT FOR INDEFINITE PERIOD." The story indicates the women would reorganize into a general club similar to city women's clubs. On November 8, the *S&B* announced that the four women's societies had voted to disband, earning the paper's congratulations. The Homecoming edition of the *S&B* told returning alums about a series of major changes on campus, including the suspension of the Women's Literary Societies, reorganization of the Student Court, introduction of Sunday dates, and the demise of the vigilante group, "Oracle."[61]

A new women's organization called the Tanager Guild replaced the Literary Societies. It was divided into sections according to interest: drama, music, journalism, and parliamentary law. The Tanager Players were to be directed by Hallie Flanagan, who later became a major leader of FDR's New Deal.[62]

It seems obvious that Hilda Mauch had hit a responsive chord, and hit it she did in edition after edition of *S&B*, achieving dramatic and rapid results that changed the social life of Grinnell women. She left the men alone for the time being, though she returned to the attack in February 1925, with an editorial wondering how long the Men's Literary Societies could last.[63] They proved more resilient, however, and nothing more was heard of the issue, especially as Hilda's editorial tenure ended in April, when she confessed that, as a woman, she had concentrated on Quadrangle matters. She added that women deserved the focus of the newspaper for a change but offered one last dig, criticizing the women for complaining but not taking positive action.[64] The demise of the Women's Literary Societies was a major event in the history of the College and it was largely achieved by one person, Hilda Mauch.

STUDENT GOVERNMENT

Today, Grinnell College prides itself on the extent of student self-government. Somewhat unexpectedly, the College of the early 1920s also laid similar claims to active student self-governance. Of course, the irrepressible Hilda Mauch had her own take in an editorial calling for students to test the self-government concept by a referendum sponsored by the Student Council (it did not happen). She charged that there was student self-government only when it agreed with the powers that be—that is, the administration and the faculty.[65]

Hilda Mauch notwithstanding, there is evidence of successful student initiatives to introduce cars for seniors after Spring Break and to allow Sunday night dating also after Spring Break, though it must be said that each initiative required faculty approval. Despite the need for faculty acquiescence, these were definitely student initiatives.[66] During Joe's senior year, there was also a lot of discussion of the organization of men's and women's government as well as the all-campus Student Council. An editorial late in the previous year suggested the Men's Senate was more responsive to its constituency than the women's governing body, the League Board. The editorial suggested women should be allowed to petition the League Board for desired actions.[67] This was Hilda Mauch urging reform in women's self-governance; a subsequent editorial pointed out that the League Board had never had legislative powers.[68] However, a news story in the same issue reported on a conference of the Midwest Section of the Women's Self-Government Association, where it was learned that Grinnell women had more power than women in most other colleges, particularly noting that few self-governing bodies dealt with cases of discipline without faculty intervention as was allowed with the League Board at Grinnell.

On the men's side of campus, power was divided between the elected Men's Senate and an elected Men's Court, which had the major responsibility to enforce college rules. Though the two bodies considered reforms that would lead to more student powers, nothing transpired. During these deliberations, Senior Joe Rosenfield was quoted in an *S&B* student poll regarding the desirability of increased student power: "I am not in favor of student government because I do not believe that any group of students, elected at large, is qualified to pass judgment on serious student misdemeanors. Trained educators should handle problems of misconduct."[69] Joe was thinking about student self-governance issues in the context of how much democracy is optimal in a college and, at that time, he opted for less student and more institutional control. The continuing effort to balance a democratic ideal with the realities of collegiate life was an enduring theme of Joe's college years, and those issues would continue to engage him during his fifty-nine years of Trustee service.

CONCLUSION

In the final issue of Joe's senior year, a *S&B* editorial emphasized the high scholastic standards of the College that had yielded Iowa's next Rhodes Scholar, the sixth in the College's history. It emphasized Grinnell's high standing, citing that Grinnell was one of only twelve schools to receive a $50,000 grant for the fine arts from the Carnegie Foundation. The College had produced an Olympic Champion and the debaters had argued creditably against Oxford. World War I had caused a "slump in campus tone," which had recently recovered fully. Almost every student carried a "sense of individual responsibility," and a spirit of trying new things permeated the campus with students seeking new and better ways of doing things even to the point of breaking with tradition.

The editorial speculates that few graduating seniors anywhere would leave feeling so positively about their College.

That final statement sums up Joe Rosenfield's feelings as he left Grinnell, and those feelings never left him. He loved his College with a passion seldom equaled and with a dedication unparalleled. Joe's love for Grinnell was almost "pathological," said his "Godson," Fred Little. Warren Buffett described Joe's love for Grinnell as "irrational,"[70] adding that all love affairs are irrational. This love, together with Joe's exceptional abilities, are what made him a Trustee who, in my judgment, did more for his College than any Trustee in the United States.

This weighty judgment would have been leavened by Joe's sense of humor were he to have had the opportunity for the last word. He would have lightened it with something like what he told the Younkers' Bettie Johnson, who wrote his profile in the *Younker Reporter* August 1951 issue a few years after he had joined Younkers full time. In reference to his college experience, he said, "[I] had a prodigious appetite and stopped nightly at Grinnell's Candyland for two chocolate sodas. [I] seemed to be habitually broke and on one occasion telegraphed [my father] to the effect that the wolf was staring me in the face. 'Please wire funds' [I said] to which [he] replied 'and not a pleasant sight for either of you,' and sent no funds." Joe added, "[My] scholastic record at Grinnell was only average." Joe never took himself as seriously nor inclined to regard himself as highly as did those of us who knew him.

PART TWO
JOE ROSENFIELD'S FAMILY

THE FRANKEL LEGACY

It may seem odd to title a section on Joe Rosenfield's family "The Frankel Legacy," but the title is apt. The primary family influence on Joe was from his mother, Rose Frankel Rosenfield. When asked in a 1998 interview about the influence of the women in his life, Joe began with his mother, Rose:

> *"Oh, God, yes. Yes, indeed! . . . Well, I guess we start with my mother who was like, I like to think of her as the original suffragette. And she just ruled the roost and called all the shots. And she was very civic minded and she'd get in her car and have a driver drive her downtown and she'd pick up money from businesses downtown . . . which took some courage 50, 60 years ago.*
>
> *And she was just—she fought like the devil for women's suffrage. Just fought—I suppose some hated her for it. So she was a big influence."*[1]

Joe's memory was echoed by his friend, Kay Bucksbaum, whose mother was a close friend of Rose Rosenfield. She described her "as a force to be reckoned with."[2]

Joe grew up on 37th Street, south of Grand Avenue in Des Moines. He was surrounded by Frankels: his grandmother, Babette Sheuerman Frankel, and his aunt, Allie Frankel, lived next door; Uncle Nate Frankel lived across the street; Uncle Henry Frankel lived two blocks away on Tonawanda Drive; and Uncle Anselm Frankel was four blocks away on 41st and Grand.[3] Joe was the lawyer for the Frankel family business, Younkers, starting in 1928; he then joined the Younkers Board in 1929, moving to full-time employment at Younkers from 1947 to 1969. He then chaired the Board from 1948–1968. Joe was awash in Frankels.

Rose Frankel, of Des Moines, and Meyer Rosenfield, of Rock Island, Illinois, were married in 1900, and Meyer moved to Des Moines to enter the Frankel retail business. Meyer and Rose had three children: Ruth (1902), Joseph (1904), and Louise (1908). Though early-twentieth-century convention prevented Rose from keeping her maiden name, she preserved it by inserting "Frankel" as the middle names of each of her offspring. It is with the third-born of these children, Louise, that we begin the story of the family of Rose and Meyer Rosenfield. We begin with Louise because in 1990 she wrote an autobiography: *Journey to Autonomy*.[4] The title reveals the theme of her memoir as she struggled to escape the overpowering presence and later, memory, of her mother, Rose.

Louise began her memoir by recalling all she could remember about her mother. Rose Frankel Rosenfield was one of the most forceful and accomplished women of her generation in Des Moines or any other American city, for that matter. Tall and dignified, as Joe said, "she ruled the roost" in the household and in Des Moines civic life. She came from wealth. The Rosenfield home was served by a cook, a cleaner, a gardener, and a chauffeur. This domestic help gave Rose the time and energy for an active civic life. She created Des Moines' first Settlement House; she traveled to Chicago to meet with Jane Addams to ask her to recommend a leader for the new Des Moines house. Addams recommended Flora Dunlap, who took the job and became Rose's best friend while she led the successful Roadside Settlement House beginning in 1905. Rose was on the Board of the Roadside Settlement House until 1940.[5]

During World War I, Rose headed the Women's Division of the War Bond drive and later headed the Women's Division of the Community Chest (women did most of the collecting). She was a charter member and the only woman on the Des Moines Planning and Zoning Commission, serving from 1926–1928. She became disillusioned when she was left staring at the meeting room walls while the chair, the famous political cartoonist Ding Darling, assembled only the male members for their scheduled meeting at a substitute location, the Des Moines club, which was enhanced by a fine dinner. Furious, Rose soon resigned. In 1931, Rose became a charter member and the first woman on the Des Moines Park Board. She served until 1933 and then again from 1937–1943 when she resigned in protest over the way Mayor McVicar handled a strike of park workers. Rose was a keen gardener, founding the Des Moines Garden Club, and, when it grew too large, she created the Founder's Garden Club. She was the inspiration for the development of Des Moines' Lilac Arboretum. Rose founded the first Parent-Teacher Association in Des Moines at old West High School. She was also a board member of the Jewish Settlement House, which later became the Jewish Community Center.

Joe emphasized Rose's devotion to the women's suffrage cause. In 1916, she helped fund an unsuccessful Iowa suffragette amendment. Her interest in public affairs propelled her to endow a lectureship in International Relations at Grinnell College in 1934 to honor her late husband, Meyer. That lectureship has survived to this day, enhanced by Joe's endowment of the Rosenfield Program in 1979. This program, which has become a Grinnell College institution, embodies Rose's interest in public affairs and international relations.

Joe probably learned his liberalism from Rose, both through her example as well as reading the books and periodicals that covered her shelves and tables. In addition to sets of classics, such as Jane Austen, Charles Dickens, William Shakespeare, and John Ruskin, the parlor tables were covered with subscriptions to liberal periodicals: *Harpers*, *Atlantic*, *The New Republic*, *The Nation*, *Foreign Affairs*, and the weekly *Manchester Guardian*. Rose's interest in the arts was lifelong; in 1956, toward the end of her life, she gave $25,000 to the Des Moines Art Center for the purchase of contemporary art.[6]

She was born in Oskaloosa, Iowa in 1873 and died in her Des Moines home of a stroke in September 1960. She was educated in the Oskaloosa public schools and attended the Loring School in Chicago for two years after her father denied her ambition to attend Wellesley College in Massachusetts.

The crux of *Journey to Autonomy* is Louise's struggle to gain independence from her mother: "People who know me today as a self-assured and assertive person are incredulous when I tell them that for a good portion of my life I was shy, insecure and lacked self-esteem . . . looming large in that picture was a very strong but unloving mother." She goes on: "Mother tried to do the right thing for her three children by seeing to it that we were educated, well dressed and well mannered, but she unwittingly cowed us in the process . . . as far as I can recall, neither my sister, Ruth, my brother, Joe, or I ever challenged mother directly." When Louise did challenge her many years later, Rose admitted that Louise was unplanned and, as Louise suspected, unwanted. Louise's birth was a difficult one, and Rose had trouble nursing her. Louise added that "we were strictly a 'hands off' family loath to reveal personal feelings to one another."[7] This family legacy reveals something about why, in Fred Little's words, Joe was "almost pathologically private."[8]

Louise's description of her relationship with Rose adds, "Praise for her children was not in Mother's nature and I grew up with a feeling of unworthiness . . . My brother was spared: he could do no wrong."[9] Further elevating Joe from his sisters was his father's promise to pay Joe for refraining from smoking until age 25; his father offered only punishments to the girls.[10]

Those of us who knew both Joe and Louise often marveled at their differences. While both were extraordinarily strong and accomplished, Louise was an intellectual, while Joe, though whip smart, had little interest in abstract ideas. Louise was a writer, but I cannot imagine Joe ever wanting to write a book, much less one as introspective and revealing as Louise's autobiography. Where Joe was defined in part by his sense of humor, as "Line-a-day Rosenfield," Louise seemed dour, with little sense of humor. Joe could be mellow where Louise was a bundle of rough edges. They agreed in their civic-mindedness and burning commitment to make the world a better place, but Joe's approach was less overtly forceful.

Louise's autobiography reveals some of the reasons for these differences beyond simple personality traits. Joe was significantly more nurtured and appreciated by their parents than was Louise, which made him much more self-confident. This differing treatment extended even to the futures that Rose and, to a degree, Meyer, planned for their children. Joe was destined for business, particularly the family business, whereas:

> *"Ruth and I [Louise] became surrogates to fulfill Mother's dreams regardless of how unsuited these dreams might be to our interests and abilities. (Joe of Course was destined for the business world). Ruth, who was to have a career in politics was sent to Vassar when she would rather have gone to school in Iowa. After finishing Vassar she was sent to Columbia University in New York City for post-graduate work in political science. Ruth dropped out of Columbia before completing her first semester . . . Meanwhile, when I was very young, Mother registered me at both Wellesley and Vassar and selected me to pursue a career in the art world despite the fact that I showed no ability or natural interest in that direction."*

Louise did in fact attend Wellesley for a year in the midst of finishing a Grinnell degree, and she earned a Masters in Art History from Harvard/Radcliffe. In later years, she worked at the Des Moines Art Center, yet she showed little interest or talent in the many studio art classes in which Rose enrolled her in the early years.

When Louise finally shook off the penumbra of her mother, she grew to appreciate Rose's extraordinary strength and accomplishment. However, the enduring specter of Rose Frankel Rosenfield is best expressed in these words: "Mother's effect on people she did not care for was amply described by her cousin, Selma Sheurerman Lyons . . . who reported that a visit to Rose Rosenfield sent chills up and down her spine." Rose was indeed, in Louise's words, a "gray eminence."[12]

Meyer Rosenfield did not come close to matching Rose's powerful influence on the family. He focused almost entirely on business, joining the Frankel retail company, Harris-Emery, when he married Rose. After Harris-Emery merged with Younkers in 1927, he became a vice president of Younkers and a member of the Board of Directors. Meyer died of cancer in 1929, the year after Joe graduated from law school at the University of Iowa, and Joe immediately was elected to the Younkers Board as Meyer's replacement. Rose forced Louise to leave Wellesley and return home during Meyer's illness. Having transferred to Wellesley after her sophomore year at Grinnell, she returned to finish at Grinnell because it was closer to her family. Louise described Meyer as a "quiet, shy person, rather short in stature, with thinning gray hair and rimless glasses . . . Unlike most of his colleagues who had lunch together at the Des Moines Club, he came home for lunch every day."[13] Louise further distinguished Meyer's personality from Rose's, saying he refused to go to evening social events or entertain guests for dinner. His only evening recreation "was to meet with my uncles several evenings a week at Grandmother's house, where they would discuss business."[14] She wrote, "My brother, Joe, told me only recently that Mother once confided to him how desperate she was during her early married years because of Father's lack of sociability. Father was primarily directed to business and let Mother run the show at home."[15] Also, Meyer did not like to travel, but Rose managed to organize two family trips to Europe following Ruth's and Joe's college graduations (1922 and 1925) and an Alaska trip in 1924.

Louise's final assessment of Meyer underlined Joe's "favored" status. She writes that though Meyer read *Alice in Wonderland* to her when she was little, as the children grew older, Meyer "paid very little attention to Ruth and me, but he had a close relationship with my brother."[16] This close relationship was also manifest during the two family trips to Europe where Joe and Meyer tended to go one way while the women went another. It is a pity Joe had so little to say about his parents. We must therefore rely primarily on Louise to reconstruct what must have been a significant relationship with his father. We know from Meyer's response to Joe's plea for money, noted in the previous chapter, that Joe must have received some of his sense of humor from his father. It is obvious this sense of humor did not originate with his mother, as Louise gave no hint that Rose had a lighter side.

The Rosenfield and Frankel grandparents lived remarkable lives, particularly the Frankels, and it was again Louise who collected and told their stories. This effort highlights another profound difference between Joe and Louise: Joe — in the experience of those I have interviewed and in my own experience as well — spoke little if at all about any aspect of his family unless directly prompted, and even then his response was sparse. Louise, on the other hand, obsessed over her mother while ferreting out stories about her grandparents, revealing in the process much about the strengths of mid-nineteenth-century German immigrants as they met the challenges of succeeding in a strange land.

Joe and Louise did not know either of their Rosenfield grandparents. According to Jewish custom, Joe could not have been named Joseph had his paternal grandfather, Joseph Rosenfield, been alive at Joe's birth. Both Rosenfield grandparents, Joseph and Henrietta May, emigrated from Germany in the 1850s. Before his emigration, Joseph served two enlistments in the military, unlike many who emigrated to escape military service. In fact, as Joe told Louise, he had learned from Meyer that his grandfather liked military service so much that he re-enlisted.[17] Joseph Rosenfield immigrated to Rock Island, Illinois, where he prospered, establishing a leather business to which he added a bank. It was not at all unusual in that period to add a bank to a retail business, often merely a small section of the store.

Joseph's brother and sister also settled in Rock Island, and Joseph and his brother married May sisters. Meyer was the third of Joseph's and Henrietta's ten children.

Since I am indebted to Louise for this story of the grandparents, a much larger attention to the Frankels in comparison with the Rosenfield grandparents signifies their far greater presence and influence in the lives of the Meyer and Rose Frankel Rosenfield family, as Louise, Joe, and Ruth grew up surrounded by Frankels.[18]

The archives of the Des Moines Jewish Federation contain extensive material on the Frankel family, especially the grandparents, Isaiah and Babette — much of which was collected and written by Louise. Isaiah Frankel was born at Ichenhausen, Bavaria, on October 14, 1832. At age 14, he was apprenticed to a cigar maker and later to a merchant for two years before emigrating at age 21 (the age of maturity) to the United States in 1853. He first settled in Washington, Indiana before moving west to Macon County, Missouri. In 1857, he took out naturalization papers.[19] In 1861, he made his next and final move to Oskaloosa, Iowa, where he peddled and opened a small clothing store.

In January 1864, Isaiah married Babette Sheurerman, whom he had met in Chicago. Their wedding was in Davenport, Iowa with a Protestant minister officiating because there was no Rabbi in the area. Isaiah and Babette had six children: Anselm (Dec. 1864), Manassa (1866), Nathan (1868), Henrietta (1870), Rose (1873), and Henry (1881). All of the children were born and raised in Oskaloosa, though the youngest, Henry, spent some of his high school years in Des Moines.

Isaiah entered into a twenty-eight-year business partnership with Emanuelle Bach and the Frankel store grew to be the largest in Oskaloosa. In 1873, they started the first bank in Oskaloosa. In 1888, Isaiah bought out Bach and took his sons into business with him. They built a new store on the town square in 1889, where the facade still bears the Frankel name. Of the business relationship between Isaiah and his sons, Louise wrote, "My brother, Joe, recalls that Isaiah required his sons to be at the store every day including Sundays and evenings. At one point, his son, Manassa, rebelled and went across the street to work with a competitor. When Manassa reported for work the next day, his boss said, 'Your father has just fired you.'"[20] In 1894, the Frankels opened a branch store in the rapidly developing capital city, Des Moines, with Manassa as the manager. Two years later, in 1896, Isaiah was paralyzed by a stroke. He never recovered and died in 1897. He sold out to his sons after his stroke and they rapidly moved their business and families to Des Moines. They acquired a Des Moines business competitor, Harris-Emery, in 1901, and then merged with an even bigger competitor, Younkers, in 1927, with the Frankels acquiring a 50 percent ownership of the merged company. The business retained the Younker name.

Beginning as a poor villager in nineteenth-century Bavaria and going on to great success and considerable wealth, Isaiah's story is an immigration classic. He became not only a successful businessman, with the aid of opportunities afforded by mid-nineteenth-century America, but was also politically successful. A staunch Democrat from 1868 to 1887, he served four terms on the Oskaloosa City Council. His obituary portrayed him as public spirited and philanthropic, "generous to a fault"; though possessed of a considerable fortune, it added, he was not a speculator. He had also reached into Des Moines as one of the founding members of Temple B'nai Jeshurun. Despite this, his funeral services were conducted by a Protestant minister, but burial at Woodland Cemetery in Des Moines was conducted by a Jewish Rabbi.[21]

Isaiah's wife, Babette, provides an equally compelling story. Babette was the lone grandparent known to Louise, Joe, and Ruth, as she lived next door to the Rosenfields until her death in February 1929, the year after Joe graduated from law school. What Louise wrote and Joe said about Babette was based mostly on personal experience; also, at Louise's urging, Babette wrote an interesting account of her early life.[22] Babette was born on October 18, 1840 in the village of Binau on the Neckar River near Heidelberg in Baden-Wurtemberg. Her mother, Sarah Lipschutz, had been born in 1797 and her father, Manassa Sheurerman, in 1792. Manassa died in 1857, triggering the family's emigration to the United States. Babette's mother, Sarah, died in 1879, well after she and the children had settled in Iowa.

As a child, Babette was not interested in school; she preferred the outdoor life. She loved to turn hay in the fields with the local peasants, often without her parents' permission. She left school at age 10 and went to work with her sisters, Rose, age 12, and Sophie, 8, in a family millinery business. She had earned money early on ironing shirts for her neighbors, standing on a stool to reach her work. Her millinery job was to deliver the caps made for neighbors, some of whom lived miles from Binau. She would also collect caps and other items for the family laundering operation. On one of her deliveries, she had to jump from floe to floe on the Neckar River late on a spring afternoon after crossing the same river in solid ice early that morning. She had to build up her courage when she walked through dark and threatening woods. She carried all of her wares in a basket on her head, and sometimes her rounds took up to eight hours.

In 1847, Babette's older brother, Abraham, emigrated to the US, settling in Muscatine, Iowa. Three years later, her older sister, Rose, joined him in Muscatine, where she worked in a millinery store. In 1857, when their father, Manassa, died, the rest of the family emigrated to Muscatine. Abraham sent Sarah, Babette (who was 17 at the time), her younger sister Sophie, and brother Leopold just enough money to book passage on a sailing ship. Babette was one of only three passengers who did not get seasick. Sarah and Sophie were laid low, scarcely leaving their beds the entire trip. Using Babette's story, Louise wrote: "By the end of the journey, their supply of food became very scanty. Babette did all the cooking for the family over an open fire in a kind of fireplace in which kettles hung on hooks. She wrote that she often was burned probably from swinging cables."[23]

On arrival in Muscatine, the family settled with Abraham and Rose. By this time, Rose was forewoman of the millinery shop and Babette and Sophie went to work for her while their mother, Sarah, kept house for the family. Two years after his family arrived, Abraham moved to Marengo, Iowa and opened a store. When he had earned enough money, he brought Babette and Leopold to Marengo; Sarah and Sophie stayed behind, while Rose had already moved to Elgin, Illinois. Babette was determined to learn English quickly and had succeeded after only a year in her new homeland.

In 1870, Abraham and Leopold became business partners, buying a woolen mill in Marengo. They moved it to Des Moines in 1882, naming it The Capitol City Woolen Mills, which Leopold continued until the Depression of the 1930s. Their logo was: "From Sheep to Shape."[24]

In June 1864, Babette left the Sheurerman household to marry Isaiah Frankel in a double ceremony in Davenport, in which her brother, Leopold, married Matilda Schwartz. Babette and Isaiah had met in Chicago, but she gave no details of their meeting. Isaiah brought Babette back to Oskaloosa where their marriage produced six offspring: four boys and two girls. Babette was a warm and caring mother whose influence extended into the neighborhood. A friend of the Frankel boys described her as:

> *"A busy hard working woman, but . . . never too busy to tie a cut finger, feel us for broken bones and heal the hurts with cookies or an apple. There was nothing too hard or too much trouble for Mrs. Frankel to do for her children. She was a kind woman and a grand good mother. She stands out as about the nicest person I knew in that period of my life."*[25]

This was the grandmother who offered a warm embrace to the Rosenfield children while they grew up next door.

In 1897, when Isaiah died, Babette and her two youngest children, Rose and Henry, traveled to Europe for a year. This was doubtless when Rose learned to love Europe. While they were there, the bulk of the Frankel business shifted to their "branch" in Des Moines, so Babette and the children settled in Des Moines when they returned in 1898. Rose told her daughter, Louise, that Babette could not wait to get out of Oskaloosa and away from Isaiah's sister, Sophie, who had lived many years with the Frankels in Oskaloosa. This was the first time that Louise, Joe, or Ruth had even heard of Sophie. Babette had erased her sister-in-law from the family.[26]

When Rose and Meyer Rosenfield built their dream home at 207 37th St., early in the twentieth century, Babette moved to the adjacent home. She continued to follow her love for travel, even taking a somewhat exotic trip to Egypt when she was 70. A few years later, she broke her hip, and until her death at age 89, she was forced to use crutches; she moved her bedroom to a downstairs room and had a bathroom put in an adjacent space. Louise's visual memory of her grandmother was as "a stalwart white haired matriarch sitting in a high-backed chair in her living room." She was a good cook, and the tight-knit Frankel family regularly gathered at her house for Sunday brunch. On hot summer evenings, they also loved to sit on her terrace, a favorite family meeting place, where they would burn punk to keep the bugs away and cover their heads with towels to ward off bats.[27]

Joe saw Babette as unusually philanthropic, with a particular interest in a Mississippi school for the children of freed slaves:

the Pinney Woods School. She hosted the Pinney Woods Cotton Blossom Singers whenever they toured the Midwest.[28] Writing about this remarkable woman, who was her lifeline while growing up, Louise said, "Grandmother never forgot the hardships of her earlier life in Germany and she was grateful for the opportunities she found in this country." Such was a fitting conclusion to her loving portrait of Babette.[29] It is easy for us nowadays to forget the opportunities this country offered to energetic and talented immigrants of humble European stock. The Frankels were an emblem of that story.

Though she inherited her drive and talent, Babette's daughter Rose lacked her mother's warmth. Babette's Sheurerman family was large and close-knit, sponsoring yearly family reunions in Iowa. These reunions featured a clever news sheet, the "Binaur Blatt." Rose was probably seen as a daunting presence; one item in this newssheet revealed, "At the Movies" featuring Rose Rosenfield in "The Weary Housewife" role. This article reminded Louise that her mother often complained of being tired when she did not have a cause to drive her. [30]

I am indebted to Louise Noun for providing so many stories about the Rosenfield and Frankel families, but she had so little to say about her famous brother, Joe. Most of what she says follows the theme that Joe was her parent's favorite while she was "tongue lashed" by her mother and mostly ignored by her father. The distance between Joe and Louise many of us noticed is certified in Louise's *Journey to Autonomy*. Joe and Louise respected one another most highly, but they did not know what to make of one another. Several times I heard Joe say, "Aw, that's just Louise." Joe and Louise lived in the same city and were both tremendous forces for the betterment of Des Moines. Both were Grinnell College graduates, but where Joe loved Grinnell with unequalled passion, Louise was largely unhappy with her campus life, so much so that she escaped to Wellesley after her sophomore year only to be obliged to return because her mother called her home to help with her father's care during his terminal illness.

Sometimes Joe and Louise cooperated on an important cause, as in 1966 when Louise, as President of the Iowa Civil Liberties

Union (ICLU), took on the Tinker Case. Seven Des Moines Middle and High School students had been suspended by the District for wearing black arm bands to school to protest the Vietnam War. Three of the students, John and Mary Beth Tinker and Christopher Eckhardt, lodged a First Amendment case in the Iowa courts that was appealed to the US Supreme Court after a negative decision by the Iowa Supreme Court and an evenly split vote in the Eighth Circuit of Appeals. Lawyer Dan Johnson successfully argued the case in 1969, with the positive majority ruling written by Abe Fortas. Louise drove the case and Joe paid for it—showing a very fruitful if somewhat rare sibling partnership.[31]

The Tinker First Amendment case was exactly the sort of cause that would unite Joe and Louise. Quite different was Louise's decision to enroll in Drake Law School following divorce from her husband, Maurice, in 1967. Joe advised her not to enroll as he was sure that she would not like the law or the law school experience. Louise did not heed Joe, but after one semester, when she was upset by the way she was treated as the only woman in her law school class, she dropped out. Thus, to her chagrin, she proved Joe right.[32]

Louise lived mostly off of her Frankel inheritance, which included a substantial block of Younkers' stock. One source of friction between Joe and Louise was that she thought he had received favored treatment in the inheritance and had once given Louise bad investment advice. Joe mentioned that he took an investment "drubbing" during the Depression: "One company that gave him a particularly bad time was the E.W. Variety Stores. Not only did he lose his own money when the company went belly up, but on his advice, Louise had invested savings she had accumulated through birthday and other gifts. 'It took years to forgive him for losing my birthday presents,' she says."[33]

Jill June, the Executive Director of Iowa Planned Parenthood, had a close, personal relationship with both Louise and Joe. Jill said that about twenty-five years ago, Louise told her that both she and Joe got a fair share of the family inheritance, but whereas Joe got his outright, her inheritance was placed in a trust. Louise was resentful about this: "Look what Joe has done with his life," Louise said, "but no, my money was tied up in that trust and I couldn't do anything with it because the bank is what made the money, not me."[34] June described the sibling's relationship, saying, "They loved each other, but did not always like each other. . . they weren't estranged, but they weren't close."

Kay Bucksbaum, who was a mutual friend of the two siblings, said, "He had a completely different personality from his sister Louise and I would say that Louise was pretty introverted and Joe was pretty extroverted."[35]

Louise mentions Joe in further anecdotes in her memoir. When Joe was about ten, he and a friend were riding ponies when the friend rushed up the driveway to announce that Joe had fallen off and been killed. Fortunately, the friend was wrong; Joe survived and by the next day had recovered completely.[36] On a family trip to Alaska in 1924, Joe was frustrated when Rose would not let him bring a husky dog home. Despite his frustration, "All in all, Joe and I remember the Alaska venture as the best family trip we ever took."[37]

Unlike Louise, Joe never talked about himself or mentioned family unless specifically asked. Joe never aspired to write a book, much less an autobiography. Fred Little, who knew Joe best, said Joe was almost pathologically private.[38] Why was Joe so reluctant to talk about himself or his family? No one seems to know. He was inherently modest, to be sure, and regarded boasting as unseemly. He was certainly proud of his family, but the comfortable circumstances of the family and the fact that they were so prominent in Des Moines essentially relieved him of any obligation and even desire to tell their or his story. Joe was a "doer," and he was content to let his "doing" tell his story. He was totally comfortable in his own skin, and that was enough for him. If we knew more about his father, Meyer, we might have a better understanding of Joe's childhood and family experience. We know so little about Meyer because he was such a private and "retiring" person. Joe seems to have been his father's son in this way.

The Rosenfields built a tennis court at their 37th street house, and it became a neighborhood gathering place until the Cowles (owners of *The Des Moines Register* and *Tribune*) built a bigger and better court just down the street. Louise said Ruth and Joe were "fairly good players," adding that tennis was the only form of play Rose allowed in her show-case yard. As a result, the rest of the children's play items, such as a playhouse and sandbox were relegated to Babette's yard.[39] Joe commented on the tennis court in his 1998 Des Moines Project Interview, recalling that another neighbor, Henry Wallace, who became Franklin Roosevelt's Vice President, frequently played with him. Joe recalled Wallace fondly adding that he was an ambidextrous player.

Another glimpse of a young Joseph Rosenfield was provided by his schoolmate Gladys Foster Davis, who said he was a shy kindergartner but a good organizer.[40] We know that "shy" boy shared a second floor open-air-sleeping porch with his sisters. Warming pans were used to ward off the cold that sometimes plunged below zero.[41]

Under Rose's guidance, the Rosenfields sought assimilation with the dominant Des Moines gentile culture, but the children were nevertheless sent to "Sunday School" at the old Temple on 8th Street, where they studied "biblical history at a self-defeating pace."[42] Louise said the Rosenfields never celebrated Jewish holidays at home and their food did not follow Jewish custom; it was German-American. Joe told Wendel Cochran of *The Des Moines Register*, for a 1981 profile, that "ours was an assimilated generation," and he made it clear that he did not practice any religion. Joe was a classic secular humanist.

Joe attended Greenwood Elementary School and West High School. He was a Boy Scout, and we have photographic evidence that he and his troop met Theodore Roosevelt.[43] There really is no evidence to suggest that Joe lived anything but a happy and comfortable life with his family at 207 37th St. In fact, he was so comfortable at home and with his mother that he returned to live with her after graduating from Iowa Law in 1928. He lived there for twelve years until his marriage in 1940. It was not unusual in the 1930s for unmarried sons to live with their parents.

Surprisingly, no one I interviewed knows much about Joe's wife, Dannie, or his son James. Even the oldest interviewees were a generation younger than Joe, so this omission was not totally unexpected. Even Fred Little and Jill June, who were closer to Joe than anyone, could say almost nothing about Dannie or James. Here is what we do know.

Joe and Dannie Burke first knew each other at the University of Iowa when he was a law student and she an undergraduate. She was from Albuquerque, New Mexico, born in Reno, Nevada in 1908. She was elected to Phi Beta Kappa at Iowa and went on to earn a Master's Degree in Social Work at the University of Chicago. Thereafter, she worked as a Psychiatric Social Worker first in Kansas and then in New Mexico. Joe and Dannie were married in 1940 and honeymooned in Hawaii.

Dannie was a remarkable woman. She served twelve years on the Iowa Board of Regents, from July 1957 until July 1969. Wayne Richey, Secretary to the Regents, gave her high praise. She was credited with beginning the era of Regents' openness, saying "of course we have to open to the people of Iowa and the newspapers of Iowa." This was instinctive for her.[44] At one time, she was a mail pilot, and she co-piloted a cross-country women's air race in 1961. She and Joe's sister Louise were close friends and leaders of the Des Moines Chapter of the National Organization for Women (NOW). She was helping Louise create a Young Women's Resource Center, Chrysalis, in 1977 when she died of a stroke in December. Dannie was an early supporter of Planned Parenthood and was active in the Des Moines Community Playhouse.[45]

Jill June said that though Joe did not often talk about Dannie, he did say "she was a quiet companion; she was his companion [and] they enjoyed each other."[46]

Joe credited Dannie with turning him into an active Democrat. She worked hard on Eugene McCarthy's 1968 presidential campaign. Joe said, "I think I would blame [my Democratic leanings] on my wife, partially . . . I like the Democratic philosophy better than the other. I'm not rabid about it. That's the way I feel. Dannie was a very strong Democrat." In the same interview, Joe described Dannie as "very bright and very interested in women's causes. Good causes. She also was interested in children's causes and mental health. She was another [woman] who influenced me greatly."

Dannie and Joe were devastated by the death of their only child, James, in December 1962. A seventeen-year-old senior at Lincoln

High School, James was popular and accomplished, and served as Lincoln's representative on the All-City Student Council. He was also a member of Lincoln's varsity swim team. James was killed in an early Sunday morning automobile accident near the State Fair Grounds. Though Joe owned the Volkswagon Beetle in which he was riding, James was riding in the front passenger seat when the car hit a utility pole while travelling too fast to navigate a turn. James's friend, and the Lincoln Student Council President, was injured while riding in the back seat and the uninjured driver was an older, non-student acquaintance of the two boys. James was thrown from the car and pronounced dead on arrival at Broadlawns Hospital.[47]

Joe's closest undergraduate friend, Bob Fell, co-author of DORIC, provided some of the only personal insight into James as a child. Grinnell alums have a quarterly "Class Letter" to inform one another of their post-graduate lives. Bob Fell was the 1925 Class Agent, and he was notorious for writing the longest and most detailed of all the class letters. Fell visited Joe at least yearly and would usually report on the lively and engaging nature of young James.[48]

Joe's friend, Bill Knapp believed that Dannie, and, to an extent, Joe, never quite recovered from James' death. He opined that Dannie lost all religious faith and that she "was pretty put down and bitter about it . . . that changed their lives when they lost their son."[49] In light of the event, one can surmise that a major motivation for Joe's penchant to reach out to mentor young men was to compensate for his lost son.

Because Joe so closely guarded his privacy, we have learned little about his family life directly from him, but we are fortunate his sister Louise was an assiduous collector and reporter on the family character and activities, particularly the Frankels. The Frankels were the critical influence on Joe. He was shaped by and continued the Frankel legacy of extraordinary German immigrants who created a family and a business that powerfully influenced Oskaloosa, Des Moines, and, eventually, all of Iowa through the expansion of the Younkers retail empire that, as we will see in the following section, was engineered by Joe Rosenfield.

YOUNKERS

Even before I undertook this biography, I felt I knew Joe, since he and I had interacted for more than twenty years when we were colleagues on the Grinnell College Board of Trustees and then when I served under Joe's Trustee direction as Grinnell's President. Even so, it was a revelation to be immersed in the Younkers' archives at the Iowa Historical Society in Des Moines. Joe's family, the Frankels, were 50 percent owners of Younkers, and both the family and Department Store were instrumental in making Joe who he was. There was serendipity between Joe and Younkers. From an early age, the Younkers culture heavily influenced him and, in turn, he was a major contributor to that culture, serving as Vice President, General Counsel, and Board Chair from 1948 to 1965.

Younkers was the product of four Jewish family retailers who, by 1927 had combined to form the largest department store in Iowa; by the 1960s, the enterprise had one of the largest customer bases in the nation. The values of those four families meshed to create a business that fostered a sense of belonging among its associates and a set of business ethics that projected integrity and quality to its customers. Dominated by the descendants of the founders, Younkers became an Iowa institution from at least the era of the Great Depression. In 1979, the company was sold to Equitable of Iowa to prevent a hostile, out-of-state takeover. No longer a family business, Younkers culture began to change; and, as we shall see, the change was not for the better.

All four families—the Younkers, Frankels, Harrises, and Mandelbaums—were Polish and German immigrants in the post-1848 revolutionary wave of European immigration to the US. The three founding Younker brothers were born in Polotzk, Poland, eighty-five miles north of Warsaw.[50] In 1856, Lipman, Samuel, and Marcus—the second, third, and fourth brothers—settled in Keokuk, Iowa. All were in their teens while their parents remained in Poland. The brothers founded a thriving peddling business in the southeast corner of Iowa where the Des Moines

River emptied into the Mississippi. At that time, Keokuk was the largest town in Iowa because the Des Moines River was navigable while the Mississippi rapids north of Keokuk prevented St. Louis steamboats from navigating on the Mississippi beyond Keokuk. Keokuk was also the embarkation port for Civil War recruits and soldiers as well as a way station on wagon train routes to the trans-Mississippi West.[51]

The peddling business soon transformed into a retail store that gradually became the focus of the Younker brothers' business. Keokuk had the largest Jewish population in Iowa, and the upper floor of the Younkers store was used for the first formal Jewish services in Keokuk and, perhaps, in Iowa.[52] The railway between Keokuk and Des Moines was completed in 1866 and Samuel Younker rode the first train to Des Moines. Des Moines was about the same size as Keokuk in 1866, but it already had twenty-two retail stores; while Samuel appreciated the potential, he counseled against expansion to Des Moines at that time. When the decision was made to open a Des Moines Younkers in 1874, the number of retail establishments had dwindled to seventeen and Des Moines had grown substantially larger than Keokuk.[53] The Des Moines store was started by a younger half-brother, Herman, who had immigrated to Keokuk in 1870. The first Younker newspaper ad set the tone for the Younkers' culture: "We have come to live here and mean to do what is right. If you want honest goods at bottom prices, call at Younker Brothers." In this case, an ad spoke the truth.[54] The original Des Moines Younkers was located at 6th and Walnut and the store caused a stir when it made the radical decision in 1899 to move out of the heart of the retail district a block to the West, building a new store on 7th and Walnut, which became the permanent Younkers location. The Keokuk store closed soon after Samuel died, and all operations were shifted to Des Moines.

Younkers' first acquisition came in 1912, when it bought the Grand Department Store. In 1923, it made a much more significant acquisition of the adjacent Wilkins Department Store, creating a block-long store. This set the scene for a merger with their chief competitor, Harris-Emery, in 1927, amid a major agricultural depression accompanied by numerous bank failures.

In 1927, the Frankel family was the owner of Harris-Emery. The Frankel stores began in Oskaloosa in 1861, where Isaiah, who had emigrated from Germany, settled as a peddler just as the Younker brothers had done in Keokuk. As business became more concentrated, peddling soon led to the establishment of a store. The Frankels established a branch in Des Moines. In 1894 two of Isaiah's sons, Manassa and Nathan, established the Frankel Clothing Company of Oskaloosa in Des Moines at 413 Walnut Street. Business was good, so in 1899 a new five-story building was constructed on Sixth and Walnut. Tragically, the store burned in 1901. The search for a new store led to the Frankels' bold purchases of its rival, Harris-Emery. Joe Rosenfield's father, Meyer, had just joined the Frankel store, having married Joe's mother, Isaiah Frankel's daughter, Rose. Meyer's cousin, Walter, had just become wealthy due to the death of his father, who was a leading Rock Island, Illinois citizen. Walter made an unsecured $50,000 loan to the Frankels and that, combined with a significant loan from banker Arthur Reynolds, enabled the Frankels to purchase the Harris-Emery store. Later, Walter Rosenfield came to Des Moines to have a look at the new store and he pitched in to help wrap packages; ironically, he was fired by a floor-walker for his clumsiness. Nevertheless, he was rewarded repayment in just over a year, along with the satisfaction of seeing the success of the new store. The bank loan was repaid in full a few years later.[55]

The Harris-Emery store had been established soon after Henry C. Harris came to Des Moines in 1886. He had come to comfort his brother, Hardy, whose wife and child had just died. Henry Harris returned to his home in Rutland, Vermont to sell his store in preparation for opening a store in Des Moines. He opened the Harris Dry Goods Store in Des Moines in 1892 at 7th and Walnut and soon joined with John S. Emery to form the Harris-Emery Co. When the Frankels purchased the store in 1901, Henry C. Harris remained a significant stockholder, and his descendants continued to own a substantial block of Younkers stock.[56] In 1916 the successful business remodeled the store so that it rose from five to eight stories and added a section to the east.

Younkers and Harris-Emery, the two largest department stores in Des Moines, were fierce competitors. Though the Younker and

Frankel families were friends and their executives socialized, the stores were intense competitors, guarding trade secrets while also employing each other's clerks and buyers. Joe suspected they were intimately acquainted with each other's "secrets" despite supposed firewalls. Iowa agriculture fell into sharp decline in the late 1920s resulting in numerous bank failures as well as depression of retail businesses. Where in 1923 both Harris-Emery and Younkers booked equal record setting profits (though Younkers had greater volume of sales), by 1926 the volume of both stores had dwindled and their profits had been halved. Late in 1926, Manassa Frankel approached Younkers President, Norman Wilchinski (Younkers president from 1921–1937), with a proposal that the rival stores merge. Sidney Mandelbaum was later quoted as saying that the Frankels were just as interested in profits as the Younkers and for this and other reasons, the Younkers executives agreed to enter into merger negotiations.[58] Joe, who became the Younkers financial guru, described the merger negotiations that were worked out by the Gamble law firm he joined a year after the merger. Though the Harris-Emery assets were substantially smaller than those of Younkers, the Frankels insisted on receiving fifty-percent of the voting stock in the merged corporation. Gamble created a unique stock arrangement whereby the Younker and Frankel interests each received fifty-percent of a special issue of 7 percent non-callable preferred (voting) stock. Of the $1,000,000 issue, Younkers stockholders received $500,000, while Harris-Emery stockholders equally received $500,000. However, to compensate for the imbalance of assets, the Younkers stockholders received a majority of the non-voting common stock (65 percent to 35 percent). This arrangement prevailed until 1948 when Younkers went public and the investment bankers insisted all stock in the corporation become voting. By this time, the distinction between Younkers and Harris-Emery interests was no longer so important.[59] The merger was registered in January 1927 while Joe was in his last year at Iowa Law School. He did not attend the Harris-Emery stockholder meeting that approved the merger, but his proxy voted "yes." Joe received 275 shares of preferred voting stock, while his father, Meyer, who became Vice President of the merged store, got 540 shares.[60]

The merged store was called Younkers; Norman Wilchinski was President and Sidney Mandelbaum Vice President and General Merchandise Manager. Henry Frankel, the youngest of Isaiah's sons, became Treasurer. Wilchinski remained President until his death in 1937, when he was replaced by Henry Frankel (1937–1944). Sidney Mandelbaum retired in 1933, though he remained a Director.

The merged store thrived; the combined profits of the competing stores in 1926 had been $300,000 and by 1927, following the merger, the profit was $500,000. The clear efficiency of combined operations had a positive effect on the business.In 1928, in a step that had been agreed upon before the Harris-Emery merger, Younkers purchased J. Mandelbaum & Sons, the last of the separate long-established department stores, built in 1899 on the North side of Walnut between 5th and 6th.[61] Julius Mandelbaum had immigrated from Germany during the Civil War, starting business in Des Moines in 1864.[62] His son, Sidney Mandelbaum, who was married to Norman Wilchinski's sister, helped to pave the way for the Younkers' Mandelbaum purchase having already become a Younkers Vice President. Two Wilchinski sisters were married to Mandelbaum brothers.

Thus, by 1928 a remarkable retail enterprise had emerged, bringing four Jewish immigrant families together—the Younkers, Frankel-Rosenfields, Harrises and Mandelbaums—who collectively shaped a highly successful and nurturing culture.

When Joe graduated with Honors from the University of Iowa Law School in 1928, he joined the firm of Gamble, Read, Howland. Graham Gamble had worked out the details of the Younkers/Harris-Emery merger a year earlier. Joe had done very well in law school, but the fact that he was a Frankel was an important determining factor in him getting the job. Joe worked at the Gamble firm (adding his name to the masthead) from 1928 until he moved, at his own request, to Younkers full time in 1947.[63] While at the Gamble firm, he handled the Younkers account, essentially functioning as their General Counsel. Joe later said at least one-third of his Gamble Firm work was on the Younkers account.[64] When Joe's father died of cancer in 1929,

Joe replaced him on the Younkers Board of Directors. He would remain on the Board for forty years until 1969, serving as Chair from 1948 until 1965, when he was moved to a specially created position: Chairman of the Executive Committee.[65]

Emblematic of Joe's importance to Younkers while he still was at the Gamble firm was the hiring of Morey Sostrin in 1938. This was an early example of succession planning. Joe's uncle, Henry Frankel, was well along in years when he replaced Norman Wilchinski as President upon Wilchinski's death in 1937. Frankel retired in 1944. By then, Morey Sostrin was well groomed to be his replacement. Joe had been sent to Cincinnati in 1938 to interview Sostrin, who, after a significant career in store management, became a relatively young president of the moderate sized McAlpine Store. Morey later told the story of his interview in a hotel room with Joe while Joe was in his underwear and reclined on his bed.[66]

Joe later told a story that captures Morey Sostrin's sense of humor, recounting an incident just after Joe had joined Younkers as Vice President and General Counsel in 1947. When asked about prospects for advancement at Younkers by a young applicant, Sostrin responded, "Well here is Mr. Rosenfield in his second day at Younkers and he is already a Vice President."[67]

The March 1947 *Reporter* (Younkers' monthly magazine) introduced Joe as the new Younkers Vice President who would continue as General Counsel, adding, "Although he has not been engaged actively in selling, he recalls one youthful experience as salesman with Norman Wilchinski as the customer. As a Boy Scout he was selling tickets for President Taft's speech in Des Moines. He suggested to Mr. Wilchinksi that he buy ten dollars' worth. To his surprise the customer replied, 'I'll take $100 worth.'"[68]

At the other end of Joe's Younkers career, an article published on his retirement details another of Joe's youthful attempts at sales. This occurred when he was working in a Christmas job at Harris-Emery well before the 1927 merger: "Joe, as he is widely known went to work at age 14 at Christmas time in the toy department at Harris-Emery; and was discovered by state authorities to be too young to work. His own uncle, Henry Frankel, had to fire him." Joe later sold pants at the Frankel Men's Clothing Store during the summers, but his color-blindness convinced him that retail was not in his future.[69]

An artifact from Joe's Harris-Emery years may have had an influence on his sense of humor when he was a student at Grinnell College. The Harris-Emery magazine, *Tips*, was replete with humor more or less along the lines of DORIC and the *Malteaser* with one-liners and cartoons. Joe would have read those magazines and doubtless absorbed their flavor as he created humor in his undergraduate years at Grinnell.[70]

During his years at Younkers, Joe was not at all involved in retail. His financial skills launched him into crafting major investment decisions as Younkers profits mounted. Through Joe, Younkers was an early and substantial investor in Heritage Cable Television, which became the ninth largest cable network in the US. As important as were Joe's investment decisions, the bulk of his time was devoted to Younkers' expansion into the cities of Iowa and adjacent states.

Joe's decision to leave the Gamble firm for full-time employment in the family business was prompted by the commercial opportunities of post-war America. When his uncle Henry retired as Younkers CEO in 1944, Morey Sostrin, with whom Joe had a special relationship, replaced him. Henry remained Chair of the Board of Directors for a while, but he retired fully in 1948 and Joe replaced him as Chair. Through Joe, the Frankel interests continued to be present at the highest level of Younkers. Equally important to Henry and Morey in attracting Joe from the Gamble firm was the opportunity for post-war expansion, which all three recognized. Joe was the perfect person to explore new markets and negotiate property acquisition. As Joe himself said, in his laconic way, "We just had a little meeting a few of us one day and said, 'We've got to start opening branch stores. If we don't we're going to be left out in the cold.' So we started opening them. I spent a lot of time getting the locations, getting the stores going . . . I didn't do any of the merchandising. I don't know anything about merchandising. But I do know where the good location for a store might be."[71] Early expansion focused on business districts in small cities. The process had begun before World War II with a store established in

Ames in 1941, followed by one in Mason City during the war in 1944. After the war, realization of the pent-up demand for housing and cars created suburban shopping centers with ample room for free parking. In 1947, Younkers built a store at the new Crossroads Shopping Center in Fort Dodge. The trend to locate stores in downtowns continued throughout the 1940s with the purchase of Davidson's in Sioux City in 1948 and new stores in Marshalltown in 1948, in Iowa City in 1949, and in Ottumwa in 1949.[72] In the process, Younkers became the first Iowa retail store to expand into numerous towns, a step that previously had been taken only by national chains, such as Woolworths and Kresges.[73]

In 1951, Joe was deeply involved in the purchase of the Innes Department Store in Wichita, Kansas. It was by far the largest department store in Wichita, and the city's burgeoning Boeing aircraft industry made Wichita an attractive retail location. The Younkers archives contain a trove of documents detailing the protracted and detailed negotiations over the price of the building and its inventory, along with payment arrangements.[74] The Innes purchase turned out to be pivotal to a dramatic shift in Younkers' acquisition strategy. The Innes store was sold only five years later, in 1956, because of the seminal decision made by Joe and Morey Sostrin to concentrate almost exclusively on expansion into shopping centers. The Innes purchase was perceived as an overreach into downtown expansion, as had a similar venture in Denver, so Joe and Morey Sostrin made a disciplined decision to focus almost exclusively on shopping center expansion.[75]

When Younkers went public on the day Harry Truman was elected in 1948, cash to fuel Younkers' expansion was created. The shock of Truman's victory created a collapse in the stock market; Younkers stock, which debuted at 26, dropped to 20 on the first day. It soon rebounded, providing the cash for Younkers expansion into Iowa small cities. It was no coincidence that the decision to go public was implemented soon after Joe joined Younkers full time in 1947.[76]

The remaining purchases in the 1950s and 60s followed the shopping center blueprint with the single exception of a downtown store in Oskaloosa (1957), the original home of the Frankel's.

All the subsequent expansions in which Joe Rosenfield was instrumental were located in shopping centers: the new stores in Omaha, Nebraska (1955); Austin, Minnesota (1958); Merle Hay, Des Moines (1959); Bettendorf (1960); Newton (1960); Spencer (1960); Des Moines Eastgate (1962); Burlington (1966); Dubuque (1968); and Cedar Falls (1968).

Joe told a story about the significant Merle Hay negotiation, a development that soon would rival the downtown Des Moines store in sales. The new shopping center was located on the site of an old Jesuit Monastery. In 1957, Joe commissioned Ralph Jester to negotiate with the Jesuits for the site, which included the monastery and its forty acres. Joe had heard that because the city had grown too close to the Monastery, the Jesuits were interested in moving, making the property available. When Jester called on the Jesuit leader, he was told they had decided to sell the property for $500,000. Joe told Jester that the price was "outrageous," and urged him to continue the negotiation. Joe said, "He did so and reported to me that the head of the Order told him that they felt that $500,000 was a reasonable price; that their order was some 1500 years old and that it would not bother them too much if they had to wait another four or five hundred years to get their price. We closed the deal the next day—price $500,000." Joe, whose business philosophy was that the other person should get a good deal as well, had to go the "extra mile" this time.[77]

The Younkers store at the Duck Creek Shopping Center in Bettendorf (1960) has special significance in the Joe Rosenfield story. This shopping center was developed by Martin and Matthew Bucksbaum of Cedar Rapids. Previously, they had developed the Town and Country Center in Cedar Rapids, having shifted into shopping center development after beginning in grocery retail. As shopping center developers, they incorporated as General Growth Properties. The relationship between Joe and the Bucksbaums, which began with Duck Creek, blossomed into a continuing business partnership and friendship. Joe later described the relationship: "We were very close to General Growth and we owned part of the deal and the public owned part of it. But the Bucksbaums ran it and were the big stockholders. They would always consult us as to where they were thinking of putting a center; and really asked us if we would be the first ones to sign up as a tenant."[78]

Joe had a remarkable capacity to recognize young talent; he often reached out to young people he met in friendship as a mentor and supporter. This quality was evident with Martin and Matthew Bucksbaum, and Younkers became the anchor for many of their most successful centers. In fact, the Bucksbaum's moved to Des Moines and adopted the corporate name, General Growth Properties, which became one of the largest shopping center developers in the Midwest. Joe was appointed to an enduring seat on the General Growth Board. In the early years, Younkers, following Joe's advice, owned one third of General Growth.[79] Joe's relationship with the Bucksbaums was enhanced by Matthew's wife, Kay, who was a 1951 Grinnell graduate and Trustee colleague. When Joe retired from Younkers in 1969, General Growth offered him an office in their Des Moines corporate headquarters, and he occupied it for over thirty years until his death in 2000.[80]

The post-war expansion Joe guided did much to make Younkers one of the top six retail sales areas in the nation and the only one that was a state rather than a city. The collective success of the branch stores was certified in the mid 1960s when, for the first time, their sales volume exceeded that of the downtown store.[81]

Joe retired from Younkers on May 31, 1969. In an article commemorating his retirement, in the June 1969 issue of the *Reporter*, he was credited with guiding Younkers' post-war expansion by being what his kindergarten friend, Mrs. Gladys Foster Davis, said of him: even though he was shy, "even at that early age [he was] a born organizer when the need arose."[82]

Younkers was an extraordinary organization that nurtured a sense of family among its employees who, in fact, "bought-in" to the vision and purposes of the company. In return, the company trained them, cared for them, and taught them civic virtue and generosity. The corporation itself not only modeled generosity, it encouraging a spirit of giving among its associates. The corporate culture was rooted in the four Jewish founding families, and Joe was simultaneously a product of one of those families, the Frankels, and of the corporate culture they helped to create.

As a researcher who, other than shopping in their stores, did not know much about Younkers, I learned to appreciate this extraordinary commercial enterprise through reading reams of its corporate news magazines: the weekly *Good Morning* and the monthly *Reporter*. The self-proclaimed Younkers vision asserted a philosophy of total service to the customer as well as a high degree of personal development for its associates. With respect to the community at large, Younkers' goal was to "build a sense of social responsibility and support for volunteerism in the communities in which we operate." Furthermore, Younkers was determined to create partnerships with its suppliers that were built on open negotiations concerning mutual business objectives.[83] This goal was another way of stating Joe's business mantra that the other person should also get a good deal. A 1974 poll in *The Des Moines Register* proclaimed Younkers the top business organization in influencing Des Moines community affairs.[84] This quality shines through in almost every issue of *Good Morning* and the *Reporter*.

Howard Lyons, a long-time employee in the days of Henry Frankel and Morey Sostrin, wrote, "I know better than most people the full depth of Henry Frankel's leadership [and] devotion to serving the people of Iowa and our nation with unselfish service that helped to improve the quality of life for all. Henry Frankel and other families which later included the Sidney and Morris Mandelbaum families set the pace in Iowa and America, not only in retailing, but in customer service." Lyons had intimate knowledge of Younkers' community service efforts; Henry Frankel asked him to lead Younkers' extraordinary successes in the seven War Bond and War Stamp sales during World War II.

Lyons concluded, "Iowa has been extremely fortunate now and in past years to have had all of these wonderful Jewish families show their knowledge and expertise and dedicated community service to help Iowa to be one of the finest places in the world to live, to grow and to raise a family, to get an education . . . to be the best one can be."[85]

In the March, 1961, *Reporter*, Younkers President Morey Sostrin amplified the Younkers vision:

Everything that we do, which we do for an ultimate profit, depends on customer satisfaction . . . People, they're the most important part of our business. The big thing that distinguishes Younkers from the average store is its people and their philosophy of friendly, courteous and helpful service; going out of the way to be considerate, and kind, and gracious and liberal with customers and each other . . . Whatever we do should be the right thing to do in our ethics and service. Temporary gain in dollars is secondary to the building and preservation of our most priceless asset—good will."[86]

Six years later, in the September 1967 *Reporter*, Sostrin quoted the great retailer, Harry Selfridge (Marshall Field in Chicago and Selfridges in London), in an article on the meaning of public relations:

To do the right thing at the right time in the right way; to do some things better than they have ever been done before. To eliminate errors, to know both sides of the question; to be courteous; to be an example; to work for the love of work; to anticipate requirements; to develop resources; to recognize impediments; to master circumstances; to act from reason rather than rule; to be satisfied with nothing short of perfection.[87]

This catalogue of aphorisms might seem typical of corporate hype, but Younkers managed to live its vision. The weekly *Good Morning* and monthly *Reporter* certify that the achievement and, more importantly, testimony of both associates and customers bear witness to a corporation that truly practiced its exemplary goals. There was abundant staff training to assure the goal of excellent customer service.

Joe personally embodied the Younkers vision and, in turn, contributed to it. In fact, even before he joined Younkers full time, he was instrumental in creating a pioneering profit sharing plan. Designed in 1944 and inaugurated in 1945, Younkers assigned 10 percent of pre-tax profits to a profit-sharing retirement plan made available to all those employed for five or more years. In other words, a non-contributing retirement plan was created as far back as World War II with corporate generosity unmatched at the time and seldom matched since. By the time of Joe's retirement in 1969,

Younkers had contributed over $12,000,000 to the retirement income of its employees.[88]

A sign of the quality and outlook of Younkers associates was the organization of a Mutual Aid Society in 1908. Employees contributed voluntarily to an ever-growing fund that provided necessary sick benefits in times of need. It flourished in subsequent years and was frequently evident through solicitations in *Good Morning* and the *Reporter*.[89] The corporation also provided health support and tips with constant reminders of the benefits of Blue Cross/Blue Shield insurance. In fact, when he was on the Board of Hospital Services of Iowa, Joe was a founder of the prototype for non-profit health insurance. Younkers periodically offered free chest X-Rays in the downtown store.[90] Several times a year, associates were urged to donate blood, and there was an annual "Younkers Day" at the blood center every March.[91] Flu shots were administered annually in the store.[92] The company offered many other services to its employees, including Income Tax Counseling, vacation tips, and counseling on safe driving.[93] They even offered tips about arranging your home and yard in such a way that it was not obvious that you had gone away on vacation.[94] Younkers was a pioneer in creating entertainment, sporting, and social events for its associates. They organized basketball, softball, and bowling teams that competed in Des Moines leagues, as well as summer golf tournaments. Joe, typical of his interest in baseball, sponsored a raffle for tickets to the Des Moines Bruins minor league baseball games. Younkers had a choir in both the downtown and the Sioux City stores. The annual Christmas party became so large that it had to be moved to the famous KRNT Theater and often featured headline performers.[95]

Of course, as a retail enterprise, Younkers offered abundant employee training, as evidenced in *Good Morning* and the *Reporter*. What seems remarkably different from what one has come to expect in corporate efforts to amplify sales was the Younkers spirit of collegiality and self-improvement. There were, of course, periodic formal training sessions in sales and other store jobs, but what stands out in the weekly and monthly publications are the admonitions about customer satisfaction and the consideration and friendliness of the sales staff. In fact, Younkers was the first Des Moines store to employ a woman, Mary McCann in 1881. Though shunned by the male clerks at first, she was able to prove that women customers naturally gravitate to a female sales associate.[96]

The aphorisms in the store publications were impressive with their focus on customer satisfaction and employee improvement. For example, one publication said, "What is a Customer? The most important person; we are dependent on him; not an interruption in our work, but the purpose of it; a partner in our business; not a person to argue with."[97] Another said, "The Real Test of the Younkers Sprit: It is when they have returns, exchanges, refunds, credits and adjustments. Do this with a good spirit and a smile."[98] And another: "Profit by the mistakes of others; you may not live long enough to make all of them yourself."[99] The September 17, 1951 *Good Morning* said, "America's productive genius always finds better ways of doing things! If you have a better idea for improving our service, please express it."[100] On June 22, 1955, *Good Morning* provided "Seven Things to Remember: The Value of Time; The Success of Perseverance; The Pleasure of Working; The Dignity of Simplicity; The Virtue of Patience; The Improvement of Talent; the Joy of Originating."[101] On April 18, 1949, *Good Morning* featured "The Art of Remembering Names: 1) When introduced, be sure you have heard the name correctly; 2) Repeat the person's name as often as possible with him as you talk to him; 3) Learn as much as possible about him. Study his features; 4) Associate the name with something; 5) Later, test your memory of the name."[102] Apart from the sexist language, this is good advice for anyone and especially valuable for sales persons as there are few customers whose hearts are not warmed and wallets opened when sales staff remember their names. The advice went on and on. I will end with a short example that embodied the essence of the four founding families: "Moral honesty is the keynote to enduring success."[103] Moral honesty was what Joe exhibited when, in the middle of an EEOC inquiry about unequal salaries for equal work, as President Chuck Duchen explained the problems created by pregnancy, Joe said, "No, you pay them the same as the men."[104]

The Younkers Tea Room was a Des Moines and central Iowa institution. It featured good cuisine for lunch and dinner as well as frequent fashion shows. In the days of Joe Rosenfield's chairmanship, it was common for women to dress up for a day of shopping at Younkers, punctuated by lunch with friends in the Tea Room. The call rang, "Meet me at the Tea Room." The joys of a day shopping at Younkers topped by lunch with family and friends was recalled in the *Des Moines Register* as recently as October, 2017, by a woman writing from New York City.[105]

Perhaps the most salient and unique aspect of the Younkers culture was its emphasis on, to use a classic concept, civic virtue. Through the forties, fifties, and sixties, virtually every election was highlighted in *Good Morning* and, often, the *Reporter*. Be it national, state, or local, employees were admonished to vote; store opening was sometimes delayed so that associates could easily find time to vote. The September 1952, *Good Morning* trumpeted, "Don't be a 'Vambie,' living but dead to his country because he is not registered to vote."[106] The following October, as the national election was imminent, *Good Morning* announced that a sample of the newly introduced voting machines would be on display at a booth in the Tea Room.[107] This was followed, in the November 3, 1952, *Good Morning*, with a front page cartoon, "See You at the Polls," announcing that the store would not open until 10:00 a.m. on election day.[108] Particularly noteworthy was the regular push to be sure to vote in city council and school board elections. Primaries also got special emphasis: "Freedom is Everybody's Business: Vote in the Iowa Primaries."[109]

There were seven War Bond/War Stamp drives in Des Moines during World War II. Younkers was the leading seller among Des Moines businesses, and *Good Morning* was the principal promotional vehicle for the sales efforts. In that period, there were no civic responsibilities more important than support of the war effort. In October 1942, Younkers donated its air conditioning refrigeration equipment to the government to be used for manufacturing synthetic rubber for the duration of the war. This was a significant gesture, as Younkers was the proud pioneer of retail air conditioning in Des Moines. Henry Frankel informed the associates that there would be two blowers on each floor to keep customers and employees as cool as possible under the circumstances.[110]

The United Campaign, the precursor of United Way, was heavily emphasized at Younkers. For example, the October 5, 1953 *Good Morning* announced an all store meeting on the United Campaign.[111] This was a sign of Younkers' exceptional devotion to the United Campaign and philanthropy in general. Joe developed a reputation as Des Moines's number one philanthropist, which was, in part, based on his philanthropic role at Younkers. Notably, Younkers was one of the first retail stores in the United States to give 10 percent of its pre-tax income to charity; during Joe's tenure, Younkers frequently gave six-figure gifts.[112] Bill Friedman, who eventually became President of Younkers, called Joe the corporation's "financial mastermind because of his oversight of investments of the very substantial profits."[113] In addition to investments, profits were converted to donations. In the April 1955 *Reporter*, Joe, under his title as Chairman of the Board, wrote an article on "Younkers—A Good Corporate Citizen." Be a good citizen and participate in worthwhile activities, Joe wrote. This has been Younkers principle for its entire history. Citizenship means building a fine city, and Younkers and Joe were devoted to Des Moines. "It is necessary for all of us to contribute generously of our time and money toward the furtherance of all community endeavors," he wrote. In fact, Joe wrote, the influence of Younkers in Des Moines is seen constantly in community projects. Annually, multiple thousands of dollars are contributed to the United Campaign, as well as other worthwhile causes in the city. Younkers donated $75,000 to Methodist Hospital for a new unit, as well as $37,500 to the Lutheran Hospital capital campaign. Also, Younkers pledged $125,000 to the Des Moines YMCA drive, as well as $175,000 to Drake University. Joe also noted there had been a contribution to the new Des Moines baseball park, a project dear to Joe's heart. Joe added that Younkers had made substantial donations in Sioux City, where its Davidson store was located. These donations were to the Sioux City YMCA and Morningside College. All of these things, Joe added, are traditional with Younkers. It is an integral part of Younkers' philosophy, and the good will that it engendered is one of their most priceless assets.[114]

This article is emblematic of the deep connection between Joe Rosenfield and the Younkers' culture. Toward the end of his life, Joe said, "I'm sure that Younkers got a lot of business based somewhat on the fact that we were good citizens and people appreciated it. You heard all these stories of returned merchandise that they took back regardless of how long it had been out."[115] As I dove into that culture through the archives at the Iowa Historical Society, I could see clearly the symbiotic relationship between Joe and Younkers. Iowa Governor Harold Hughes provided contemporary testimony to that relationship. In December 1967, Joe was inducted into Younkers' 20 Year Club, but he was absent because he was attending a Governor's Conference at Hughes invitation. Hughes wrote the following letter to honor Joe and Younkers:

> *Few Governors, if any, are as interesting as Joe Rosenfield . . . No one I know has done as much for so many worthy causes and done it so quietly. Joe has successfully avoided attention or praise behind the façade of a big cigar and his own special curve-ball sense of humor. But the special thing that has impressed me is the loyalty and sense of belonging that the employees of this company have toward the organization. Younkers is not just a place where they work. It is THEIR store. And the people of this community also have a friendly and proprietary feeling about Younkers. It seems to me that this tells us a lot about the character of Joe Rosenfield and all the fine people past and present who have built this great retail enterprise into a Midwestern institution . . . So I send my personal congratulations to Joe and Dannie, [and] to the entire Younkers organization.[116]*

Harold Hughes and Joe were very close friends, and Hughes knew Des Moines and Iowa as well as anyone. His certification of the intimate connection between what Younkers was and who Joe was is utterly convincing. Without Younkers, Joe would not have been fully "Joe," and without Joe, Younkers would not have been fully Younkers. Years after he left Younkers, Joe's eyes would "light-up" when he and Fred Hubbell talked about Joe's years at Younkers.[117]

In January 1979, 122 years after its founding, Younkers was sold to Equitable of Iowa, the holding company spun off by

Equitable Insurance Company. James W. Hubbell Jr., Chair of the Board, and Kenneth Austin, CEO, represented Equitable, and Charles Duchen, Chair of the Board, and William Friedman Jr., President, represented Younkers. Joe Rosenfield no longer had an official role at Younkers, and because he was on the Equitable Board, he took no direct role in the sale, though some feel that nothing this momentous would have happened at Younkers without Joe's imprimatur.[118] Fred Hubbell, who became the President of Younkers under Equitable of Iowa in 1985, said that though Chuck Duchen brokered the deal on behalf of Younkers, Joe was also involved.[119] At the time of the sale, Fred's father, James W. Hubbell, said "Joe had the feeling that the two companies would make a good marriage."[120] Typically, Joe later joked about the Hubbell's acquisition of Younkers, quipping at a black tie function with impeccable timing, "It's so nice to see all these Hubbell women here so nicely dressed tonight and the good thing now they're in Younkers they don't have to take the dress back tomorrow like they used to."[121] We do know that Joe received $923,208 for his share of the $71.5 million sale of Younkers stock to Equitable.[122] By this time, *Good Morning* had disappeared and the *Reporter* had been cut back from monthly to quarterly issues. The decline in traditional Younkers culture is evident in the continual thinning of the *Reporter* and its increasing focus on hard selling and prevention of customer and associate theft. In fact, an article in the September/October 1983 *Reporter* detailed $1,269,850 in losses. Fifteen-hundred associates had been surveyed and 94 admitted theft, with 198 having given unauthorized discounts or let other persons use employee discounts. Five-to-ten year employees (from the old Younkers) were much less likely to have been involved than were those who had worked there from six months to five years.[123]

The sale to Equitable of Iowa was prompted by fear of a hostile take-over allied with the desire to keep Younkers local. Equitable also had the cash to support expanded operations. Younkers bought Brandeis in 1987, went public in 1993, and by 1996 had merged with the Proffits chain, which made Younkers part of a 107 store conglomerate located in 16 states. In 1998, Proffits merged with Saks.[124] Though certainly still an Iowa institution, Younkers was no longer locally owned, nor was it the organization of which Joe Rosenfield was such an integral part. In fact, in 1998 Joe said of chain stores, "They're detached from the home office and they may send in a check or do this or that, but you've got to have somebody on the scene that sees the value of business and the community and go from there."[125] There could be no better assessment of what Iowa lost when Younkers ceased to be a family business firmly rooted in Des Moines and Iowa.

POSTSCRIPT

It turns out Iowa has lost even more than when I first penned the words above. It has lost Younkers entirely. On April 19, 2018, *The Des Moines Register* announced that by the end of August 2018, all 49 Younkers stores will close, including the 17 remaining in Iowa. Bon-Ton Stores, the current Younkers owners, had filed for bankruptcy and their entire chain of 256 stores, which include Bon-Ton, Carson Pirie, Herberger's, Berger's, Boston Store, and Elder-Beerman, as well as Younkers, will shut completely.[126]

A follow-up *Register* feature in the Business Section on Sunday, April 29, remembered what Younkers once represented in the lives of Iowans:

> *If you grew up in Des Moines there's a good chance you visited Santa, had lunch in the Tea Room or bought your first formal gown or suit at Younkers department store. Many people have a memory of the iconic Des Moines department store chain that after 152 years and a handful of owners will close all of its stores by the end of August.*[127] *In the days since the news broke, Iowans have memorialized the store online—posting shots of everything from Tea Room cookbooks to black-and-white toddler portraits taken in the old studio. Morbid curiosity has led many to visit the everything-must-go sales that will extinguish the brand for good.*

This "memorial" article goes on to quote some of the online

reminiscences. Betty Tiernan remembered the Christmas displays and riding the trolley to ride the state's first "moving stairs;" closing with, "To me, it is the biggest pain in the neck I've ever experienced. I'm just heartbroken." Jane Buck, who visited the store from childhood and frequented both the Tea Room and lunch counter, pronounced, "My memories are so vivid. It was well-kept and very organized, the whole nine yards—just up-scale, top notch." Buck, who opened her first charge card in the 1940s, closed by saying, "All I can say is goodbye to my old friend. It's a big loss. It's the end of an era. 162 years. I really did grow up with Younkers." Jeanie Hopcus recalled that as with others who grew up in Des Moines, she took the trolley downtown to shop at Younkers and loved the Younkers elevator with the friendly operators who would announce each floor and the departments. The downtown store "was so vibrant . . . and such a friendly store" with everything under one roof.

Connie Boesen, a Des Moines City Council member, worked at Younkers for 34 years when she left the store in 2003 and her position as a buyer of sweaters and knits. She believes that Des Moines is losing "an institution." "It did mean a lot to this community.[128] It was part of what developed this community . . . Younkers was the store you went to sit on Santa's lap. That was the place you went. It was part of the fiber of the community."

There could be no more appropriate summary of what the Younkers culture meant to Des Moines and Iowa communities. Joe Rosenfield helped to build that culture, and that culture helped to build Joe Rosenfield. We said "good bye" to Joe in 2000, and now we say, "Good Bye, Younkers."

Joe Rosenfield as a baby. *Iowa Jewish Archives*.

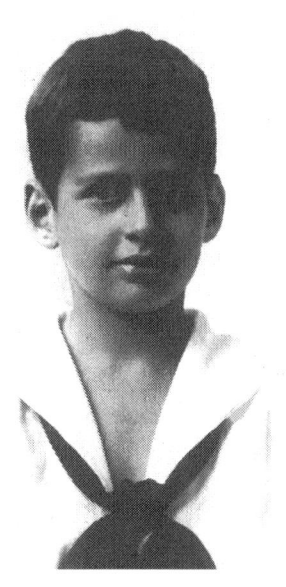

Joe Rosenfield as a child. *Iowa Jewish Archives*.

Undergraduate photo of Joe Rosenfield.
Grinnell College Archives.

Boy Scouts meeting with President Teddy Roosevelt, 1918.
Iowa Jewish Archives.

82 MENTOR

> "My devotion to Grinnell has been undiminished since 1921 and will continue until the end of my existence."
>
> JOE ROSENFIELD
> OLDEST ON RECEIVING AN HONORARY DEGREE
> FROM GRINNELL COLLEGE, 1994

Joe as a boy. *Grinnell College*.

Joe Rosenfield, third from the right. *Grinnell College Archives.*

To All Men To Whom These Presences Shall Come, Greetings

B. BLANCHARD TALBOTT

After searching for countless hours, reporters finally located Mr. Talbott in the vicinity of the local brick-yard, where he and other gentlemen-of-high-order were playing at dice. The astute editor of The Malteaser proved to be less loquacious than Mr. Rosenfield and for a time declined to be quoted on the subject of this year's outlook.

However, he did not dismiss the reporter with cursory treatment. He was inclined to be facetious and playfully tossed a newly-yarded brick at him, saying æ$!&!!*) :.

Refusing to give a description of himself, Mr. Talbott gave his consent to the reporter to do the same.

Intensely unhandsome, the author's sugar-bowl face surmounts gable-like shoulders and at times half smiles, half scowls at those who stand by in awe at its passing. Glittering, bottle-green eyes of his hold multitudes with the sheer beauty of them. Unquestionably with this subtle description in mind, no one will allow this brilliant to pass without at least giving information that he is known.

According to late statistics procured from the author, he is without question one of the greatest men who ever attended Grinnell college. In fact, he was perfectly willing to give verification to this fact, and even declared that it would probably be years before this institution might see another as great as he.

J. FRANKEL ROSENFIELD

(Bertillion Measurements on Request)

Mr. Rosenfield, better known in social circles as High Jackin' Al, Gus the Galute, and other alias-like cognomens is herein mentioned as manager of business of this pamphlet.

His qualifications are sterling. They are below catalogued.

Enjoying temporary sanity.

Never convicted of a felony.

Is well rated in the society register of Des Moines' 400 (his official number in this body of selectmen being 14,348.)

Stays out of jail frequently.

When interviewed at his villa yesterday on the outlook of The Malteaser, Mr. Rosenfield declared:

"I hope that the school year of 1923-24 will afford my co-inmates the greater privileges of association with me. However, I earnestly beseech curious co-eds to refrain from sending me flowers and candy and to devote less of their attentions to me than in the past. ...I have come to realize my high-most position in the life and society of Grinnell and I shudder when I recall how I have been pursued by college women, who have deliberately designed to subvert my bachelorhood. I hope that during this school year I shall be able to accommodate all who wish to gain the benefit to be had from knowing such an unusual and interesting personage as myself."

.....4.....

Spoof Biographies from the *Malteaser*.

Rose Rosenfield. *Jewish Archives*.

Ruth Rosenfield, Louise Rosenfield Noun. *Jewish Archives*.

really mean something if they hit, rather than buying 100 stocks and doing modestly well with them.

"In 1929 I bought a couple of stocks, the first I bought, in companies that both went broke. After that it was several years before I got back into the market, and it's been kind of an off-and-on thing ever since—periods of time when I was out of the market and periods of time when I was very much in the market," Rosenfield said.

The fact that Rosenfield managed Grinnell's endowment as though it were his own was by design, not by chance.

"When Grinnell started getting a meaningful endowment, I would spend much more time on the Grinnell endowment than I would on my own, probably because most of my own money was going to Grinnell eventually," he said.

The Great Spectator

Born May 16, 1904, to Meyer and Rose Frankel Rosenfield, he was raised with two sisters, a younger sister Louise Rosenfield Noun '29 and an older sister Ruth.

Rosenfield's devotion to philanthropy was nurtured by the early influences of his life, including his mother, an early suffragist and the impetus for the Rosenfield Lectures; his sister Louise Noun, a 1929 graduate of Grinnell College and a well-known champion for women's rights and the namesake of Grinnell's Noun Program in Gender and Women's Studies; and his wife, Dannie, a member of the Iowa Board of Regents.

His decision to attend Grinnell College after graduating from West High School in Des Moines in 1921 was mysterious, even to Rosenfield himself.

"On getting out of high school, I really didn't know where I wanted to go to college," he said. "I entered Grinnell in the fall of 1921, not knowing exactly what I'd find there. But after I had been there about three weeks, I had fallen in love with the place and you couldn't have driven me out of there with a team of horses.

"I just took to Grinnell right away. Whether Grinnell took to me, I don't know, but I certainly took to Grinnell the whole spirit of the institution, partially the quality of the instruction, but the dormitory system, the lack of fraternities, sororities, the kind of people you found there, and the rather liberal atmosphere—the whole thing, some of it quite intangible. I just liked it."

Although law became the focus of his career, while a student

MONEY MAGAZINE FEATURES JOE ROSENFIELD '25

Joseph Rosenfield '25 and the financial wizardry that he used to help Grinnell College build its large endowment was featured in the June 2000 issue of Money magazine.

The article, which discussed the investment strategies that helped Grinnell build an endowment of more than $1 billion, hit the newsstands on May 15, less than a month before Rosenfield's death.

"Allow me to introduce you to the man who turned one of the finest small colleges in the country into one of the richest," wrote Jason Zweig, senior writer and columnist for the magazine. "Full of charisma, wisdom, and wisecracks, he retains a mind as sharp as a razor. He decks himself out in dress slacks and a Chicago Cubs shirt. ... Rosenfield personally owned 3 percent of the team, and in his 70s he vowed to stay alive until the Cubs win a World Series—which may explain the air of immortality that surrounds him." Sadly for Grinnell College and the Chicago Cubs, that was not to be.

The article highlighted Rosenfield's investment brilliance. By investing in such little-known opportunities as Berkshire Hathaway and NM Electronics for Grinnell College, Rosenfield built an incredible portfolio for his alma mater. Berskshire Hathaway is owned by Rosenfield's close friend Warren Buffet, while NM Electronics was a company formed in 1968 by Grinnell alumnus and trustee Robert Noyce '49. It later became Intel Corporation.

"I just wanted to do some good with the money," Rosenfield stated in the article. Zweig adds, "That's a lesson for all of us. Instead of blindly striving to make our money grow ... each of us should pause and ask: What good is my money if I never do some good with it? Is there a way to make my wealth live on and do honor to my name?"

Rosenfield graduated from Grinnell College in 1925 with a B.A. degree. Elected to the board of trustees in 1941, 16 years after his graduation, he served as chairman of the board from 1948–1952.

"From the mid-'60s through the mid-'90s, Rosenfield was the key member of the investment committee at his alma mater," Zweig wrote. "It is for Grinnell, not for himself, that Rosenfield has worked most of his investing magic."

And, he adds, thanks to Rosenfield, Grinnell College has the largest endowment per student of any private liberal arts college in the United States.

Money Magazine.

Rosenfield Honored by Sertoma

Des Moines Tribune, Tues., Dec. 17, 1974

Joseph F. Rosenfield Tuesday was presented the Sertoma Club's Service to Mankind Award at the club's Christmas luncheon.

The award is given each year to an outstanding citizen who is not a member of the club, in recognition of meritorious service to the community.

Rosenfield was honored for his contributions of time, effort and financial assistance in a wide area of civic activities, including service as a member of the Board of Trustees and treasurer of Iowa Methodist Hospital and past director of Blue Cross Hospital Services of Iowa.

He is a former chairman of United Campaign, has served as a director of Willkie House, and has been president of Des Moines Enterprises, the sports-promoting branch of the Greater Des Moines Chamber of Commerce, the group that brought professional baseball to Des Moines.

Rosenfield is now serving as trustee of the Iowa Law School Foundation and recently helped the foundation raise more than a million dollars in endowment funds. He is also a trustee and past president of the Board of Directors of Grinnell College, and served on the advisory committee for the new building of the Des Moines YWCA.

A lifelong resident of Des Moines, Rosenfield is a former chairman of the board of Younkers, and a former vice-president and general counsel of the company.

Following retirement, he has remained as a consultant and chairman of the company's executive committee. He is also a trustee of General Growth Properties and an honorary life member of the Greater Des Moines Committee. He makes his home at 3060 Grand Ave.

Mr. and Mrs. Rosenfield

Des Moines Tribune

Mr. and Mrs. Joseph Rosenfield are shown aboard the S. S. Lurline on which they sailed Friday from San Francisco, Cal., for their wedding trip to Hawaii. Before her marriage, Aug. 11, Mrs. Rosenfield was Miss Dannie Burke of Albuquerque, N. M. They will be at home in Des Moines after Sept. 15.

Dannie.

Louise Rosenfield Noun. *Jewish Archives*.

Rose Rosenfield. *Jewish Archives*.

Sketch Shows Younkers in Shopping Center in Bettendorf

The above architect's drawing shows Younkers branch store which will occupy 60,000 square feet at the new Bettendorf shopping center at Kimberly Highway and Middle Road. The building, at one end of a mall, will be a modern one-floor operation. The store project will cost $1½ million, the developers announced. A 30-year lease has been completed by Younkers with the developers for the largest unit in the center. Sketches on this and the opposite page were made by the developers, M. Bucksbaum Co. of Cedar Rapids.

Credit Union Elects Six New Board Members

Six directors were elected to the board of the Credit Union at its annual meeting held in the training classroom on Monday morning, April 7.

Ruth McGlothen, auditing; and Gretchen Mullins, secretary in the Glynn merchandising office, were re-elected to the board. Others elected for three-year terms were Jon Fitch, cosmetics; Marcella Hunt Young, credit office in the Store for Homes, and Nelson Mossholder, window display.

Golda Wyatt, employees' cafeteria cashier, was elected to fill a one-year unexpired term. Bruce Mossholder, electrician, was elected alternate.

Directors with one-year terms to serve are Margaret Lally, Thelma Goreham, Eddie Johnson and Beatrice Burrell.

Directors with two-year terms yet to serve are Lucile Wallett, William Temple, William Carlson, Myrtle Baker and Joe Shelledy.

Eddie Johnson, president, called the annual meeting to order with 63 members present, compared with 46 the previous year.

Lucile Wallett, treasurer, reported that the Credit Union has $93,494 invested in government bonds. 27 new members have joined since the first of the year, and 21 loans were made in March. Approximately one third of the share accounts is loaned to members.

Elda Bull, jewelry, enjoyed Easter week entertaining her daughter, Beverly of Miami, Fla. Beverly is a personal appearance director of stewardesses for Eastern Air Lines out of Miami.

Joyce Mortensen is helping out as secretary in the Store for Homes in place of Lillian Conard who returned to work for the government.

Ina Wheeler, payroll office, and husband, spent the week end of March 22 with their daughter and family, Mr. and Mrs. Melvin Springer, at Orchard.

Violet Ballard, toys, proudly reports that her granddaughter, Marcia Beals, age 8, won first prize for her bird house at Meredith School.

William Jefferson, porter on second floor, west, and his wife, Ada, rest room maid, were called to Sioux Falls, S. D., Friday, March 28, to attend the funeral of Mr. Jefferson's niece. They returned to work on Monday, March 31.

Understand Your Social Security
Arranged by Lucile Wallett from Information Supplied by Local Social Security Office.

There is a tendency among all of us to take our Payroll Deductions for Social Security as something we must pay, and not give too much thought to the benefits that we will, or can eventually receive.

This is the first of a series of articles that the Reporter will run, to help all of us to a better understanding of the benefits that we may expect to receive.

Last year, in addition to the amount that each of you paid into the Social Security fund, the store also paid $175,767.82. Thus, this payment by the store when added to the amount that will be paid to the Trustee for the Profit Sharing Plan, makes approximately $498,767.00 that the store paid last year to assist employees when they retire or when for some reason, if it is necessary to stop working.

THE YOUNKER REPORTER
April 1955

Younkers Archives, Iowa Historical Museum.

Younkers Signs Lease for Store in Bettendorf Shopping Center

Reprinted from The Daily Times, Davenport, Wednesday, Feb. 12

Younkers Department Store, with headquarters in Des Moines, will be part of the new shopping center at Kimberly Highway and Middle Road in Bettendorf.

The announcement was made today at a luncheon meeting at the Plaza in Bettendorf, attended by Mayor Arnold Kakert of Bettendorf, city officials, top officials of the Younkers firm and the shopping center developers.

The store project will cost $1½ million, it was announced by the developers.

Joseph Rosenfield, chairman of the Board of Directors of Younkers, and Morey Sostrin, president of the firm, attended the meeting.

A 30-year lease has been completed with Younkers by the M. Bucksbaum Co., Cedar Rapids, developers of the new center. The store will occupy 60,000 square feet and will be the largest unit in the center.

One-Floor Operation

The building will be a modern one-floor operation and will be one of the largest and most up-to-date department stores in eastern Iowa, the developers reported at the meeting.

It will be located at the east end of the center and at the end of a covered mall. There will be automobile parking spaces on three sides of the building.

Sostrin said the store will have the same departments as the Younkers unit in Rock Island, only on a larger scale.

"The single floor design," he said, "will offer facilities for more suitable operation."

Air-Conditioning

He reported that the store will be completely air-conditioned and that all of the fixtures will be of the latest design.

Sostrin said the latest merchandising techniques will be employed in the operation of the store.

The officials of the Younkers firm told Bettendorf city officials that the new store is an additional expansion in the Quad-City area for the company. They said they would continue operation of their Rock Island store.

Expressing themselves as being "well pleased" with the Quad-City area, the store executives said the unit in the Bettendorf shopping center is part of their program for "complete coverage of the area." They said they were impressed with the growth of the Bettendorf area and that the new store is part of their state-wide system of units in shopping centers.

30 More Stores

Martin and Matthew Bucksbaum, the developers, reported that they were "well satisfied" with the progress being made in the development of the center. They said the plans provide for an additional 30 stores in the area, covering 200,000 square feet in addition to the Trio roller skating rink on the 25-acre plot.

Parking space will be provided for approximately 2,000 automobiles, it was reported at the meeting.

Martin Bucksbaum is in charge of the leasing of space in the center. He said leases are now being negotiated with other national chain stores and that there also will be space for lease to Quad-City area merchants.

Among the stores planned in the center in addition to Younkers Department Store are a super-market, drug store, women's speciality shops, fashion shoe store, family shoe store, a large variety store, linen-drapery shop, hardware and appliance store, music record shop, food speciality store, paint and wallpaper store, children's wear shop, jewelry store, millinery store, men's wear store, women's sports wear shop, and a restaurant.

The Bettendorf Shopping Center developers built the Town and Country Shopping Center in Cedar Rapids and recently completed improvement projects in the business district of Burlington. The firm is also planning a new shopping center near the airport in Des Moines.

Omar Franklin, store architect, and his wife left Wednesday, March 5, for Phoenix, Ariz., where they will visit for two weeks with their daughter, Elizabeth, and family.

Studying an architect's drawing of the Younker department store branch which will be part of the new Bettendorf Shopping Center, are, left to right, seated: Morey Sostrin, president of Younkers; Joseph Rosenfield, chairman of the board of the firm; standing: Mayor Arnold Kakert of Bettendorf; Matthew Bucksbaum and Martin Bucksbaum, the developers of the shopping center.—Photo by courtesy of The Daily Times of Davenport.

Credit Office Notes

CATERING to a convalescing husband is Priscilla Brown, while Mr. Brown recovers from recent surgery at Iowa Methodist Hospital.

RETURNED to work and recuperating nicely from their operations are Elsie Mann and Mardy Barman.

ENDURING pain with a smile, Jessie Warner is some improved from an arthritic condition which has beset her this winter.

DISCOURAGED not, by threatening weather, Hazel Smith and her husband drove to Iowa City recently to visit with their son-in-law and daughter.

INDOCTRINATED in a limited fashion to the general procedure of a credit office, have been Terry Mankowski and Carolyn Aller, of Drake and Des Moines Tech respectively. The girls have been working in the office a few days a week for the past month.

TRYING to reduce or trying to gain weight—seem to be occupying the interest of most of the girls in the department—but for some strange reason, the thin folks get thinner and the plump ones ("fat" has been cut out of our dictionary) get heavier.

Mrs. Flo Holcomb, millinery, spent several days in Kansas City, Mo., recently visiting her daughter and family, Mr. and Mrs. George Shipley.

THE YOUNKER REPORTER — *March 1958*

Younkers Archives, Iowa Historical Museum.

Chairman of the Board Gets Shopping Center Underway

Joseph F. Rosenfield, chairman of the board of Younkers, spread the first shovelful of cement poured at the Merle Hay Plaza shopping center at Merle Hay road and Douglas avenue on Monday, June 30. Building construction began at the multi-million dollar project with the setting of columns for the Younker building. Ground clearing had been underway for some time.—Photograph is by courtesy of the Register and Tribune.

Personnel Promotions, Transfers and Changes

The personnel office has announced the following advancements, promotions, transfers and changes:

Nancy Thompson, who graduated in June from Iowa State College, started June 17 as a trainee-assistant in the basement girls' and infants' departments. Nancy first started to work for Younkers in 1952 while going to East High School working in clerical and selling jobs during vacations as she went on to college. Last summer she spent her time in notions doing detail work and selling.

Pat Delin has transferred from the messenger group to a helper's job in the display department.

Norman Bates, messenger, has become a packer in the delivery department.

Larry Evans, who has been selling children's shoes, changed to second floor women's shoes.

Jacqueline Griffith, who has been on leave of absence and formerly was in statement mailing, took a job in accounts payable on her return in June.

Kathryn Strait, who has been selling since March in the College Shop, transferred June 30 to the French Room detail job.

Extras to Regulars

The following extras have become regulars during June in the departments named:

Paul Meeks, messengers; James Shafto, Penberthy stock; Mary Dennis, basement corsets; Shirley Kahn, basement; and Sandra Cooley, women's alterations.

Also Gary DeSomber and Karen Vander Meede, Cremona Room; Leona Riley, draperies, Store for Homes; Christine Henry, notions; David Kauzlarich, first floor shoes; and Opal Climie, women's alterations.

Marietta Dickey, statement mailing, spent a week of her vacation visiting relatives in Kansas City, Mo.

Mildred Thompson, buyer of budget dresses, was given a surprise vacation send-off by the ladies of her department on Friday, June 20. She is enjoying a trip through Canada with friends.

Miss Glenda Rees, ready-to-wear merchandise office, has left the store and has moved to Omaha. Members of the office wish her the best of everything she undertakes in the future.

Florence Taylor, credit office, says the excitement of a pleasant vacation trip to Michigan with her mother, Mrs. Bessie McGlocklin, was scarcely over when her mother was faced with an unexpected trip to the hospital for an emergency appendectomy. Last week she was recuperating at home.

Ruth Gutteridge, Kardex files, spent the week of June 26 at Owatonna, Minn.

LaVon Lindblom, decorating studio, with her daughter Kathy, drove to Grand Island, Neb., for the July 4 week end. She and her sisters from Omaha, Nebr., and Topeka, Kans., visited their father.

THE YOUNKER REPORTER

July, 1958

Younkers Archives, Iowa Historical Museum.

Country Club Blvd., daughter of Mr. and Mrs. F. E. Tappen.
Valley High School: Wendy Hanes, 1820 Vine Street, West Des Moines, daughter of Mr. and Mrs. O. W. Hanes; Connie Edge, 1213 Locust Street, West Des Moines, daughter of Mr. and Mrs. Marvin A. Edge.
Roosevelt High School: Susan Hamborg, 6826 Colby Avenue, daughter of Mr. and Mrs. Richard R. Hamborg; Cheryl Scanland, 2100 80th St. Court, daughter of Mr. and Mrs. J. E. Scanland, Des Moines.
Technical High School: Janet Lillie, 2014 44th, daughter of Mrs. Clara Lillie; Sharon Cook, 3827 E. Douglas, daughter of Mrs. Ralph E. Cook.

My Trip to Europe
By Mabel Kutch

When someone asks, "What was the highlight of your trip to Europe," I truthfully must say, "Everything." Each day we enjoyed new experiences in countries unfamiliar to us, where people were friendly and kind. And too, Jeannette Midgorden, a long-time friend, was always a congenial traveling companion.

We sailed on May 3 from Pier 90, in New York. It was most exciting; the bon voyage activities prior to sailing, the hundreds of people calling and waving to passengers, the band playing and the ship photographer snapping group pictures. As the New York skyline faded out of sight, I suddenly remembered I was "scared to death" of water, but that soon passed when we returned to our stateroom and found flowers, gifts and messages from friends.

The five days of leisurely living on the Queen Mary were all we expected, and more. We were pleased with our dining room assignment—the six people at the table couldn't have been nicer. There was a delightful couple, Standard Oil people who after living in many countries, were returning to England. I'll always remember the story about their unusual house pet, a six foot boa constrictor that bothered no one until the day they accidentally shut the door on its tail, then it promptly bit her. There was a charming Englishman with a tremendous sense of humor, who shared a dish of snails with me; a young man from Scotland who ate quantities of corn on the cob, in salute to the gals from Iowa; and an interesting woman from New York. Our host was the most handsome purser on ship, and the nicest. Our group "clicked" when we first met and our table seemed to have the most fun, and perhaps was the noisiest.

As the days flew by, we participated in all the activities, went to the movies, shopped and relaxed on the deck. We met lots of people, including the Gerald Millers, formerly of Des Moines, and were invited to tea, cocktails, parties etc. We played bingo (Jeanette won $40.), bet on the horse races, and took cha-cha lessons.

We both were prize winners (travel clocks) at the Saturday night gala hat-parade party. The theme was songs and I made Jeanette a "Bicycle Built for Two" hat out of cardboard and a Younker sack. For myself, I chose, "I Ain't Got Nobody," and created a tall model out of coat hangers, a towel and my hat. After clearing customs at Southhampton, we discovered we couldn't use an APO number to call Jeanette's nephew, a jet pilot (you can in the states). We had visions of being stranded there, but the American Consul came to our rescue the next morning. The nephew and wife met us in London and we saw a great deal of one of the largest cities in the world in four hours.

Like all tourists we were interested in Westminster Abbey, Parliament, Big Ben, the Thames, the Buckingham Palace. We saw the evening change-of-guards which now takes place inside the gates, far away from curious visitors. Later, after we watched one of the guards lock the doors of the horse stables, he came striding down the walk directly toward us. We had to jump quickly out of his way or be pushed aside as he had no intention of deviating from his course, straight ahead.

Darel and Janet lived seventy miles from London in a quaint little village, near Flinchingfield air base. Their modernized thatched-roof cottage was built in 1600. The original ceiling beams, made of logs from sunken ships that had been washed ashore, were still intact. There was a huge fireplace, with space for chairs on the hearth, where people used to sit to keep warm. The yard was a gardener's dream, with a formal garden, a Chinese tea house, patches of wild flowers and a beautiful fence of roses.

After two days of getting acquainted (I soon became a new relative), packing and getting the baby settled with his "sitter," the four of us took off for a twelve day auto trip. Luggage space in the Jaguar was limited so Jeanette and I had to make a quick decision about dividing our clothes. We kept three complete outfits, only what would fit in one bag, and sent everything else home, air freight. To our dismay that bag came through weeks later at a cost of $53 plus another bill of $23. (More next month).

Mrs. Evelyn Knotts Stark, travel bureau, returned July 11 from Setauket, N. Y., where she attended the christening of her grandson, Peter Kaiser Stark. He is the third child of Mr. and Mrs. John T. Stark, jr. The christening was Sunday, July 9, at Caroline Church of Brookhaven. The day before Mrs. Stark attended the wedding of Ross Michael Carrell, formerly of Des Moines, and Helen Ruth Collins in Haddonfield, N. J.

Miss Donna Ables, elevator operator, spent one week of her vacation at home and the other visiting her grandmother, Mrs. Ida Ables, at Humeston, Donna's home town.

How We've Grown Since Sixty Years Ago!

Younkers Main Store has grown considerably since the above picture was taken sometime between 1898 and 1909, about sixty years ago! Then, it was only a five-story building, and did not extend to the alley on Seventh st., and only to the alley on Walnut. Now it is seven stories high and extends to the north alley, as well as to Eighth street. The above picture was reproduced from a colored postal card issued the early part of the century. The card was discovered by Wally Lundgren, well known stamp collector and insurance man who once worked at Younkers while going to school. He loaned the card to The Reporter for reproduction.

THE YOUNKER REPORTER Fall 1961 (now quarterly)

Younkers Archives, Iowa Historical Museum.

James Rosenfield
1946-1962

We, the Senior Class, dedicate this book to the memory of James Rosenfield, our classmate, whose friendliness will always be remembered.

Lincoln High School Dedication. *Online Lincoln High School Annual.*

New Henry Frankel Memorial Terrace Dedicated at Art Center

Reprinted from the Des Moines Register, June 16.

By Julie Zelenka

A Japanese theme was used Sunday (June 15) to dedicate the Henry Frankel Memorial Terrace at the Des Moines Art Center.

Dwight Kirsch, art center director, wore Japanese kimono and sandals as he told of the interest of the late Mr. Frankel and his wife in Japan, and how they traveled to Japan in 1956.

Mr. Frankel headed the center's planning board just before his death on July 22, 1957, and the last project he recommended was the terrace. The new terrace joins the art center on the south side of the east wing.

Symbolism in Design

"The symbolism of this terrace is in its design," Kirsch said. "The semi-circular walk that goes to the reflecting pool is designed to tie in with the rectangles of the building. It is a symbol of the name 'center'.

"The shape of the spiral (a tree-shaded grassy plot) is the sign of growth and it is surrounded by grass and growing things."

A bronze tablet engraved to commemorate Mr. Frankel is to be added to the terrace later. Kirsch said there wasn't time to have the tablet made.

That is why the Japanese theme was used. Kirsch, and Mrs. Tomoko Yamamoto, widely known Des Moines flower arranger who was born in Japan, did a pantomime. Mrs. Yamamoto also wore a native costume.

Memorial Scroll

At the end of the pantomime, they had created a scroll that read: "To Henry Frankel, our friend and patron—with affection and gratitude."

About 100 persons attended the dedication, including Mr. Frankel's widow. Mrs. Frankel returned to Toronto, Ontario, Canada, her birthplace, after her husband's death. She is visiting here.

Other relatives included Mr. Frankel's sister, Mrs. Meyer Rosenfield; nephew Joseph Rosenfield, and his son, James; niece, Mrs. Maurice Noun, and her daughter Susan; great-nephew Robert Mrs. Milton Lubetkin, of Los Angeles, Cal.

Mr. Frankel was a trustee of the Edmundson Art Foundation, Inc., which operates the center. Foundation funds were used to build the terrace.

Mrs. Meyer Rosenfield, left, sister of the late Henry Frankel, and mother of Joseph F. Rosenfield, chairman of the board of directors of Younkers; and Mrs. Henry Frankel, of Toronto, Ontario, Canada, widow of the late Henry Frankel, look at the scroll prepared Sunday, June 15, during the dedication ceremonies of the Henry Frankel Memorial Terrace at the Des Moines Art Center. It says, "To Henry Frankel, our friend and patron—with affection and gratitude."

Jewish Archives.

Introducing Younkers 1965 Junior Fashion Council at Sioux City

DATESETTERS, U.S.A., 1964, TEEN FASHION SHOW AT YOUNKER-DAVIDSON'S

On Saturday, Nov. 14, a teen fashion show presenting exciting new date fashions made with versatile Celanese contemporary fibers was viewed by an enthusiastic audience at a 2:30 showing. Younkers 1964-65 Junior Fashion Council, in their introductory appearance, modeled fashions from the pages of the November issue of Seventeen magazine. Gladys Parker, Celanese representative, was the guest commentator. Balloting was held to select "Miss Datesetter" from among the Junior Fashion Council members. The winner was Miss Jeanne Marx, East High School.

COLLEGE BOARD ADVISOR APPOINTED TO MADEMOISELLE'S 1965 COLLEGE BOARD

Miss Anne Gleysteen has been appointed a member of Mademoiselle Magazine's 1965 College Board.

The board is composed of winners of the magazine's annual College Board Competition, a contest designed to rec-

Carol LeMaster — Advisor, Leeds
Jeanne Aldrich — Heelen
Linda Brophy — East
Micki Haley — Heelen
Connie Hanlon — Heelen
Nancy Jonas — Leeds
Mary Jacobs — Central
Jean Lund — Riverside
Jeanne Marx — East
Marian Mikelson — Leeds
Kathy Miller — East
Jane Olson — Central
Linda Pocnut — Central
Barb Stoneberg — Central
Audrie Tracey — East
Diane Walding — Heelen

SIOUX CITY AT YOUNKER-DAVIDSON'S: Gladys Parker, Celanese representative, presenting a Younker gift certificate to Miss Mary Mikelson of Leeds High School, winner of the Miss Datesetter, U. S. A. title at the Datesetter fashion show.

THE YOUNKER REPORTER

March 1965

ognize young women with talent in art, writing, editing, photography, layout, fashion design, merchandising, retail promotion or advertising.

Board members, from the United States, Canada, and abroad, were selected on the basis of entries they submitted showing ability in one of these fields.

All College Board members are eligible to compete for the 20 guest editorships awarded by the magazine each May. The 20 lucky guest editors go to New York to spend the month of June as salaried employees of Mademoiselle, and help to write, illustrate and edit the magazine's August college issue. In addition they are photographed for the August issue and receive consideration for future staff positions.

The 1964 guest editors enjoyed a special bonus—a flying trip to England, where they visited Stratford and Oxford between stays in London.

Miss Gleysteen is a junior at the University of Nebraska at Lincoln, and we found her to possess unusual talent and ability during her term as college board advisor. We wish her luck on the final competition!

Iowa Historical Museum.

Members of Younkers Newly Enlarged Board of Directors

Younkers Board of Directors posed for this exclusive Younker Reporter photograph at the annual meeting on Monday morning, May 26, in the executive office. Members of the board are, from left, seated: Charles Duchen, president and member of the executive committee; Morey Sostrin, chairman of the board and member of the executive committee; and Joseph F. Rosenfield, chairman of the executive committee. Standing: J. Stuart Kirk, consultant; Kenneth McCarthy, branch store director who was named a vice president; John A. Griner III, Chicago, Ill.; Joseph M. Ginther, secretary-treasurer; Frederick A. Glynn, vice president; Stanley H. Krum, vice president; Stanley B. Friedman, consultant; William Friedman, Jr., who was named vice president of administration; William Friedman, consultant; Robert Mandelbaum; and Robert Lubetkin.

Younkers' Six Months Report Ending July 31, 1969

By Charles Duchen, President

Retail sales in our area continue at a record level as indicated by the following report.

The City of Sioux City Urban Renewal has purchased our Martin Store in Sioux City, Iowa, and it was recently closed. Also to be closed shortly is the downtown Kilpatrick's Store in Omaha. We will concentrate our effort in the two growing suburban stores in Omaha and the Younker-Davidson Store in Sioux City. On a long-range basis, these store closings will not measurably affect our earnings.

It appears that Younker's performance for 1969 will continue to be a good one.

	2nd QUARTER 1969	1968	Increase	1st SIX MONTHS 1969	1968	Increase
Net Sales	$19,689,000	$17,804,000	+10.6%	$37,384,000	$34,119,000	+9.6%
Earnings Before Income Tax	973,000	856,000	+13.7%	1,778,000	1,594,000	+11.5%
Earnings After Income Tax	452,000	402,000	+12.4%	815,000	727,000	+12.1%
Earnings Per Share Of Common Stock (Unaudited)	.35	.31		.65	.57	

Earnings per common share based on average number of shares outstanding (adjusted to reflect 100,000 shares issued in May 1969)

United Way Drive

(Continued from page 2)

tees to study and review the budgets of 39 co-operating agencies.

Other Younkerites, Joseph Rosenfield, chairman of the store's executive committee, and J. Stuart Kirk, recently retired secretary-treasurer, always have been active in United Campaign work. Mr. Kirk presently is doing volunteer work for the YWCA, an agency of the United Community Services.

Mrs. William Friedman, wife of a store board member, has been a board member of the Polk County Assn. for Mental Health, and has served on the budget and program panels for the Legal Aid Society, the Transient Shelter of Bethel Mission, and six Salvation Army agencies.

Chairman Lubetkin needs your cooperation in making the store campaign a success. The campaign slogan is "Good Givers feel BEST!"

Miss Nancy Malmberg, gloves, returned to work the week of July 1 after spending a week in Las Vegas, Nev. She visited relatives and took in some shows.

Mornetta Skipper, assistant in handbags and gloves, was surprised by the girls in both departments with a cake and coffee party on her birthday, July 3.

Mary Jane Shaffer, a new member of the jewelry department, works at Younkers during the day and attends Grand View College for evening classes.

THE YOUNKER REPORTER

Sept, 1969.

Iowa Historical Museum.

LIFE AND LEGACY OF JOE ROSENFIELD 97

Younkers is 114 Years Old; 96 Years in Des Moines

Anniversary time at Younkers comes in the fall, and each year the Younker Reporter notes the passing years with selected historical notes.

By William A. Temple

YOUNKERS has come a long ways, baby, in its 114 years of existence; most of the progress has been made in the present century. Founded in Keokuk in 1856, a Des Moines store was opened 18 years later in 1874, and the Keokuk store was discontinued in 1879 following the withdrawal of one of the three founders, and the death of another of its founders.

The remaining founder and the widow of the deceased founder then moved to Des Moines and were active in the store until it was incorporated in 1904.

The store always was located on Walnut street and one of its main competitors was J. Mandelbaum & Sons, the latter joining operations with Younkers in 1924, and the closing of the Mandelbaum store in 1928 when the stock was moved to Younkers.

Before the turn of the century, Younkers first occupied a small store room where the Woolworth store is now located. It outgrew the quarters in three years and moved to Fifth and Walnut where the Bond store is now located. The Bond building this year is 99 years old.

Following a fire in its former McCain building, Younkers moved back to the new and larger building in 1881 where it remained until 1899.

It was in 1881 that Younkers employed the first woman clerk in Des Moines, and it was in 1893 that Norman Wilchinski began work at age 15 and moved up in the organization to become president in 1921.

What the store has done in the 70-year period of the 20th Century is found in its enlargement, expansion, moderniza-
(Continued on page 5)

Above — YOUNKERS SECOND LOCATION in Des Moines about 1880. View shows the north side of Walnut street looking east from Fifth street. Younkers had moved into this larger building in 1877 just three years after opening a Des Moines store in the McCain block less than a block west. The store was opened by Herman Younker and his nephew Aaron Younker. — Photo furnished by Paul Ashby, vice president of the Central National Bank and Trust Co., who is an authority on early Des Moines history.

Left — YOUNKERS THIRD LOCATION in Des Moines about 1898. The store sign can be seen at upper right over the street booth during the annual Semi Om Sed (Des Moines spelled backwards) celebration when downtown streets were filled with booths of various organizations and concessioners. This Younker location occupied a new McCain building to which Younkers returned in 1881. The original store occupied a smaller portion of this building from 1874 to 1877. While Younkers were at the Fifth and Walnut store pictured elsewhere, the old McCain building burned and this building replaced it. In 1890 a third floor was added to the two story building. Younkers moved out of this building in 1899 to a smaller version of its present store at Seventh and Walnut. Additions were made to the present store in 1909 and 1923. — Photo furnished by Paul Ashby.

THE YOUNKER REPORTER
Sept. 1970

3

Iowa Historical Museum.

Directory of Younker Branch Stores
Corrected As of March 1, 1971

Opened	Location	Address	Sq. Ft.	Floors	Manager
1941	Ames	323-325 Main Street	15,000	2 & B	Hank Gilman
1944	Mason City	Second and Federal	24,780	1 & B	Robert Taggart
1947	Fort Dodge	Crossroads Shopping Center	27,000	1	Warren Gentile
1948	Marshalltown	22-24 East Main Street	22,680	2 & B	Richard Henning
1949	Iowa City	111-117 E. Washington	38,250	2 & B	Donald Crum
1949	Ottumwa	127-129 East Main St.	14,650	3 & B	Ervin Thompson
1957	Oskaloosa	118 High Ave. West	8,000	1, M & B	Vera Ewing
1958	Austin, Minn.	Sterling Shopping Center	22,000	1 & B	John Mueller
1959	Des Moines	Merle Hay Plaza	181,000	2	John Coolidge
1960	Bettendorf	Duck Creek Plaza	60,000	1	James Atha
1960	Cedar Rapids	Lindale Plaza	100,000	2	William Hayes
1960	Newton	Shopping Center	15,000	1	Jack Rynes
1960	Spencer	Shopping Center	15,000	1	Arta Peterson
1962	Des Moines	Eastgate Shopping Center	40,000	1	Joe Hamand
1966	Burlington	Fairway Shopping Center	30,000	1	Gary Harris
1968	Dubuque	Kennedy Mall	60,000	1	Ron DeBo
1968	Cedar Falls	Waterloo College Square Shopping Center	60,000	1	Gene Kuebler

to draperies; Florence Jensen, from draperies to gloves; Rosemary Patterson, cosmetics to luggage, sporting goods and toys; Lois Johnson, linens to draperies; Linda Eiler, boys' to cosmetics; JoEllen Cannon, budget accessories to linens; Marie Kleekamp, stationery to linens; Leslie Enos, gift wrap to lamps, sporting goods and toys; Eleanor Rhodes, handbags to fine foods; and Evelyn Hopperstad, from auditing downtown to furniture office.

Engaged: Mary Frances Chase, personnel and training, to Stephen Doyle, men's shoes. Fran now is a student at Urbandale High and will graduate this May. Stephen is employed by the Wohl Shoe Co. They plan to be married in the future.

Wilbur Johnson, luggage, is joined by Mrs. Johnson in thanking his many co-workers for the gift certificate and beautiful gold plate presented to them in observance of their Golden Wedding Anniversary on February 7.

NEWTON

Our annual Christmas party was held at the Holiday Inn. The evening was spent having a gift exchange, dinner and dancing.

Marie Conklin, children's dept., was happy to have her husband, Capt. William Conklin, home from Vietnam for the holidays.

Evelyn Wicks replaces Lorna Adams in men's dept. Lorna's husband was home on leave from the Navy for Christmas and she returned with him to California.

Mike Covault, stock room, made the Dean's list at Community College.

Ella Mae Stienberger, cosmetics, had surgery Feb. 12 and last week was re-

THE YOUNKER REPORTER

March, 1971

WATERLOO-CEDAR FALLS: Above shows how Younkerites looked at their Christmas Party.

covering nicely at home.

Debbie Richards, daughter of Janet in notions, finished her term as Worthy Adviser in Newton Rainbow Assembly in January.

The recent Farm Show brought people from many surrounding communities to the shopping center and into our store. Departments should be complimented for the many pretty displays of the traditional red and white for Valentine's Day.

Ruth Graham is new in our millinery dept.

WATERLOO-CEDAR FALLS

Recent transfers in our store: Steve Risvedt, stock, to sporting goods and luggage; Diane Ryan, from children's to ready-to-wear; Joy Neiderhauser, from sports shack to juniors; and Marge Mixdorf, stationery and Linda Morgan, infants', to cosmetics.

Alan Kennedy, who formerly worked in men's while attending Ellsworth College is back with us in the manager trainee program.

Larry Heck, shoe dept. manager, is a new father. The baby has been named Anthony Ray.

Carol Charley, office, gave birth to a daughter in November. She has been named Brenda Jo.

Maxine Wagner, lingerie, returned to work after a long illness following surgery.

Betty Mangels, housewares and Nancy Kepler, sports shack were hospitalized recently. Both have returned to work.

Iowa Historical Museum.

Purchase of Geo. Innes Co. Announced by Store Officials

Principals involved in announcing on Saturday, Dec. 29, the purchase of the Geo. Innes Co. of Wichita, Kan., by Younker Brothers, Inc., are pictured above in Wichita. They are, seated, J. F. Rosenfield, board chairman of Younkers; and standing, left to right, Morey Sostrin, president of Younkers, Walter P. Innes, Jr., vice president of the Innes company; and Walter P. Innes, Sr., president of the Geo. Innes Co.

Legal Representation

Max Skeer, prominent Kansas City, Mo., real estate broker, who has handled a number of large transactions in Wichita and throughout the nation for firms of national standing, acted for the Innes company in the lease and purchase negotiations.

Also representing the company were Walter Innes, Sr., Walter Innes, Jr., George Spradling of Lilleston, Spradling, Gott and Stallwitz, Wichita, and Ellis D. Bever of Bever, Dye, Mustard and Belin.

Representing Younker Brothers were Rosenfield, Sostrin and Milton O. Riepe of the law firm of Gamble, Read, Howland, Gamble and Riepe of Des Moines.

Accounts payable department had their Christmas department party in the Tea Room Dec. 19. The party was given by May Hunter and Vera Pearlman. Following the dinner, gifts were exchanged.

SECOND PRIZE WINNER

Hans Carstens, display manager of Younker-Davidson's in Sioux City, was awarded $50 for second prize in the annual national window display contest sponsored by the Millinery Fashion Bureau for windows installed during November.

Saint Nick presented every girl in art needlework with a nice gift Dec. 13. Who was Saint Nick? Why Mrs. Bryan, art needlework buyer. Miss Manville, the instructor, also gave each girl a lovely gift. The girls presented their buyer with a new pair of satin house slippers.

The sixth floor houseware girls took invoice Sunday, Jan. 6, and celebrated the birthdays of Bertie Hogan and Esther Lindquist with a chicken dinner and birthday cake.

Lucile Foster is taking a leave of absence from her duties in the auditing department to be at home with her husband, Fred, who is ill.

Mutual Aid Benefits

The following Younkerites received benefits from the Mutual Aid Association during the month of December:

Ethel Marchant, daytime frocks	$46.67
Vera Hanson, Marshalltown	48.00
Elmer Stuart, Cremona Room	48.00
Marie Grabau, bas. corsets	20.00
Icis Doud, silverware	13.33
Minnie Caskey, delivery	10.67
Hazel Junger, Tea Room	14.67
Nadine Edwards, Marshalltown	48.00
Della Chapman, furniture	9.33
Delbert Gilfillan, window display	9.33
Vera Whitney, Tea Room	8.00
Estelle Riley, girls' dept	48.00
John Schroeder, Cremona Room	24.00
Jessie Warner, adjustment dept	40.00
Mayme Harris, notions	14.67
Rowena Sloan, bakery	8.00
Marjorie Glanville, Mason City	13.33

Mary Miner is the new office cashier who started work in November.

THE YOUNKER REPORTER

Mid 1950's. *Iowa Historical Museum.*

JOSEPH F. ROSENFIELD, a director of the Younker corporation since 1929, formerly chairman of the board and now chairman of the executive committee, retired from active daily participation as of May 31. He will continue in his role as chairman of the executive committee and acting as a consultant.

Joseph F. Rosenfield

Under Mr. Rosenfield's direction Younkers has expanded into new markets, established a unique profit-sharing plan for its employees and has enjoyed solid financial stability and growth.

Considering the retailing background of the Rosenfield and Frankel families, it seems only natural that the Younker organization should claim him as an executive despite the fact that he was educated for, and active for many years in the legal profession.

Mr. Rosenfield's grandfather, Isaiah Frankel, opened the original Frankel store in Oskaloosa, in 1861. His father, Meyer Rosenfield, was an executive of the Harris-Emery Co. department store which merged with Younkers in 1927. His father was a vice president in the combined organization. His mother, Rose, was a sister of Henry Frankel, president of Younkers from 1937 to 1944, and first chairman of the board from 1944 until he retired in 1947.

A native of Des Moines, Mr. Rosenfield was born May 16, 1904. He was the only son of Meyer and Rose Rosenfield. He had two sisters, Ruth Ransome of New York City and Louise Noun of Des Moines.

Mr. Rosenfield attended Greenwood School and old West High. From the age of eight he became an avid baseball fan, a sport which he thoroughly enjoys and is actively interested in to this day.

Joe, as he is widely known, went to work at age 14 at Christmas time in the toy department at Harris-Emery's, and was discovered by State authorities to be too young to work. His own uncle, Henry Frankel, had to fire him! One summer he sold pants at the Frankel Clothing Co.

In 1921 Joe enrolled at Grinnell college and received a B.A. degree in 1925, an average student who could be found at any sports event.

He was granted a degree of Juris Dicto in 1928 from the University of Iowa at Iowa City. He was admitted to the Iowa Bar in 1928. He returned to Des Moines and joined the law firm of Sargent, Gamble and Read. Later he was made a partner and the firm then became known as Gamble, Read, Howland and Rosenfield, a firm that has been the legal counsel for Younkers for many years.

In 1929, upon the death of his father, Mr. Rosenfield became one of the directors of Younkers. As an attorney he spent much time and energy on the legal and business aspects of Younkers, and in 1947 gave up his law practice to join Younkers on a permanent basis. He became vice president and general counsel at that time and in 1947 was elected chairman of the board, succeeding Henry Frankel.

Much of his store activities have been directed towards the locating and leasing of the branch stores.

Mr. Rosenfield was married in 1940 to Dannie Burke, a school acquaintance at the University of Iowa. Her home had been Reno, Nev. Mrs. Rosenfield is a member of the State Board of Regents.

40-Year Director
Rosenfield Retires
But Remains as Chairman of the Executive Committee

The Rosenfields live at 3660 Grand. He is a member of Temple B'nai Jeshurun.

Mr. Rosenfield has been generous with his time and talents. At one time or another he has been requisitioned to serve on almost every civic enterprise and is well known in the city and througout the state for his many and varied activities.

He is a director of the Bankers Trust Co.; the Iowa Power and Light Co.; and Northwestern Bell Telephone Co.; trustee and past president of the board of trustees of Grinnell College; president in 1948 and now honorary life member of the Greater Des Moines Committee; and a past chairman of the United Campaign.

He has been a member of the board of trustees and the treasurer of Iowa Methodist Hospital; a past director of Blue Cross Hospital Service which he helped found; a member of the board of directors of Willkie House; and served as president of Des Moines Enterprises, the sports-promoting branch of the Greater Des Moines Chamber of Commerce.

At the annual meeting of the board of directors on May 26, Mr. Rosenfield was presented with a silver plaque honoring his store service; and the framed original painting of himself which appeared in this year's annual report.

Mrs. Dorothy Chastarn, basement accommodation desk, and husband recently spent a week's vacation at their cabin near Fayetteville, Ark.

Service is the Word in Iowa !

Lewis E. Kaplan, publisher of CLOTHES, news magazine of the fashion industry, published in New York twice a month, wrote the following editorial concerning Younkers in the April 15 issue of the magazine.

"Every so often it dawns on us just how large this United States of ours is. We become aware that the entire world does not revolve around the latest happenings in New York or Los Angeles and that there is still an America out there where the mores of the people are linked to the good virtues even if personal lives don't necessarily measure up to such credos.

"One could not find a better example of this other, less frenetic way of life than in the fertile, rolling Iowa farmlands—lands that were tamed first by the sweat of the immigrants and later by the machine age to become the corn belt of the world. But, though it is comparatively sparsely settled, this farmland state does have its cities, its industries, and, of course, the retail stores to service its people.

"Service! There is a word that has almost disappeared from the vocabulary and the thinking of most merchants. And yet, it still does exist . . . even if it is necessary to go all the way to Iowa to find it. And find it you will—in spades—literally as a fundamental tenet for doing business.

"But, if Iowans, generally, are more service-minded, nobody out there has been more successful at parlaying this ingredient into big business—more specifically, into a better than $70 million business blanketing the state—than the subject of this issue's cover story—Younkers.

"This 113-year old store has proven that, in its corner of America, there is more to retailing than buying and selling merchandise. Younkers has demonstrated that there are customers who remember the way they are treated when they spend their money—and that this memory, carried forward from one loyal generation to the next, can—and has—built sales and profits that any major store in America would like to carry on its balance sheet."

THE YOUNKER REPORTER

Jun, 1969

Iowa Historical Museum.

Younkers Profit Sharing Plan Distributes $1,126,475 to Members

By J. Stuart Kirk, Secretary-Treasurer

Statements from the Bankers Trust Co. were received by all members of Younkers Profit Sharing Retirement Plan in July. The statements showed each participating member's share of the company contribution, the amount of earnings based on each participant's balance in the Plan on February 1, 1964, and the total amount in each person's account as of January 31, 1965.

The funds distributed came from the profits of the store in the amount of $448,817, and from the earnings of the Plan in the amount of $677,658 making a total of $1,126,477. This is the largest amount that has ever been distributed to members of the plan.

You will be interested to know that since the conception of the Plan, the store has paid to the Bankers Trust, as Trustees, a total of $6,778,933. During this same period, the earnings distributed to the accounts of members of the Plan amounted to $2,807,256.

The growth of the store business over the years that the Plan has been in existence has resulted in substantially larger annual credits to the members of the plan as evidenced by the schedule of total credits as shown at the end of this article.

The operating statement covering all income and expenses is shown in the box herewith:

As of the end of the Trust year (January 31, 1965) the assets held by the Trustees representing amounts that are due to members of the plan were as follows:

Cash	$ 55,410.99
Bonds	4,837,881.93
Stocks	2,105,958.85
Contributions due from Younkers and Kilpatrick's	76,899.37
Accrued Interest and misc. items	51,490.82
Total Assets	$7,127,641.96

The Bankers Trust Company advise us that last year they paid $224,302.09 to former employees. A large part of these disbursements are paid former associates who receive a specific amount each month. At present there are approximately 100 former employees receiving regular monthly checks from their account.

Explanation of the Operating Statement

1. Most of the Trust income comes from interest received on bonds, but we do own some preferred and common stock from which dividends are received.

2. Each year the Trustee is required to re-value all securities that are held on January 31. On January 31, 1965, the market was up compared with the previous year and thus we had a substantial gain in the value of securities amounting to $405,891.

3. Often it is advisable to sell securities that we are holding and invest the funds in other securities. Last year the profit from such sales amounted to $70,360.53.

4. Amounts forfeited by participating members who severed their connection with Younkers before 15 years of service, or having reached 65 years of age, amounted to $17,435.49. This amount is redistributed to remaining members of the plan.

5. For keeping records, making payments and the many other duties performed by the Trustees we paid $15,239.28.

6. It is important that we have expert advice in connection with the investment of a fund of this size and the fee of $7,500.00 is paid to Lional D. Edie & Co., who advise us in connection with the purchase and sale of securities.

7. The Trustee and the Advisory Committee find many occasions where it is necessary to have the advice of attorneys who specialize in plans such as ours. For this service we pay $1,200.00 a year.

8. Persons who continue to work after 65 and those who retire and take their payments each month or year do not participate in the interest, dividends or other earnings of the plans, but they do receive interest on the balance of their account. The interest paid last year on these determined accounts amounted to $42,134.87.

Membership in the Plan

In accordance with the Trust Agreement that conforms to U. S. Treasury Department regulations, all employees who have been continuously employed by Younkers Brothers on their regular payroll for more than five full years, automatically become members of the Plan.

New members in the plan receive credit based on earnings from the beginning of their sixth year of employment to December 31 of that year. After this initial year, total annual earnings are used as the basis of computing each individual's share.

Employees not already in the Plan will be eligible after they complete five years of regular employment with Younker Brothers.

This is a Profit Sharing Plan

Under our Plan, all co-workers who qualify share in the success of this business. Not only do we share in the profits, but the amount that each person receives
(Continued on page 8)

Operating Statement of Profit Sharing Plan

Income	
Received from interest and dividends	$252,867.20
Gain from revaluation and securities	405,891.45
Gain on sale of securities	70,360.53
Forfeitures	17,435.49
Other income	287.17
Total Income	$746,841.82
Expenditures	
Trustee's fee	$ 15,239.28
Investment Council fees	7,500.00
Legal fees	1,200.00
Interest on determined accounts	42,134.87
Corrections of employees' accounts prior years	1,622.14
Insurance (Bond)	899.58
Miscellaneous	588.05
Total Expenses	$ 69,183.92
Profit distributed to members of Plan	$677,657.90
	$746,841.82

Total credits to members of the Profit Sharing Retirement Trust since the plan started:

For Fiscal Year Ending Jan. 31

1945	$ 166,410.96
1946	201,709.17
1947	235,418.08
1948	237,825.62
1949	335,955.55
1950	396,657.53
1951	335,644.66
1952	334,784.78
1953	384,225.71
1954	526,326.41
1955	588,636.94
1956	467,553.51
1957	192,751.61
1958	496,616.97
1959	653,886.56
1960	386,865.10
1961	690,188.06
1962	537,278.47
1963	459,945.20
1964	831,082.42
1965	1,126,474.90
Total	$9,586,188.21

THE YOUNKER REPORTER
September, 1965

Iowa Historical Museum.

Joe Rosenfield, 1980's. *Jewish Archives.*

Joe Rosenfield, late 1980's. *Jewish Archives.*

Joe Rosenfield, 1990's. *Grinnell College*.

of political science at Grinnell Rosenfield tested his journalistic talents, reporting for the *Scarlet and Black* and later writing a column called "The Doric" (see sidebar, right).

"We called it 'The Doric: A Column of Pure Beauty,' which was kind of a scandalous sort of thing. Then there was *The Malteaser*, which was a humorous magazine of which I was business manager for three years. I also was the business manager of the school annual and finally I had to take over the editorship when we found that the editor hadn't been doing his work," Rosenfield recalled.

"Beyond that I was a great spectator. I don't think I ever missed a sporting event. I was no athlete at all, but I don't think I missed a football game or a basketball game or a track meet, and I would go out and watch football practice and basketball practice and got a big kick out of it, although Grinnell was not doing an awful lot of winning."

A Remarkable Man

Rosenfield was part of a well-established Des Moines retailing family, but it was not assumed he would take over the family business. "I hadn't decided on anything beyond Grinnell at that time. I guess probably the spring of my last year, I decided to go on to law school. My father was very determined that I not come into the store at that time. And he was right," Rosenfield remembered. "I was not cut out to go into the store and buy and sell merchandise where I would have been a flop. I don't like to shop, and I don't like merchandising. So I agreed to take a shot at Iowa for one year and see how I liked it."

Rosenfield received a J.D. from the University of Iowa in 1928 and practiced law with a Des Moines law firm until 1947. Upon the death of his father in 1929—Meyer Rosenfield, director of Younker's—Rosenfield joined Younker's department store, which had merged with the family retail business. He retired in 1964 as president and chairman of the board.

An enthusiastic spectator of sports while at Grinnell, his love of baseball led him to become the chief minority stockholder of the Chicago Cubs baseball team, a team he supported with a passion for most of his life. Following the purchase of the team by *The Chicago Tribune*, Rosenfield donated the proceeds from his portion of the sale to Grinnell College.

– Doric –
A Column of Pure Beauty

Editor's Note: The following are excerpts from the column titled "The Doric" written by Joe Rosenfield and his cohorts for the Scarlet & Black in November of 1924.

Quien Esta?

Sir: The rumor that Joe Rosenfield was late to class because the freshman just in front of him reading a letter walked so slowly, is false. ... It wasn't a freshman.

The Girl in My English Class says that she is glad Grinnell isn't all mixed up in politics the way that horrid old Electoral college is. —Denver Red

---

On the Banks of Old Grinnell

Aristotle, our demon reporter, brings news that the Merchants National Bank opened yesterday ... to let three directors out the back door.

As an added attraction for Homecoming, a cowmilking contest will take place between the halves of the Ames-Grinnell game, three Grinnell professors to oppose three Ames deans. The odds now favor the "Farmers," but before Saturday they may shift to Ames.

The Girl in My English Class says that she supposes that steel wool comes from hydraulic rams.

The lowest mortal in school, according to one of our literary lights, is the nefarious derelict who cribbed out of the Bible while taking an exam in Religious Problems.

We the editors, urge that the student body get behind the movement to SEND THE BAND TO OMAHA ... or someplace.

Howard Wicks went to Omaha last Saturday to scout the Creighton-Oklahoma game for Grinnell. He reports that the cabaret business is fine.

The Girl in My English Class says that she reads in the paper that it took 34,000 muskrats to make all the Hudson Seal coats worn last year and that she thinks it's just wonderful how those dear little animals can be taught to do such work.

This column of spasms is the result of the two real columnists of the Doric going away for the week-end and leaving the Office Dog to write the column.

We have chewed up three pencils trying to think of another witty paragraph to fill this column. We can not think of one. Our brain (silence in the galleries, please) is exhausted. And besides: lo! it is filled

Grinnell College Archives.

LIFE AND LEGACY OF JOE ROSENFIELD 105

Grinnell College Archives.

PART THREE
JOE ROSENFIELD, COMMUNITY CATALYST

DES MOINES' CATALYST

Webster's New Collegiate Dictionary defines "Catalyst" as "an agent that induces...significant change." There can be no better definition for the actions of Joseph Rosenfield in Des Moines during the second half of the twentieth century. Often without acting as the visible leader, he made multiple things happen in Des Moines, and his remarkable impact often stretched into the rest of Iowa and beyond.

You can hear it in the words of acknowledged Des Moines icons. Developer Bill Knapp asserted that "he was just a catalyst to have a lot of things happen...very much respected by everyone." Knapp said, "His word was his bond and [he was] probably respected more than anyone I've ever known in Des Moines ... I've never known anyone that had more love and honor and respect than him. Joe was solid...I've never known anyone to say a bad word against him. He's one of the best business people and highly respected as much as anyone ever has been in Des Moines."[1]

Michael Gartner, former editor of *The Des Moines Register* and current Iowa Cubs owner, described how Joe inspired others to do good: "Joe was the guy who instilled in a lot of [Des Moines leaders] and I think especially Bill Knapp, this sense of...doing good, and also the sense that just because you're rich there's a lot of people who aren't and you're just lucky...So that's why so much has been done and the people responded...What's the common thread? The common thread there is Joe." Gartner adds, "He made an enormous number of people rich in this community [with investment advice and investments]."[2]

One of Joe's closest friends, icon John Ruan, erected a Boy Scout statue at Camp Mitigwa in Joe's honor as evidence of Joe's inspiration to others to "do good." Among other things, Joe's advice that Ruan invest early in Intel helped to supply the funds Ruan used to endow the World Food Prize.[3]

Premier Des Moines leader Dick Leavitt said Joe "just had great leadership qualities. It would have been tough to say no to Joe...he had to have been among the best at passing the hat ... I think he was just a towering human being."[4] Jon Batesole, an executive with General Growth for many years, saw Joe as a leader of leaders: "I feel that he took ownership of the community; he was pushing the people who were leaders." Batesole's colleague at General Growth, Stan Richards, said: "[Joe] was a leader of leaders ... he shaped people ... He brought a feeling of total integrity to any discussion...It didn't take much for Joe to get people to respond to him."[5]

Former Meredith CEO Bob Burnett, who knew Joe from serving with him as a Grinnell Trustee and through interactions with him in Des Moines, said, "Joe was very much a behind the scenes guy and there is no doubt in my mind that ... his footprint was involved in almost everything that happened in Des Moines. But unlike some of the other names...you didn't often hear of any of these events or projects that were in the name of Joe Rosenfield."[6]

Developer Jim Cownie, who has underwritten the cost of this biography out of the sense of an unmet tribute to the man he felt had first helped to launch and then saved his business career, said, "Anytime I could be with Joe, I would be with Joe. He was just that great of a human being...he ran under the radar in Des Moines ... he did a lot of things quietly...Joe was on top of the list as far as I'm concerned, ethically, economically."[7] Bill Friedman, former Younkers CEO, thinks one of the reasons for Joe's influence was his accessibility: "He would meet almost anyone who wanted to talk to him," including representatives of all the charities.[8] Accessibility was just one of the attributes that garnered respect from all who knew Joe. Iowa Attorney General Tom Miller testified, "All people that knew him respected him, [he was] incredibly well respected ... you could just sense the respect that people had for him." And, he added, Joe was "humble more than anything."[9]

John Bucksbaum, the son of one of General Growth founders, Matthew Bucksbaum, knew Joe quite well when he was growing up. He summed him up definitively: "Few people have had the kind of influence on institutions that Joe has had: Younkers, Grinnell, General

Growth, etc."[10] It is the plethora of institutions that Joe "influenced" that are the spine of this section. Beginning with Joe's student days at the University of Iowa Law School and continuing with his nineteen-year career at the Des Moines law firm, Gamble, Howland, and Rosenfield, this section focuses on Joe's life as a businessman, investor, philanthropist, and member of the Jewish community in Des Moines. Joe was rated by *The Des Moines Register* as Des Moines' leading philanthropist, and his concern for others led him to mentor a significant number of young men and women. Joe's mentoring of Jim Cownie and Jim Hoak as they struggled to establish Heritage Communications was one of his greatest contributions to the business life of Des Moines. Equally, he played a major role in helping Martin and Matthew Bucksbaum establish and enhance General Growth Properties, one of the largest developers of shopping centers in the Midwest. Joe's interests were broad and deep, propelling him to play a major role in the Iowa Democratic Party, Planned Parenthood of Iowa (later the Heartland), Living History Farms, and the Chicago Cubs. Quite naturally, his many interests and contributions placed him on the governing boards of a "Who's Who" of Iowa and national institutions.

THE UNIVERSITY OF IOWA LAW SCHOOL

After graduation from Grinnell College in June, Joe entered the Law School of the University of Iowa in the fall of 1925. He joined approximately 200 students, mostly from the state of Iowa, with a majority being University of Iowa graduates. Most joined the Iowa Bar and practiced throughout the state after three years of legal studies.[11] Whereas Joe had concentrated on his extra-curricular activities, principally publications, during his undergraduate years, at Iowa Law School he was a serious and successful student. He retained clearer and even more positive memories of his law school teachers than of those at Grinnell. When asked in a Law School Campaign Brochure about what stood out at Iowa, he responded:

My Professors. I was fortunate to have some outstanding ones and I'm very appreciative of the kind of legal education I got there. My professors were exceptional teachers and I remember them vividly, especially O.K. Patton, who I thought was one of the finest teachers I ever had. He just drilled the law into us. [12]

Joe described another professor, Wayne Cook, who was a practicing lawyer and then practiced again after a stint at Iowa: "He used to come charging into the classroom bellowing out questions." Cook taught criminal law and bills and notes. "I got a fine education!" Joe pronounced, though he judged that legal education in the 1920s was much narrower than later in the twentieth century. He was taught "contract law, straight constitutional law, etc. Now there's an increasing variety of subjects being taught. There's an element of public service in law." Students are encouraged to consider public service and other service as opposed to going straight into a law office. "I enjoyed my years there," Joe said, "I worked diligently and I didn't have a nervous breakdown doing it. I enjoyed the companionship of my fellow students. We had a lot of fun together."[13]

Many years later, after Joe had become an exceptional lawyer, businessman, and philanthropist, he joined the Law School Foundation Board and was a leading member of the Iowa Law School Second Century Campaign Committee. He endowed a scholarship in 1966, and ten years later, Joe was recognized with a Distinguished Alumni Achievement Award. His fundraising was not limited to the Law School; he gave excellent investment advice to his friend, Dick Levitt, a member of the University Foundation Board, saying, "I'll tell you what Grinnell is doing." The University of Iowa made a profitable investment in the Sequoia Fund based on Joe's advice.[14]

Joe was a financial supporter of Iowa football in the Forest Evashevsky era, but he became disillusioned with Hayden Fry and, as Kay Bucksbaum said, "that was the end of his support for University of Iowa Football."[15] In 1990, Joe expanded on his disillusionment:

"[Iowa football] got too commercial; too money conscious; too much buying of these players. Too much letting students through that don't deserve to...It's too professional. I sometimes think it ought to be either made strictly professional and tell the players you can go to school if you want to, if you want an education, or if you

don't, you can stay here and play football. Either that, or abolish it. Pretty radical, but I don't know that at this stage you can stop all the, or even a big part of the money end of it. You've got the alumni to deal with; the alumni and the whole state of Iowa that are more interested in Iowa football than they are in Iowa University.[16]

Many would argue that Joe got it right.

Reflecting on his decision to go to law school seventy years after his 1928 graduation, Joe said, "I think probably I had no idea what I was going to do until I was in the middle of law school. And I found at that time, I began finding that I liked the law very much. I did well in law school and by the time I was through law school there was no question in my mind or my family's mind that that's where I should be."[17]

THE GAMBLE LAW FIRM

Following graduation with honors from The University of Iowa Law School, Joe joined the Gamble, Read, and Howland law firm as an associate and later became a partner. The senior partner, Graham Gamble, had worked out the details of the 1927 merger of Younkers with the Frankel's Harris-Emery store. The creativity of Gamble had allowed the smaller Harris-Emery enterprise an equal share of voting stock with larger Younkers interests. It was good business for Graham Gamble to recruit a member of the Frankel family to his firm as they were the lawyers for the highly successful merged retail store. The Gamble firm was one of the well-established legal practices in Des Moines, having been founded just after the Civil War. At that time, the Rock Island Railroad, extending across Iowa, needed legal representation. The founder of the firm was a lawyer for the Rock Island in Alabama, and the railroad brought him to Iowa as its lawyer for trans-Mississippi expansion. Rock Island remained a major client until its demise in 1979 after struggling through three bankruptcies in that decade.[18] At Gamble, legal work for Younkers gradually grew larger than the work for the Rock Island, and Joe was quite naturally assigned to that account. Younkers business eventually consumed about a third of Joe's time. He also did the legal work for John Ruan's trucking company, founded in 1932, often doing its filing with the Iowa Transportation Commission. Joe was particularly busy with Ruan's many military contracts during World War II. This business association led to one of Joe's deepest friendships. Though they had quite different personalities, and were profoundly divided in politics (Joe a staunch Democrat and Ruan an equally dedicated Republican), Joe and John were devoted to each other. Chris Green remembers their intimacy. Talking about one of his friends' appearance, Ruan said in front of both men, "I just wish we could take Hoak's body and Joe's brain in it and we'd have somebody that was worth something."[19]

Joe also represented banks, particularly during the Depression, and he did work for his alma mater, Grinnell College, until he became a Trustee in November 1941, which led to frequent trips to campus on "heavy" legal business.[20] National By-Products was another of Joe's clients, leading to a friendship with Bob Fleming, the CEO. Joe even did work for the Hubbells, filing their estate will. "It was like two pages ... which said, everything goes to the Trust."[21]

Joe left the Gamble firm in 1947 to join Younkers full time as a Vice President and General Counsel, adding the Chairmanship of the Board in 1948. He continued to do legal work for Younkers, and his principal interest was in negotiating the expansion of Younkers to multiple Iowa communities and the investment of Younkers' considerable profits. Lawyer Fred Little, who knew Joe as well as anyone, did not believe Joe was a lawyer at heart:

"I don't think Joe's interests were really in the law. Law can be confining ... and he was a bit of a buccaneer. Joe liked to take risks. I think he was a superb businessman and superb businessmen don't make very good lawyers often ... Joe's traits and interests leant themselves much more to business and [his other] primary interests. [The law] was nothing that I think meant much to Joe ... as his life unfolded it clearly wasn't as a lawyer, I'm sure of that.[22]

Joe's "buccaneer" tendencies were certified by John Ruan who recalled in a profile by *The Des Moines Register* that during World War II he and Joe would sometimes shoot craps in the old Mainliner

Bar across from the Des Moines airport. Ruan said, "He would play the longest odds and lose his money."[23] In the same profile, Chicago sportswriter Jim Enright opined, "At least I think he is a hunch player. I've never been to a race track with him when he didn't bet on the seventh horse in the seventh race."

Joe obviously had interests and abilities that extended far beyond the law, yet he was a full-time lawyer for nineteen years and all the evidence points to his having been a very good one. After all, he came alive intellectually at Iowa Law after having been somewhat indifferent to his studies at Grinnell. Joe may not have been a lawyer through-and-through, but the 1930s and early 1940s were an important time in his life, and he acheived considerable legal accomplishments. There is ample evidence that he enjoyed the law and his career as a lawyer.

DES MOINES' CATALYST

Joe gradually evolved to play a major role in Des Moines while he practiced law. After two decades of legal practice, he assumed the chairmanship of Younkers, one of the city's leading businesses. Born in Des Moines to one of its most prominent and active families, he evolved quite naturally into leadership, but his version turned out to be a subtler brand than usually is associated with the term.

It is unlikely anyone knows Des Moines better than Michael Gartner, former *Register* editor, current owner of the Iowa Cubs, and regular columnist in the Des Moines newspaper *Cityview*. Gartner describes Des Moines as a city "that has never run on political leadership." According to Gartner, it has always worked because there is great respect for business leadership because most of the businesses are locally owned: Meredith, Principal, insurance companies, Younkers (before the 1990s), Pioneer, and the Hubbell enterprises and, until recently, the newspaper. Executives of these corporations have allegiance to Des Moines and to Iowa. They assumed they weren't going to be transferred to other cities or corporate headquarters. The Levitts, Cowleses, Merediths, etc., and their executives assumed Des Moines was where they were going to raise their children and access the schools.

According to Gartner, this local spirit was behind the great wave of development from 1973–77, which included the Civic Center, skywalk system, and Botanical Center. A bond issue for the Civic Center had been voted down, so David Kruidenier, Jim Hubbell, and William Brenton raised $9-11 million for the project in 90 days. Michael Gartner gives a specific example of how the system of leadership worked. One day, while he was *Register* editor, he got a phone call from Bill Knapp, who asked what he was doing. "I'm putting out the greatest newspaper in the world, what are you doing?" And Knapp said, "I'm on my way to pick you up [because] we have to save Tiny-Tots," which was a day care center. Knapp said, "We have to raise $250,000 this afternoon. I'm in for $25,000 and so are you."

Gartner said, "Okay," so he and Bill Knapp went out that afternoon to raise the money, telling donors, "These kids are the kids of your workers and most don't have fathers. If this place closes, your workers will have to quit their jobs to tend to their kids; that would be far more costly than putting up $25,000 now." They got the power company to forgive a $15,000 bill, and by the end of the afternoon, they had their $250,000. This illustrates why "Des Moines is such a great city."

Joe had an indirect role in this story as, according to Michael Gartner, "Joe was the guy who instilled in a lot of people and, I think, especially in Bill Knapp this sense of not only doing, but you do well by doing good; and also a sense of just because you're rich there's a lot of people who aren't and you're just lucky. And there by the grace of God, go do it." According to Gartner, Joe similarly influenced others in the leadership of Des Moines:

"Joe is one of the larger strands that runs through here. First of all, he made a lot of people rich (with investment and investment advice). He made an enormous number of people rich in this community; and some of us rich are pretty grateful. So, if he makes a call and asks somebody for money [they respond]...So, he had this great sense of... great social conscience and he kind of inculcated people with it in various ways. One, by his example; one by being the benefactor; one by being their business strategist; one by being an investor at a key time when they might have

gone belly-up. I think that Jim Cownie would tell you that Joe saved him."

Gartner believes John Ruan felt "a sense of obligation, a sense of 'I don't want to let Joe down.'" Gartner continued, "I think that Bill Knapp felt the same way," adding that the Bucksbaums had similar feelings. Michael Gartner tells a story that solidifies some of the reasons for Ruan's sense of obligation: Archie Brooks managed the Ruan building and parking in the underground garage was always a problem. "So, one day, Archie says to John III, the young John, 'dammit, John, we need these spaces. Why does Joe Rosenfield have a space to park down here?'" John's response to Archie was, "If you made my father $300,000,000 in a deal, you can have a space to park here too." This remark was about the Intel stock Joe had urged John Ruan to purchase: "And that way, Joe had a big stake in the World Food Prize. His fingers are everywhere," because Ruan had used his Intel investment to endow the World Food Prize.

Michael Gartner ended by speculating that Joe's Jewish heritage had done so much to shape him into a Des Moines catalyst, a quiet shaper of Des Moines. Joe "just wanted to do what's right...He was the town's smart guy and the town's conscience. It's hard to exaggerate how important knowing the community is."[24]

Other key figures corroborate Michael Gartner's observations of Joe's special place in Des Moines. Connie Wimer, CEO of Des Moines' Business Publications Corporation is a long-time community leader who knew Joe well and is exceptionally familiar with Des Moines. Speaking of the time when Joe was active, she said,

"In those days the big things that happened in the city happened because of a group of about ten or twelve men; and they'd get together in a meeting and decide some major thing needed to happen and somebody'd say, 'Well, I'll put in $100,000 and somebody else would say, well, 'I'll put $500,000 in.' It would go around the table. Everyone had to be able to put in a meaningful amount; and I refer to it [as] the benevolent dictatorship. It was a group that dictated what was going to happen in Des Moines and I think Joe was a big part of that. But it wasn't out in public. You didn't exactly know unless you knew one of those persons how or why it happened."

According to Wimer, John Ruan, Bill Knapp, Fred Weitz, David Kruidenier, and Fred Hubbell Sr. were part of the group, along with Joe.[25]

Jim Cownie called this group "The Breakfast Club." He, Randy Duncan, Chris Green, and Bill Knapp would pick up Joe, Bob Fleming, and the rest and take them to a place Jim had west of town every couple of months where they would discuss community issues. Jim felt Joe was the linchpin of the "Breakfast Club."[26]

A consistent theme of all who speak of Joe's role in Des Moines is that he seldom was out front. Bob Burnett, former CEO of Meredith and fellow Grinnell Trustee, said, "Joe really had his fingers on what was going on in Des Moines. He was...a behind the scenes operator in many ways; and he provided influence with other business leaders of Des Moines far beyond what was ever known publicly." He added that though it was difficult to detect Joe's footprint, "it was there for many things."[27]

Stanley Richards, long-time General Growth executive, described Joe's influence this way:

"He brought a feeling of integrity to any discussion. In other words, people so respected his counsel, his advice, because they knew his track record in everything. He was a leader of leaders. I think he shaped people like Bill Knapp, who jumped on the bandwagon with him; and he used his wealth very substantially to help the City of Des Moines. He just brought statures to any gathering. He was just a pure gentleman and such an honest individual that nobody ever questioned his motives."[28]

Another General Growth executive Jon Batesole said, "I feel Joe took ownership of the community. He always wanted to see things improved...He maybe didn't stand up to be the leader, but he always pushed the people who were leaders and supported them."[29]

Connie Wimer agreed: "Everyone respected Joe. They knew he was brilliant and he had a great sense of humor; so when you have that much respect in the community you can accomplish a lot. And, of course, he had money to go with that; so he made a huge difference [for Des Moines]."[30]

John Bucksbaum, Mathew and Kay's son, joined General Growth after college graduation. He grew up revering Joe, and he expressed his family's judgment best when he said, "Whenever anyone in Des Moines needed something, they came to Joe."

Joe's footprint was absent from some projects, such as the Civic Center, Blank Park Zoo, and the Art Center,[32] but he was almost certainly involved in the Marriott Hotel project in 1981. Joe's close friend, John Ruan was the driver of the project, but the Hubbells' Equitable of Iowa and Younkers were the big funders. Both Fred Hubbell and Jim Cownie are certain Joe played a major role because Younkers would not have acted without his approval and because he partnered with Ruan in many ventures.[33]

Catalysts make things happen even though they are not always visible while they act. This is the perfect description for Joe's impact on Des Moines. There is consensus among Des Moines leaders in the 1960s and 70s that Joe was their catalyst.

JOE ROSENFIELD, BUSINESSMAN

A special section of *The Des Moines Register* published in 1976, titled, "The Powers that Be: The Most Powerful People in Des Moines," listed Joe number eight on the twenty-five person list, and that was seven years after he had retired from Younkers. He was the oldest person on the list that took the Register six months to compile. On December 5, 1979, Joe was the fourth member elected to the Iowa Business Hall of Fame. His fellow inductee was Frederick M. Hubbell. The three predecessors in the Hall, which was inaugurated in 1975, included the first inductee, Joe's Grinnell College classmate, John Norris of Marshalltown (Lennox Furnace), and those inducted in 1976, Ellis Leavitt of Des Moines and Lt. General Hanford MacNider of Mason City.[34]

The focus of Joe's business career was his twenty years as Chairman of the Board and Vice president of Younkers. In 1981, Wendell Cochran chronicled Joe's business career, paying particular attention to his role at Younkers after the 1948 public offering that greatly enhanced capital for expansion. Joe's negotiating skills were instrumental to Younkers' expansion across Iowa and neighboring states. As Morey Sostrin said, "He loved to negotiate anything." Cochran wrote that the success of Younkers in the "go-go-years of the '50s and '60s gave the company a pile of cash to invest, which Joe managed. [Joe] used the money to build up Younkers chain and to foster businesses. The outstanding example is General Growth."[35]

Younkers was Joe's principal business, but he was active in so many other ways. Joe and Bill Knapp became friends and occasional business associates through their mutual support of Governor and later Senator Harold Hughes. In 1972, Bill bought the apartments at 3600 Grand from Joe and his partner, Arthur Sanford. Joe had earlier agreed that if he sold, he would sell only to Bill. Knapp agreed to let Joe stay in his 3600 Grand apartment, promising never to raise the rent. Joe assured Bill he was not likely to live many more years, but when he was still living, not dying until 2000, Knapp joked that he had subsidized a millionaire.[36]

In 1976, Bill Knapp, John Ruan, and Joe tried to buy Merle Hay Mall, where Younkers had built a major store in the late 1950s as the anchor for Des Moines' first shopping mall. Purchasing the mall was Joe's idea, but when the partners were unable to secure a controlling share for $1,750,000, falling short of their 35 percent target, they dropped the idea.[37]

Their mutual interests in business ventures and democratic politics brought Joe and Bill Knapp into a close friendship from at least the early 1970s. Knapp believed Joe was the quintessential businessman: "He loved Des Moines and he made money here...Des Moines was his anchor...Business was his life. He studied the stock market, he studied business. I never knew him to go to a movie. He just focused on business and that was his fun. I just don't remember him doing a lot other than focus on business."[38] Bill heard Joe say, "The greatest thing anyone can do if they want to be successful would be a lawyer, and best, if you could be a lawyer and an accountant. If you had those two things, nothing could stop you."[39]

John Ruan, another of Joe's intimate friends, was listed number one in *The Des Moines Register* "Powers that Be" survey in 1976, where Joe was eighth. Joe started doing legal work for Ruan in 1937 handling some of Ruan's labor cases, as well as various transportation commission filings. Joe and Ruan partnered in some business ventures and Joe gave John extraordinarily successful investment advice. In the early 1940s, Joe and John McGinn, part owner of the Hotel Fort Des Moines, convinced Ruan to buy liquor in Chicago and transport it to Des Moines. Since the State of Iowa was the sole liquor wholesaler, Ruan's plan was illegal. He carried the liquor hidden in the nose of a Ruan trailer.[40] As far as can be determined, this was the only illegal advice Joe ever gave a friend.

Joe offered John more legitimate advice when he urged him to buy the struggling Bankers Trust in 1965. Ruan eventually owned 80 percent, and its assets had increased 179 percent by 1975, making Bankers Trust the second largest bank in Des Moines.[41] Ruan persuaded Joe's good friend John Chrystal to run Bankers Trust, and when Chrystal moved from Carroll to Des Moines, he became Joe's permanent roommate at 3600 Grand Avenue.

One of the more intriguing Rosenfield/Ruan partnership projects was their investment in the *Boston Herald Traveler* newspaper. In 1964, with the paper losing money, they attempted to gain a controlling interest as well as a majority of seats on the board. Their focus was actually on the paper's profitable TV station, WHDH. Not only did Joe and John fail to achieve a controlling interest, but in 1969 the FCC forced the *Herald Traveller* to sell the TV station. The partners eventually prospered because in 1973, John Blair and Company bought the paper; this company, through an earlier merger with Hearst already, had acquired the *Boston Herald-American*.

Both Joe and John reaped a large profit from the ten-million-dollar sale (at $33 a share).[42]

Joe also invested in Broadway plays. According to Wendel Chochran, "A friend recommended that Rosenfield should get in on a New York play, 'as sure way to lose money as has been invented.' The play was '*Hello Dolly*,' and Rosenfield still gets checks; he also owned part of '*The Man Of La Mancha*,' another huge success. He says he's forgotten the losers among the forty or so plays he's backed."[43]

Joe also got John Ruan to join into some of these Broadway investments.[44] In the early 1940s, Joe and John were also partners in a chain of radio stations, including KIOA in Des Moines.[45]

Joe led John to several extremely profitable investments, particularly Intel and Heritage Communications. When Intel went public in 1971, Joe, who was part of the startup investment, along with Grinnell College and Sam Rosenthal, another Grinnell Trustee, encouraged John to buy Intel, which he did after some hesitancy. By 2001, after frequent additional purchases and stock splits, Ruan had roughly four million shares. These shares helped him endow the World Food Prize. Following Joe's urging, John also invested in Heritage, an investment that eventually ballooned to a nearly $20,000,000 profit for him.[46] As Michael Gartner said, Joe helped to make many people rich, and his close friend John Ruan certainly was one of them.

The Wendell Cochran interview, "Joe Rosenfield, Patron of Iowa Business," in the May 10, 1981 issue of *The Des Moines Register* affords an intimate glance into Joe's business career. Joe, who always wanted to fly below the radar, was a reluctant participant, but Cochran managed to produce an interview gem, capturing not only Joe's accomplishments but also his unassuming nature. Near his 77th birthday, when the interview was conducted, his car was a nine-year-old American Motors Rambler; his wardrobe, according Younkers Executive Bill Friedman, was not a good advertisement for the store; and his friend, Tom Hutchison, said Joe kept on having his shoes repaired rather than purchasing new ones. Cochran, himself, observed that Joe's color-blindness showed in his choice of clothes. On the other hand, Joe was a devastating bridge player who was capable of keeping track of all 52 cards in the deck.

Turning to Joe's accomplishments, Wendel Cochran writes, "One week away from his 77th birthday, Joseph Frankel Rosenfield is the patriarch of the Des Moines business community. Old men value his friendship, young men seek his advice. A few years ago you couldn't have done much in town without asking him; today you shouldn't." Cochran then quotes John Ruan: "His friends admire him for his intellect, his engaging sense of humor, and above all, for his overwhelming sense of fairness in his personal business dealings." Cochran opines: "Nearly every business in Des Moines bears his imprint, nearly every business leader has been nurtured by his side." When Cochran asked Ruan why he continued his close friendship with Joe after he became the principal funder of Harold Hughes, an enemy of big trucks, John answered, "Opposites attract." The Ruan friendship underscored Joe's remarkable capacity to remain friends with staunch Republicans while being one of the chief funders of Democratic politicians.

The Ruan/Rosenfield partnership is the main thread through Cochran's article, underlining Joe's support of John's downtown development efforts. Ruan often persuaded Joe to join him at a six o'clock breakfast or for lunch at the Des Moines Club where many an idea was hatched. The Cochran article underlines, of course, the importance of Joe's twenty-year leadership of Younkers during its greatest successes in the 1950s and 1960s. Joe was indeed the patron of Des Moines' business for a generation, and his ethics were at the very heart of his leadership. All who knew him recognized that Joe "lived" his business mantra that the other person should get at least as good a deal as you do. This was why everyone trusted Joe implicitly. Such ethics are always good business.

JOE ROSENFIELD & THE DES MOINES JEWISH COMMUNITY

Joe's maternal grandfather, Isaiah Frankel, was one of the founders of Temple B'nai Jeshurun, a Reform Jewish congregation on the west side of Des Moines. A locus of German immigrant Judaism, it became a strong and prosperous congregation. Though Joe's parents, Meyer and Rose, were active members, Joe, who was a fully paid member, was not very active. The testimony that Joe was not at all religious is virtually unanimous; nevertheless, Joe was very supportive of the Des Moines Jewish community.[47] Joe's sister, Louise, was non-practicing also and went in another direction, joining the Park Avenue Unitarian Church.[48]

Joe supported the Temple because it was important to the Jewish community and because it was part of his family's tradition.[49] He was also a strong supporter of the Jewish Federation, a key institution for the support of Jewish culture and life in Iowa. In 1948, he served as President of the Federation, and he was a consistent financial supporter, leaving the Federation $600,000 in his estate.[50] Stanley

Richards, who was a pillar of the Federation, felt that Joe was one of its primary supporters.

Joe's strong support of Des Moines' principal Jewish institutions certifies his identity as a Jew, and yet, he claimed a broader identity as a citizen of Des Moines. Fred Little said, "Joe crossed the border all the time between the Jewish and non-Jewish community."[51] Bill Knapp opined that "he just wasn't in with the group of Jewish people; he was his own man. I don't think he looked at it as Jewish or Christian, he looked at everything the same."[52] Dick Levitt, commented that Joe was not a religious person and added, "And I think that he arrived at that intellectually." However, Joe respected those whose lives were driven by faith: "I think he identified himself as a Jew, although not in a religious sense...Joe was not a self-hating Jew."[53]

Stanley Richards, who was a devout Jew, told a story that illustrates how deeply Joe was respected by the broader Des Moines community:

Joe was never ashamed of his Jewishness, that's for sure; and one of the reasons why Wakonda changed its policy [was] because when his name came up [for membership with] one other lawyer...there were a number of the members of Wakonda that said, "They are coming into the Club, because if they don't, we're out" —and because of this decision early on, they kept Wakonda from being a closed Country Club."[54]

Joe grew up in a much more anti-Semitic environment than he faced later in life. Even when Kay Bucksbaum grew up in Des Moines a generation later, she felt "not entirely accepted by others," but when she went to Grinnell College "that was not the case." She believes Joe had a similar experience and that this was an important reason for his devotion to the College.[55] Stanley Richards agreed, saying that Grinnell's "hospitality to Jews" was part of the reason for his choosing to go there "and helped to account for his love of Grinnell."[56]

Joe was deeply influenced by his Jewish heritage and he embraced it in many ways, but Judaism did not shape his life. He was a citizen of his community in the deepest possible sense and that drove him. His Judaism blended into his citizenship. Bill Friedman put his finger on the essence of what Judaism contributed to Joe's life when he said Joe's Jewishness had a lot to do with Joe's generosity and concern for others.[57]

JOE ROSENFIELD, PHILANTHROPIST

If I were to choose one title for Joe Rosenfield, it might be "Philanthropist." On October 8, 1976, *The Des Moines Register* published a follow-up article to an earlier story published the same year, titled, "The Powers that Be." Arnold Garson, the author of the follow-up, focused on Des Moines' top philanthropists, headed by Joe: "There was a time when you could raise money for anything in this town by having lunch with Joe Rosenfield and getting him interested. One of the city's all-time fundraisers, he says he lacks the energy now, but he still believes he could raise a couple of million dollars over the telephone if he wanted." Referring to the earlier "Powers that Be" article, Garson continues that one of the reasons the retired, elderly man still ranks number eight among younger "powers" is his ability as a fund raiser, since fundraising is important to power in Des Moines.

Joe told Garson, "The first principle of the art of raising money is to be generous yourself. If you and your business have not made a generous commitment, you are not a very good person to go around asking for money. Access to personal wealth is very important to fundraising." In fact, Joe, who was a childless widower at the time, was intent on giving away all of his wealth before he died.

Joe Rosenfield was not on every community bandwagon; most notably, he was not part of the drive to build the Civic Center, which was led by a fellow Grinnell Trustee David Kruidenier. Joe finally conceded a $5,000 gift on the theory that the power structure should be supported. Despite the interests of his mother Rose and sister Louise, and his own Broadway investments, Joe was not a big fan of the arts and did not contribute to the Art Center, an act of major philanthropy for his mother and sister. Some in the Jewish community thought Joe should have been more generous since he did not give money for Israel. Joe admitted that he did not give to Israel, saying, "If I gave money to Israel, I couldn't give it elsewhere."[58]

Nor was Joe always guileless in his giving. Jim Cownie tells the story of going to Joe's office at General Growth with Father Mike Hess, President of Dowling High School, Jim's alma mater. Joe knew they were there for a donation and he "grabbed his phone and said,

'Hold my calls.'" With typical Rosenfield humor, he looked up and said, "Nobody ever calls me; I just do that to feel important." Joe then grabbed his checkbook and wrote a check for $10,000. In Cownie's telling, he and Hess had planned to ask for $50,000, but by giving before being asked, "Joe saved himself $40,000."[59]

One surprising act of philanthropy was Joe's essential support of Living History Farms. Joe had never met Bill Murray, who had just been defeated for the governorship by Harold Hughes, the candidate for whom Joe was the principal donor. Defeated at the polls, Murray turned his energy to creating Living History Farms west of Des Moines. Rollo Bergson had planned to develop a golf course on his land, but when Interstate 80/35 split it, he decided to sell. Murray knew the land would be suitable for his project, and it was available at a reasonable price. Consequently, he approached Joe for help, saying, "You defeated me for governor, so now you owe me." What Joe "owed" was his famous fundraising ability in the service of Living History Farms. Murray needed $250,000 to get started and more to develop the project. Joe agreed to help, giving $250,000 of his own money and touring downtown for additional funds. He got $25,000 each from *The Des Moines Register*, Younkers, Iowa Power, and Light and Pioneer. A lot of people thought the idea was crazy, but Joe was persuasive, especially as he had made a significant personal commitment.[60] Dick Leavitt was one of those who thought the idea crazy, "but Joe presented its value," so Leavitt contributed.[61] Joe and Murray became close friends and Joe continued raising money as the project materialized.[62]

In the 1981 profile, Wendell Cochran underscored that his desire to give away money had been Joe's chief motivation for making money. "Joe can be compelling as a fundraiser, as a great many people have discovered. But giving away money is a compulsion; in fact it seems that he tries to make money so he can get rid of it. Rosenfield is the rare philanthropist whose gifts continuously exceed his income, actually reducing his net worth." Joe's friend, John Chrystal said, "Rosenfield 'would be happy' if he gave away his last penny as he drew his last breath." Joe, himself, confessed to Cochran, "I don't think I'll come out even," adding "if I didn't have something I wanted to do with the money, like [giving it to] Grinnell, it would take the zip out of it...Grinnell is where I've made my most effective contributions so far."[63]

In 1991, Joe received the "Outstanding Philanthropist Award" from the Central Iowa Chapter of the National Society of Fund-Raising Executives. The evidence that produced this award is contained in a file of materials kept by Joe's Assistant, Pat Gessman, and can now be found at the Iowa Room of Burling Library at Grinnell College. Among Joe's lesser known gifts were those to The Des Moines Symphony, Homes at Oakridge (near the University of Iowa), the University of Iowa, the Jewish Federation of Greater Des Moines, Dowling High School, the I Have a Dream Foundation, the Iowa Peace Institute, and the Des Moines Metro Opera. Much more known among Joe's philanthropies was Planned Parenthood of Iowa. Executive Director Jill June noted that in 1983, Joe spearheaded the committee for construction of a new Planned Parenthood headquarters. Joe's personal gift allowed for enhanced clinical operations to expand the range of women's healthcare services in Iowa. Joe recruited his friend Warren Buffett to support the cost of a new Planned Parenthood clinic in Iowa City. In 1983, Joe gave a challenge gift that attracted another $160,000 for Planned Parenthood. Allied with Joe's support of Planned Parenthood were his gifts to the Bernie Lorens Recovery House, enabling it to open its doors to serve chemically-dependent women.[64]

The philanthropy award materials also includes letters from Bill Murray, testifying to Joe's crucial role in making Living History Farms a reality, and former governor Robert Ray, who wrote in praise of Joe's continuing role as a founding Trustee of the Iowa Natural Heritage Foundation. Joe's $1,200,000 gift to Grinnell College to endow scholarships awarded to Des Moines high school students is also noted, along with his $33,000 stock gift to the Des Moines Chrysalis Foundation, which was founded by his sister, Louise. Joe's 1966 gift endowed scholarships at the University of Iowa Law School and was but one of a series of gifts to his law alma mater.

As generous as Joe was to an impressive array of Iowa organizations, including as the principal donor to Planned Parenthood for Iowa,[65] Joe's premier philanthropic commitment, by far, was to Grinnell College. All told, including an estate gift of over $26,000,000, Joe gave at least $77,000,000 to the College that he rescued from penury.[66] Joe's will ensured that his estate would be exhausted through philanthropy.

One of the more revealing insights into Joe's laser focus on giving is from his assistant, Pat Gessman, who regularly visited his Grand Avenue apartment in Joe's last years. Joe, in his ninety-sixth year, was failing, so he asked Pat to write his checks. Joe generally appeared easy going, but he was serious about fulfilling his charitable commitments; he worried about how his death would affect them. He brought his attorney to the apartment to discuss some of his commitments, and he told Pat that he was concerned his unpaid pledges could be affected by his death. Pat confessed that she sometimes became annoyed with Joe's fixation on his pledges. In retrospect, nothing could be more revealing about the centrality of philanthropy to Joe's very being.[67] It dominated Joe's concerns about his impending death.

Almost as important as Joe's personal generosity was the way in which he taught others the importance of giving. Bill Knapp testified that Joe taught him how to give; Joe told him, "You're going to enjoy giving it away more than making it." "It's the truth,"[68] Bill asserted. Later, Joe counseled Planned Parenthood's Jill June about how to solicit Knapp, whom she thought was not giving to his potential. "What I will tell you to do is tell him what I do and why I am doing it. I'll tell him how much the need is and then he's going to have to decide for himself. I shouldn't have to ask."[69] This is how a master of fundraising, himself a leading donor, raises money.

His close friend John Ruan, of course, attests to Joe's influence over his philanthropy, and and John Bucksbaum testified that his parents, Matthew and Kay, learned much of their philanthropy from Joe. Chuck Duchen, former Younkers CEO, who knew Joe for fifty years, summarized Joe's influence succinctly: "He taught many others, in his own modesty, how to give."[70]

JOE ROSENFIELD, MENTOR

Joe was an instinctive mentor, a tendency that was intensified by the tragic death of his only child, Jim. Joe frequently reached out to young men and women of promise. One of his mentees, Fred Little, said that Joe "really relied on his intuition. He really, really trusted his intuition; some cases to his detriment, but in most cases [not]. I mean, Joe would meet with somebody, would find out a little bit about him and make a decision [about whether] this person was someone he wanted to help or not." Fred said he didn't think Joe was a lawyer at heart; "A lawyer would never act like that; he would want to see papers and check on people."[71]

Joe mentored Fred from when he was a child, so Fred was in a good position to judge this quality. Fred's father, a 1916 Grinnell graduate and Chair of the Board of Trustees in the early 1940s, was Joe's close friend; in a Des Moines elevator conversation, he asked Joe if he would like to be a Grinnell Trustee. Joe's positive response led to his fifty-nine-year tenure as Grinnell's greatest trustee. When Fred was ten, his father died tragically, and Joe stepped in as a mentor and surrogate father. Joe had continuous contact with Fred and on several occasions took him to Chicago for Cubs baseball games. Looking back on a time when Fred seemed "lost," he believed Joe's support was critical and that his mentoring was sustained into Fred's legal career. Fred was an SEC expert, so Joe used Fred's legal services for Younkers public offerings. Fred also did work for Equitable, which he attributed to Joe's influence. In 1976, Fred became a Grinnell Trustee through Joe's urging and influence, and later, when he considered resigning, all Joe needed to do was remind Fred of how he himself had become a Trustee through Fred's father's influence. Ultimately Fred, like his father, served as chair of the Trustees and testified that his devotion to Grinnell was a "mirror of Joe's devotion."[72]

Another mentoring connection centering on the College was Joe's connection to Bob Noyce, a 1949 graduate who invented the integrated circuit on a silicon chip and founded Intel Corporation. Joe, himself, was the best source of information about their relationship:

"I have a particular feeling for Bob, who first came to Grinnell not as a trustee [but as a student]. [Later] we had a kind of junior board of some kind...He wasn't working for the college, but they would meet sometimes when the trustees met and do various things for the college. And I remember almost the first time I ever saw Bob, I was just highly impressed with his intelligence and pride. It occurred to me, here is the kind of guy we would like to have on the

> *board...I talked to a couple of other trustees about it; they got acquainted with Bob; over a period of time we got him on the board and he proved to be better than we thought he would be...That is the kind of thing that just delights me, [what] a boy like Bob Noyce did for the college."*[73]

In the same 1998 interview, Joe reflected on the role he and the College played in the founding of Intel:

> *"One thing we did, several of us urged Bob to leave the company he was with (Fairchild) and go into business for himself. And Sam Rosenthal, a fellow trustee, and I took it upon ourselves to tell Bob that we would raise money or put up the money to help start the company. And he said, "We're working on it. Someday we'll do it." I remember one [trustee] meeting he came to me and said, "Well, we're ready to launch a new company and if you fellows are interested, we would like you as part of the group:" which he was allowed to do. And that was a great thing for the college. We didn't know how great; it could have been greater if we'd have kept our stock a lot longer."*

Joe further explained that he, Sam Rosenthal, and the College invested a total of $300,000, one tenth of the Intel start-up, eventually selling the Intel stock for $16,000,000, a remarkable profit; but the College would have been much better off had it kept the stock instead of following Bob Noyce's urging that the College not have the bulk of its endowment subject to the fortunes of his company.[74]

Joe mentored several of his friends in the value and joy of giving, including his contemporary, John Ruan, and younger friends, Bill Knapp and Martin and Matthew Bucksbaum. He also had a strong influence on Stanley Richards, telling him he should give while he's alive so he can see the good his contributions do. Stan became a big donor to the University of Iowa and the Des Moines Jewish Federation where he served as president for twenty years.[75]

Joe also reached out to young women who showed promise. He tried to convince Connie Wimer to run for the Des Moines City Council when she was in her thirties. She says at that time she never would have thought of running for office: "So, I look back and think what in the world did he see in me that he thought I could do that? I think he saw a passion on issues in me." Only one woman had served on the City Council at that time (1964).[76] Of course, Connie went on to become one of Des Moines' most significant leaders and the founder and CEO of Business Publications Corporation.

Joe Rosenfield was definitely a mentor to Jill June, the Executive Director of Planned Parenthood of Iowa. Jill says her relationship with Joe "started off like a rocket leaving the launching pad. It was just that powerful and immediate." When Jill began at Planned Parenthood in 1985, she learned they had planned to ask Joe for a five-figure gift. Though her staff advised against her making a personal appeal, Jill called Joe and asked him if she could visit to thank him for previous gifts. Joe encouraged her to come right away and "off I went." When she arrived, she told Joe that her staff had advised her that Joe didn't like to be bothered. Joe responded, "I wondered why no one ever came down here to thank me. You can bother me anytime you'd like." That was the beginning of an extraordinary relationship. "I just think we immediately touched each other's hearts," Jill said. "He cared for me in a way I just don't think I deserved, you can't help caring for him. He's such a wonderful man and I think about him very often and obviously get choked up when I think of him...Our friendship was long and deep and we were in each other's thoughts quite a bit." From the time Jill began at Planned Parenthood, Joe was a mentor she could turn to under any circumstance.[77]

David Clay served Grinnell College as Treasurer for over a decade, and in his later years Joe and the Trustees trusted him to become overall manager of the College's endowment. Clay provides an intimate look into how Joe mentored young people who showed promise. Joe was, in Clay's words, "A real mentor to me." For example, when Joe was working on the transition of the portfolio as he anticipated his death, he made David feel that he, David, was the decision maker. David says Joe helped him as a young man to grow over the years into the treasurer Joe thought he could be. Often, Joe would call him asking, "Anybody given us any money today?" Dave would respond, "Well, no," and Joe's retort would be, "Okay, maybe we better figure out how to make some money today." Joe would "bird-dog" the budget, and when there was an end-of-year shortfall, he would step in to make up the difference. When David began in the job, if Joe disagreed with him, he would advise David to "think a little longer," and he knew that he had missed something. Regarding negotiations on behalf of the College, Joe advised, "Don't take their last nickel, we want to be partners on this project. Both sides need to be satisfied to do a job well."

David "had never met anyone in an organization you could put that much faith in," and the Board of Trustees understood this as well. This was the very core of Joe's influence on David Clay and all others with whom Joe interacted. Typical of his focus on others rather than himself, in 1999, a year before his death, Joe participated in the planning for management of the College's investments when he would be gone. This was, in a sense, Joe's final step in mentoring the College he loved so deeply. Joe's blanket advice was to be consistent to core principles. Decide what is best for the College and then apply those principles across a variety of managers. At the time, Grinnell, following Joe's investment principles, had become the first liberal arts college in America to earn an AAA bond rating. According to Clay, the specifics of Joe's investment philosophy, which Joe's mentoring passed on to him, were:

1. Keep things simple; 2. You have to know why you're investing and that drives your investments [In Grinnell's case, the reason was the College]; 3. Be consistent; 4. Invest "from the bottom up"; 5. Commit meaningful capital to good ideas and manage risk with due diligence; 6. Be patient with the portfolio; 7. Don't let market volatility bother you; and 8. Relationship building and partnerships should be of mutual benefit. [Examples of this philosophy Clay cited were Heritage Communications and General Growth.][78]

David Clay points to Joe's extraordinary mentoring relationships with Jim Cownie and Jim Hoak, founders of Heritage Communications, and Martin and Mathew Bucksbaum, creators of General Growth. He also mentioned Joe's overwhelming support of Planned Parenthood of Iowa and its director, Jill June.

HERITAGE COMMUNICATIONS

Jim Cownie, one of the founding partners of Heritage Communications, is the sponsor of this biography. He feels that he owes his successful business career to Joe and Joe's involvement with Heritage. Jim described his support of this project as "unfinished business:" a tribute to Joe Rosenfield.[79]

The partnership that became Heritage Communications began with the friendship of two Des Moines high school students: Jim Cownie, of Dowling Catholic, and Jim Hoak, of Roosevelt. They became acquainted when they both served on the All-City Student Council in the early 1960s. Hoak went to Yale University and Stanford Law School, then briefly practiced in Chicago, where he got acquainted with Newton Minnow, John F. Kennedy's FCC Chairman. After a short stint with the FCC in 1969–70, Hoak moved back to join a Des Moines law firm. Jim Cownie graduated from Notre Dame in 1966 after finishing Dowling in 1962. He quickly became a partner in Becker and Cownie, a small investment banking company in Des Moines. When Cownie and Hoak reconnected in their mid-twenties, they decided to become partners and apply for the Des Moines cable television franchise. Iowa was the only state in the Union that required an election to authorize a franchise, and all of the previous elections had failed. The network stations successfully lobbied against cable, succeeding partly because the citizenry were satisfied with the status quo. People could watch network TV at no cost, and the advantages of cable in urban areas were limited; in the early 1970s, there was little good cable programming. On the other hand, rural areas, located too far from urban areas to receive signals, appreciated the potential cable offered.

Cownie and Hoak created Des Moines Cable Network in early 1971 and vied with Bill Knapp for a local cable franchise. The story has several twists and turns. Knapp was the local representative of the interests of Paramount-Gulf and Western of New York, a well-established organization compared with the youthful Cownie/Hoak partnership. Cownie and Hoak had created a local board composed largely of business friends and associates of their fathers, who themselves were Des Moines business leaders. Unsurprisingly, the

Knapp and Paramount-Gulf and Western interest won the City Council franchise vote, but it was by a narrow four to three margin.

As Cownie tells the story, he and Hoak went to their board with the intention to liquidate the operation of Hawkeye Television Network (as the organization was known at the time). One of the board members, Jim Cooney, who had seldom spoken at previous meetings, said: "Hold on. Don't give up so easily. Find a way to present the Board with a plan for victory, not defeat." His admonition and the agreement of his Board colleagues encouraged them to find a way to reverse the City Council vote. The only way to get another vote was to get twenty-five people in each of Des Moines' ninety-nine precincts to sign a petition demanding a new vote. Cownie and Hoak got more than the necessary signatures from all ninety-nine precincts, but when the City Council took another vote, the result was the same, even though Mayor Dick Olson supported Hawkeye. By this time, however, Paramount-Gulf and Western had recognized that they would face strong local headwinds raised by the petition drive, so they decided to bow out, leaving the field to Cownie and Hoak and their Board. Hawkeye was awarded the franchise in a 1972 vote of the Des Moines City Council.[80]

The new franchise needed capitalization; that's where Joe was introduced into the story. In 1970 when the company was chartered, Hoak, who had just earned his brokers license and would concentrate on finances while Cownie focused on operations, began approaching potential investors. Hoak's father, a prominent citizen in Des Moines, was a good friend of Chuck Duchen, Younkers President, and Joe, who at that time had moved from the Chairmanship of Younkers to chair the Executive Committee. Cownie's and Hoak's fathers had already helped to organize the Board and had contributed capital when Hoak met with Joe and Bill Friedman to "pitch" Des Moines Cable Television in the fall of 1970. The initial sale was for $1,000,000 in $20,000–$50,000 stock blocks.

Hoak said that when he met with Joe and Friedman, Joe was in a rumpled shirt and his tie was not well tied: "He certainly was not an imposing figure." Hoak knew Joe was knowledgeable about communications and that he was partial to budding entrepreneurs, which gave him some hope. Hoak, who was 28 at the time, was buoyed by the presence of his father:

"I had my slides and the whole thing. I'm talking to Joe and he had his head down...and I'm talking to the top of his head—and it's hard to make a presentation when you can't see their eyes. I'll never forget that. So, I make the presentation; I'm making it and I finished it and Joe's head is still [down] and I'm like—what's going on? And Bill Friedman—it seemed like five minutes, but probably thirty seconds; there was a pause and Bill said, "Well, what do you think Joe?" And Joe said, "Take all you can get." Those words stuck in my mind more than any other words ever. Then I knew, WE HAD OUR COMPANY. We had Joe's name; Joe made a snap judgment [on] the business [and] likely on me and [those] were kind of magical words...And so that began our relationship with Joe. Younkers bought 25% of the company on day one...And Joe did not buy any stock himself...though he ended up buying a large amount stock himself over the years."[81]

With Younkers' $250,000, they had then raised a total of $525,000 and were well on their way to their $1,000,000 initial capitalization goal in the fall of 1970. Through Joe's influence, John Ruan invested $500,000, and Des Moines Cable Network was incorporated in January 1971. In 1972, after the tremendous battle with Bill Knapp, Paramount-Gulf, and Western, they won the recently approved Des Moines cable franchise, but it was exceedingly difficult to make a profit at the outset.[82] Laying cable is capital intensive, and cable programming was severely limited before the development of satellite transmission in 1974. From 1970 through 1973, the balance sheet was consistently negative. The stock, which had debuted at $1 and then rose to $8 in 1971–72, began to plunge and by 1974 had fallen to $.34 a share. By this time, the company changed its name to Heritage Communications, since it now extended well beyond Des Moines through acquisition of several other cable networks, particularly in rural areas of Iowa and Kansas. Jim Hoak was meeting with Joe weekly to get his advice. Hoak wanted Joe to connect him to people like Bill Bradley and Ernie Banks, hoping they would offer expansion to St. Louis and Chicago. Joe made those particular contacts happen along with many others, some of which led to expansion and funding.

In early 1974, when Heritage was barely hanging on after several years of expansion but continuously negative balance sheets, Joe approached his broker, Jon Gaskell, about purchasing Heritage stock. Gaskell did not want Joe to know that the stock had "gone begging," so he told him he would check on it for him. Every time Gaskell "found stock," Joe would buy until he eventually acquired 530,000 shares at a cost of under $1 per share, often as low as $.34 per share. When it became profitable, Heritage, which had grown to the ninth largest cable network in the United States, was sold in 1987 for $34 a share. Joe later told Cownie he made more money from Heritage stock than any other stock he owned. Joe saved the company by buying all that stock. Cownie and Hoak are eternally grateful to him for that.

Equally important to Hoak was the weekly advice that Joe gave him for at least ten years. Throughout that time, both Hoak and Cownie saw Joe as their mentor and feel that much of their success was because of Joe's advice and investments. As Heritage expanded, buying and trading cable franchises, Hoak says Joe's counsel was essential. Some of the deals included assets beyond cable; for example, at one point Heritage had the fifth largest outdoor advertising business in the U.S. Joe guided them in all of their moves, and his guidance was always "ethically A-plus," says Hoak. Hoak is another among the many to testify that Joe told him, "Always make sure [in] the deal you're doing that the other side has got a good deal. Otherwise, it will come back to bite you." Heritage cable systems stretched from San Jose, California, through Dallas, Texas, to Wilmington, Delaware, and New Haven, Connecticut, with, of course, Iowa as the anchor. Some years, Heritage added 10-20 franchises. From 1976 until it was sold in 1987, the company made substantial yearly profits.

Heritage was a pioneer in satellite programming with the advent of communications satellites in late 1973 and early 1974. In February 1974, Heritage was the second cable company to contract with HBO. Soon, Heritage had ESPN, MTV, Turner, CNN, and Discovery, plus many old movies. For the first time, cable was as attractive to urban areas as it was to rural areas, and Heritage's previous expansion put it in a position to be the ninth largest cable company in the United States. It grew to be the second largest banking customer of Goldman Sachs, second only to Ford.

Riding the crest, Cownie and Hoak, who had done a remarkable job of structuring and managing the company, sold the company in 1987 to embark on fresh ventures. They were still in their mid-forties and anxious to embrace new business challenges. Joe received $34 for each of his 530,000 shares, totaling $18,020,000. He had bought all his shares for considerably less than one million dollars, making this his most profitable personal investment. As he helped save their company through investment, he also invested his time and attention into the lives of two young entrepreneurs who went on to extraordinarily successful business careers.[83]

JOE ROSENFIELD & GENERAL GROWTH

When he retired from the Younkers Chairmanship in 1968, Joe moved his office to General Growth Properties, which became his most visible business association for the remainder of his life. He had served on the General Growth Board since 1964, becoming a constant adviser to the founding Bucksbaum brothers, particularly Martin, the partner most focused on finance. When Joe died in June 2000, Mathew Bucksbaum sent this memo to the General Growth Board: "Joe was our hero and mentor and a friend. He counseled us all and kept up his interest in General Growth until the very end. We shall miss him."[84]

John Bucksbaum, Matthew's son, grew up around the General Growth offices and later worked for the company. He provided the following outline of the origins of the Corporation: Martin and Matthew, who were in a small family grocery business in Marshalltown, Iowa, after World War II, planned to create a supermarket chain. Then, they learned about a proposed shopping center in Cedar Rapids, which would be the first in Iowa to realize this new, post-war phenomenon. Their plan was to make a proposed grocery store the anchor; so they successfully set out to "beg and borrow, but not steal" enough money to buy the land and develop the project. This development soon monopolized all of their time, so they decided to find another owner for the grocery store as they shifted from retail to development. John said: "They would tell you that they made almost every mistake in the book. So, they learned and they built a second shopping center in Cedar Rapids and it was a success. So, they decided to build more of them."[85]

The third shopping center was established in Bettendorf, Iowa, in 1960. Planning began in 1958 and, searching for an anchor, they went to see the Younkers Chair and expansion planner, Joseph Rosenfield. Younkers was in the midst of rapid expansion, which Joe oversaw, and that led to the long Joe and Bucksbaum association. Joe decided that Younkers should anchor the new Duck Creek Center in Bettendorf. Joe assured the brothers, "Wherever you want to build the next center in Iowa, Younkers will be part of it."[86]

Joe went further, suggesting the Bucksbaums move their business to Des Moines. In Younkers' efforts to develop Des Moines, Joe headed the River Hills Redevelopment Group, concentrating on the West Side. One of the entities engaged in this process was the General Growth Development Corporation. Joe convinced the Bucksbaums to merge with that corporation and move to Des Moines in June 1964, assuming the General Growth name. They acquired an existing real estate trust that included the Windsor Court apartments, Fleur Apartments, Wakonda Village Apartments, and the adjacent Wakonda Shopping Center.[87] General Growth went public in 1970, enabling it to issue stock, and Younkers, at Joe's direction, bought $2,000,000 worth, giving them one-third ownership of General Growth Properties.[88] In a 1998 interview, Joe described this relationship:

> *"We were very close to General Growth and were close to the Bucksaums who ran General Growth. And we owned part of the deal and the public owned part of it. But the Bucksbaums ran it and were the big stockholders. They would always consult with us as to where they were thinking of putting up a center and really asking us if we would be the first ones to sign up as a tenant."*[89]

Younkers became the anchor for many General Growth shopping centers.

Fred Hubbell, who became CEO of Younkers during Equitable of Iowa's ownership, described the relationship in this way:

> *"Where Younkers went, General Growth could build a mall; and where Younkers didn't want to go, there was not enough demand for General Growth to build a mall. So*

[Joe] just liked the family connections and the personal people; the business proposition on both sides, and the fact he thought it was the right thing to do for the customer... not just the real estate developer, but the people who use the malls."[90]

When General Growth went public in 1970, Joe persuaded his friend Warren Buffett to join the Board, along with Walter Heller, who was formerly John F. Kennedy's Economic Adviser. "Those titans on the Board helped to shape the public company from 1970–1985. They gave quality advice."[91] General Growth Properties was the public company, and its subsidiary, General Growth Management, operated the centers. Most important, however, to both expansion and profitability was Joe's constant mentoring, particularly with Martin regarding financial structuring. "Martin always talked with Joe about financial markets."[92] Kay Bucksbaum, Matthew's wife, thought the brothers' relationship with Joe had a deep foundation: "[Joe] kind of adopted Mathew and Martin in the wake of losing his son,"[93] Pat Gessman, Martin's and Joe's assistant, agreed with Kay's assessment, saying Joe always referred to Martin and Matthew as "the boys."[94]

Martin Bucksbaum said General Growth would not have been what it was without Joe; he exercised a light touch in his mentoring: "Joe was easy to work with...He isn't always second-guessing. He has a great financial background, a good business background and he understands you can't win every game."[95]

At its zenith, General Growth expanded to be the "largest investment real estate trust of its type in the country...[with] assets of over $450,000,000." When Younkers was sold to Equitable of Iowa in 1979, its initial General Growth stock purchase of $2,000,000 in 1970 was realized for $23,000,000.[96] In the 1990s, General Growth moved to Chicago, where it eventually encountered headwinds. Some thought it had invested too narrowly in the Midwest when a national strategy would have been more productive.

Without Younkers, and Joe especially, it is clear that General Growth would not have been nearly as successful as it was in the 1970s. Joe was the guiding genius of the organization, as he immersed himself in the company for over twenty years.

JOE ROSENFIELD & PLANNED PARENTHOOD

"While Joe was alive, he was Planned Parenthood's largest donor, and he left Planned Parenthood $1,000,000 in his will, said Jill June, Executive Director of Planned Parenthood of Iowa for thirty years.[97] In 1998, Joe said that though Grinnell College was "far and away the number one project, Planned Parenthood would be ... second on the list."[98] In 1990, Joe indicated that his interest had sprung to the fore over the last few years, "coupled with the big fight on pro-choice and pro-life. I happen to be pro-choice, and [we] have a fine chapter of Planned Parenthood here. I'm very much interested in what they're doing, and I'm supporting them."[99]

Des Moines business leader Connie Wimer, relates that Joe made "a huge difference to Planned Parenthood...because the opponents are so vocal, and a lot of people in those days would give money and be supportive of Planned Parenthood, but they wouldn't put their names out there. So, Joe doing that so visibly had a tremendous impact and taught me a good lesson, that if you believe in it and are willing to give money, you ought to be willing to give your name." Connie continued, "I would say that Joe's great reputation [and] respect got Planned Parenthood through some tough times." When Planned Parenthood happened to move into the house where Joe was born, he paid the mortgage, a gift that made a huge difference to the success of the organization.[100]

Joe and his wife, Dannie, were contributors to Planned Parenthood for over thirty years. In 1983, Joe spearheaded the honorary committee for a capital campaign to construct a new headquarters. By 1983, Fred Hubbell, who had returned to Des Moines in 1981, was the chair of the Planned Parenthood Board. He was just 31 and didn't know a lot of the potential donors, so he went to Joe, who happened to be in the hospital at the time. Joe readily agreed to be the Honorary Chair, and, Fred said, he "gave a very generous gift."[101]

In 1988, Joe made another special gift to enable Planned Parenthood to expand clinical operations into the south side of Des Moines, as well as expand the range of reproductive health services in the region generally. A specially named "Joe Rosenfield Fund" was established in 1989 as a statewide funding challenge. In just a few weeks, it had raised $160,000 and continued to be a successful funding source. The Fund Brochure reads:

The Joseph Rosenfield commitment to reproductive choice, to self-determination and freedom from government interference on matters of birth control and child bearing makes him a friend indeed to these women. Unable to afford an abortion, the compassion and financial assistance of Joseph Rosenfield makes real the constitution and the promise of personal freedom beyond the means of the poor.

The following year, Joe joined with his close friend Warren Buffett to establish a new Planned Parenthood clinic in Iowa City. This cooperation was a prelude to the merger of the chapters in Nebraska and Iowa, creating Planned Parenthood of the Heartland.

Jill June, the long-time Executive Director, knew and loved Joe as had few others. Jill feels that Warren and Susie Buffett had a lot to do with Joe's interest in Planned Parenthood. The Susan Thompson Buffett Foundation focuses entirely on empowering women through contraception and family planning. Jill June believes Warren and Joe had a deep grasp of the complex dynamic of how to manage both the need for and criticism of Planned Parenthood services. Just as Warren influenced Joe, Joe influenced Bill Knapp, who became one of the strongest supporters of the Iowa chapter. Connie Wimer, another of Bill's friends, supported Joe, telling Bill, "Planned Parenthood would be a cheap date for him."[102]

Jill remembers a particularly important event that revealed the depth of Joe's commitment and understanding. Pioneer Hybrid had been giving $25,000 a year to Planned Parenthood to subsidize pap smears for women who were living in low-income situations. The women were harassed from 1988 through 1990, and Pioneer was threatened with public exposure. Pioneer decided to withdraw its support. "Joe was furious," so he and others stepped in to reestablish the annual $25,000 gift. "So that told me right away, Joe, your name and your support is worth more to us than your money. So, I need to get your name out there in a profound way if you'll let me. He did, but he didn't want the women to be thanking him. Joe didn't want anyone to feel as though they owed him anything." The fact that Jill June persuaded Joe to let the group use his name is a landmark in the Joe Rosenfield saga—the story of a man who was determined to help but to remain in the background. Joe understood that an organization he really cared about but that was on a political hot seat would benefit tremendously by his publicized support.[103]

Throughout the time of Joe's support, Planned Parenthood was increasingly targeted by abortion opponents. Though the Iowa chapter never suffered violent attacks, it was repeatedly threatened. Joe paid for bulletproof glass to be installed in the reception area of the Des Moines headquarters.[104] A particularly touching story is the time when Joe knew that the news of an abortion doctor's murder would deeply upset Jill; he called her and urged her to spend the afternoon at his apartment. Susie Buffett was in town, and the three spent the afternoon together over drinks and supportive conversation. The afternoon "restored my spirits," says Jill.[105]

By almost any standard, Joe Rosenfield was a feminist. Jill says: "Joe Rosenfield was a stronger feminist than most women ... He was particularly concerned about women who were destitute ... and would be turned away from service that would have life-changing prospects to it." She thought the origin of Joe's feminism was similar to Warren's: "Why wouldn't you want full equality for half of the world? It's just good business; it's good public policy and human rights. Why wouldn't you do that?" She added, insightfully, that Joe's humility makes it hard to criticize him, and, particularly relevant to his public Planned Parenthood support, "even his political opponents did not [criticize him]." His clarity of purpose was "a true north compass, and even if you disagreed with him, he was a hell of a guy."[106]

Fred Hubbell thinks "Joe and Joe's sister always felt that women didn't have a lot of rights and didn't have a lot of control over the decisions that affected their lives." He also added that Louise probably influenced Joe's feminism.[107]

The capstone to Joe's willingness to let Planned Parenthood use his name was his 90th birthday celebration, organized by Planned Parenthood and Connie Wimer in June 1994. It was also the 60th anniversary of Planned Parenthood. Jill was happy that Joe agreed to the birthday celebration, and Planned Parenthood "raised a lot of money." Connie Wimer and her committee raised major contributions from a Des Moines "Who's Who" list of large donors, including Myron Blank, both Bucksbaum families, the Gordons, Bill Knapp, John and Mary Poppajohn, and the Hubbells, plus a Grinnell friend, Kappie Spencer.[108] Fittingly, each guest was asked to contribute $90. Bonnie Campbell spoke about Joe's role in Iowa politics and another woman told Joe, "You're a Rhett Butler in a room full of Ashley Wilkeses."

Warren Buffett told Joe they would be back for his 100th, and Jill thought: "You better hang in their old man, I'm counting on you; I need the fundraiser."[109]

Joe's response was vintage Joe: "I don't know exactly why I should live to be 90 years old. A few years ago, I said I was determined to live until the Cubs won the World Series. After watching a few games of the opening season, I have now discarded that ambition." After thanking all for coming, Joe invited them to return for his 100th birthday, adding, "Incidentally, I won't be here, but have a good time anyway."[110] Joe lived to be 96 years old.

DEMOCRATIC POLITICS

Jim Enright, a Chicago sports writer with whom Joe vacationed in Arizona, told *The Des Moines Register* reporter Wendel Cochran that Joe was a gambler who played hunches. He said, "It's no surprise that [he] ended up playing politics, a natural setting for a serious gambler."[111] Joe's General Growth colleague Stanley Richards provided a soberer assessment: "I just think he saw right from wrong; for whatever reason, he was the underdog's man. He always felt responsible for those who had less, and I think the principles of the Republican Party towards the wealthy was something that didn't sit right with him. He backed some pretty liberal people, like Senator Hughes."[112] Michael Gartner called Joe "an instinctive liberal."[113] Fred Little attributed Joe's concern for the underdog to his family. In response to the question, "What made Joe so liberal?" he said, "I think, family. I think Joe had a great interest for and empathy for the underdog...He was attracted to liberal causes and people."[114]

Joe told Iowa Attorney General Tom Miller that his father was a nominal Republican and his mother "an ardent Democrat."[115] Near the end of his life, Joe said his wife had much to do with his becoming a Democratic activist. Joe liked the Democratic philosophy, but it was his wife's work for Eugene McCarthy in the Vietnam era that propelled him to action.[116] He fulfilled his political identification with the Democratic Party that began toward the end of the Roosevelt era.[117] Jill June provides the most intimate insight into Joe's liberal activism. She and Joe loved Winston Churchill's quote about the fact that the atrocities of the moment are made possible by the complacency of the benevolent:

Joe believed you cannot disengage—bad things happen when people do nothing. You give what you can and you live by example and you raise up your voice. So, that was his view of politics. You had your duty and you couldn't avoid it ... You were affected by it every day in every way. So, be engaged and get people into public office.[118]

Joe helped place a generation of promising Democrats into public office, including Harold Hughes, Tom Harkin, John Culver, Tom Vilsack, and Tom Miller.

Joe's support of Harold Hughes landed him on President Richard Nixon's "Enemies List." It came as a surprise:

"Well, that was as big a surprise to me as anybody. It just appeared in the paper one day that [the] Nixon enemy list was made public containing 200 names and I was there, I think, because they had two from Iowa. Harold Hughes, Governor and Senator, who should have been on the list because he battled Nixon right down to the wire. But I was a big supporter of Hughes and I think they described me as a lawyer and money man for Harold Hughes. As far as I know, Nixon never heard of me and probably has never heard of me yet. It was a sloppy list. They had people on there that had no business being on it. It had Joe Namath the football player and I don't think he even knew who the President was. But, I was on the list; got a lot of kick out of being harassed about it...Nothing ever came of it.[119]

Harold Hughes was a two-term Iowa Governor (1963–69) and one-term United States Senator from Iowa (1969–75); in addition, he ran unsuccessfully for the 1972 Democratic presidential nomination. Joe was the principal donor when Hughes was Governor and Senator. Hughes paid Joe weekly visits in his General Growth office, often so that Joe could hand over a check, which according to office rumor, often reached $10,000.[120] Wendel Cochran described their relationship: "If Hughes was the person who consolidated Rosenfield's political feelings, the [Vietnam] war was the issue. Even today, he is bitter about Lyndon Johnson's policy of trying to fight a war without restraining the domestic economy. He calls the war 'the cruelest blow of all,' the culprit for inflation that was crippling the nation." Joe was also very disturbed about the urban riots of the 1960s, which he blamed on minority unemployment. Joe, in typical form, took action, raising $100,000 from Des Moines businessmen for a jobs program.[121]

Hughes described Joe as his "Iowa Angel." Joe and Bill Knapp collaborated to raise money for Hughes' 1972 presidential run.[122] Joe admired Hughes' humble beginnings but was put off by his born-again Christianity. Nevertheless, he saw Hughes' charismatic personality and policy positions as just right for the presidency, so he urged him to make a presidential run. Midway through Hughes' 1971 presidential campaign, Joe and Bill Knapp got cold feet. One cause was an incident with Jewish donors in New York, where Hughes was asked about his Israel policy. "Let me tell you this, I'm not going to rubber-stamp anybody," Hughes replied. Knapp rolled his eyes and looked at Joe, signaling, "We're dead, let's get out of here."[123] Ultimately, it was Hughes' views about the afterlife, which included séances with the dead, that led both Joe and Bill to drop their support. Hughes folded his campaign when these views became public in *The Des Moines Register* on July 15, 1971.[124]

Though not nearly as involved as he was with Hughes, Joe was also a strong supporter of Tom Harkin. Harkin served five terms in the House from 1975–1985; he then succeeded Republican Senator Roger Jepsen, serving five terms from 1985–2015. He had one loss in 1972 when he first ran for the House.

Joe and Tom Harkin first met in 1968, after Harkin had left the military. Joe was involved in Hughes' Senate campaign at the time. Four years later, Joe gave a "good contribution" to Harkin's unsuccessful run for the House even though he knew Harkin's chances were slim.

Joe's roommate John Chrystal was a major financial supporter of Harkin's successful 1974 House campaign, and he got Joe "hooked in to it." Joe proved to be "very helpful," according to Harkin. Another connection came through Harkin's wife, Ruth, the attorney for Story County, who was a good friend of Joe's sister, Louise. By 1988, Joe had become a major donor to Senator Harkin, and during the 1990s, once every year or so, Harkin would have lunch in Des Moines with Joe and John Chrystal. Over time, Joe developed great respect for Tom Harkin. Jill June says that Joe, early in Harkin's political career, asked her if she thought Tom would grow in office. Some folks shrink, Joe opined. Of course, says Jill, both she and Joe ultimately agreed that Tom Harkin "had become a giant." For his part, Harkin saw Joe as a "Progressive Liberal."[125]

Another of Joe's Democratic protégés was John Culver, who served five terms in the U.S. House from 1965–1975 before moving to the Senate for one term, 1975–1981, when he was defeated by Iowa's current senior senator, Republican Chuck Grassley. Culver always found Joe to be "very helpful and generous; always available to share his views." Joe and John Chrystal invited Culver to their Grand Avenue apartment and to the Des Moines Club for lunches when he was in town. During his entire political career, Culver has seen "only a handful who matched Joe." "Wisdom" is the word he used to describe Joe: "You didn't find people like Joe in knowledge and wisdom."[126]

Tom Miller, Iowa's Attorney General, started his political career working on John Culver's campaigns. Culver was Miller's mentor, and through that connection, Miller met Joe when he launched his own political career. "Culver talked to Joe and Joe became a big supporter," giving significant amounts of money both to Miller's unsuccessful 1974 run against Dick Turner for Iowa Attorney General and again in 1978 when Miller defeated Turner. Miller has served as Iowa's Attorney General from that time until today (with a four-year hiatus 1991–94 when he left office to make an unsuccessful run for Governor). For Joe to have supported him when he was first running, at the early age of 29, and then when he became Attorney General at the age of 33, was, according to Miller, "a huge deal in terms of my campaign and a big deal in terms of confidence building. He always was very supportive and very generous in contributing to me."

Miller garnered Joe's support through frequent visits to his General Growth office. "He gives his own money and his recommendation to other people is very important." Joe did not intervene in policy, but he gave fundraising and more general advice. Miller felt he was part of a Democratic wave and that Joe was a critical component in that wave. One of Miller's sharpest memories is of his early encounters with Joe, who did not put Tom through a "Question and Answer" grilling. "He had decided he was going to support me," and that was all that was needed. Today, the glow on Tom Miller's face at the mention of Joe is all one needs to appreciate Miller's gratitude, respect, and love for a man who reached out to mentor him when he was just a novice politician.[127]

Tom Vilsack, Iowa's two-term Governor, from 1999–2007, and Barack Obama's Secretary of Agriculture, from 2008–2016, completes the covey of Democratic politicians mentored by Joe Rosenfield. Vilsack's relationship with Joe was not as close as it was for the others, but Joe was an important supporter through funds and occasional advice.

Bill Knapp says one of the reasons Joe was such an influential political supporter was because he was a moderate: "There are Republicans and Democrats, but they are so far out one way or the other that they have no effect."[128] Another reason was that Joe did not ask for favors. This trait is so unusual that almost everyone who knew him has commented on it; Harold Hughes said that Joe "wasn't demanding," recalling that Joe never objected when Hughes raised taxes even though he was personally affected. Hughes said, "He never asked for anything for himself." Never was there a quid pro quo for Joe's support.[129] In 1973, when Tom Harkin was working for the Legal Aid in Des Moines, he pushed for a credit card interest limit of 10 percent, which would have adversely affected Younkers. He and Joe had an amicable conversation about it, and Joe steered clear of any threats to withdraw funding or other support as Harkin was launching his political career.[130] Despite frequent interaction over a career that covered almost four decades, Joe never tried to influence any of Tom Miller's decisions as Attorney General.[131] This chain of agreement to Joe's political selflessness would be startling but for the unanimous agreement about Joe's generosity of spirit in all things.

About the only thing missing in Joe's political activism is municipal government. Joe himself admitted he did not do much regarding city government; he left that to his sister Louise, who was heavily involved in Des Moines city management reform. Joe did, however, raise money for that initiative.[132] What is most definitely present in Joe's history as a political activist was his deep involvement in state and national politics, mentoring a generation of extraordinary Democratic politicians, and, in the process, drawing the enmity of President Richard Nixon.

JOE ROSENFIELD & THE CHICAGO CUBS

The story of Joe Rosenfield's passion for the Chicago Cubs is an appropriate conclusion to the larger story of Joe's catalytic impact on Des Moines in the second half of the twentieth century. Joe once told George Will, the famous columnist and fellow Chicago Cubs fan: "The Cubs have given me something to live for...I have determined to live until the Cubs win the National League Pennant. As a matter of fact, I am making a note on my perpetual calendar to invite you to my 100th birthday party."[133] Even if Joe had lived until his 100th birthday, it would not have been enough as the Cubs did not win the National League Pennant (and the World Series) until 2016, when Joe would have amassed 112 years.

Joe owned 274 shares of stock in the Chicago Cubs, making him the largest minority owner with three percent of the total until the Wrigley family sold the team to the *Chicago Tribune* for $20,500,000 million in June 1981.[134] The Wrigley family owned 8,000 of the outstanding 10,000 shares of Cubs stock and the other 2,000 were spread among fans, which included Joe and me. All stockholders were obliged to sell their stock to the Tribune in 1981, and I knew Joe would give the proceeds to Grinnell. So, as Grinnell's president and a fellow stockholder, I called Joe and suggested the proceeds be used to establish a Cubs Room in the College's Physical Education Complex. He enthusiastically agreed and even got Cubs icon Ernie Banks to come to Grinnell to dedicate the Cubs Room. Joe had, of course, made money on the sale, which brought $1,500 a share with Joe's cost basis at $500 a share. Joe recalled this in a 1990 interview, saying: "I don't have any Cubs stock anymore; the *Chicago Tribune* bought the thing out and I gave my stock to Grinnell and they turned it in and spent it for a Cubs Room."

In Jill June's words, "Joe was crazy about the Cubs."[135] Joe became a serious baseball fan at age eight and his interest increased as he matured.[136] He attended Cubs games in the 1930s when in Chicago on legal business. In 1947, as President of Des Moines Enterprises, a branch of the Des Moines Chamber of Commerce, he spearheaded the drive to draw Minor League baseball to Des Moines in the form of the Des Moines Bruins, a Cubs farm team in the Class A Western League. Joe told the story of how there was no baseball in Des Moines, and "they started the Western League in 1947 and we got the Cubs out here and I got acquainted with the Cubs management and accidently when in Chicago when I was in a brokerage office, I bought ten shares of Cubs stock. Someone yelled out...'10 shares of Cubs stock for sale.' So, I said, 'I'll take it.' So, I bought it and continued to buy until I had 274 shares."[137] Joe spearheaded the successful effort for Des Moines to build the necessary stadium: "In 1947, we persuaded the Cubs to start a farm team out here. A couple of friends and I had to raise the money in a matter of a week or ten days because the stadium had to be ready when the season opened."[138]

Dick Levitt says the only ego Joe exhibited was over being part owner of the Cubs. He often told people "that he and the Wrigley family owned the Chicago Cubs."[139] Joe was indeed proud of his ownership, and, in typical Rosenfield humor, he poked fun at his role with the Cubs. He wrote George Will:

"Some thirty-five years ago, I was in a broker's office in Chicago and a trader who knew my interest in the Cubs told me ten shares were available, which I bought as a kind of lark. However, I soon discovered that it was like taking your first shot of heroin and I could not wait to increase my holdings. Every time stock appeared—two shares, three shares, six or what—I bought it and I kept pounding the brokers for more.

At the end of two years I had accumulated 274 shares and was otherwise bankrupt. After two unsuccessful hold-up attempts in order to get additional buying power, I managed to kick the habit through sheer iron will and the help of a

> *nationally known psychiatrist. My holdings have therefore been fixed at 274 shares, although my fanatical attachment to the Cubs remains...The Cubs have given me something to live for."*[140]

George Will, in a column called, "Life is Just a Baseball Game," wrote in the same spirit, using as examples both Joe and his good friend Warren Buffett. The column has Will, a Cubs fan, telling Buffett, a Cardinals fan, that he wants a share of Cubs stock. So, Warren writes to Joe:

> *Dear Joe: George Will, an otherwise quite competent young man, shares your irrational regard for the Cubs. I mentioned to George that in this case it is possible to put your money where your aberrations are; and that it would be possible for him to buy stock in the club. Considering that you and Phil Wrigley are the two largest shareholders, I don't see how he can help but upgrade the present membership. Why don't you write George directly and explain to him precisely how to get aboard the gravy train.*

Joe wrote Will:

> *If I were you, I would not consult Warren about the stock as he will give you a long, learned treatise on price-earnings ratios, return on capital and, and a bunch of other hogwash that has no place in a transaction between two sportsmen.*[141]

Though it was difficult being a part owner and dedicated fan of a perpetually losing (108 years between World Series championships, the longest drought in U. S. major sports history), Joe's obsession was always peppered with humor. When he was placed on Nixon's "Enemies List," the baseball writers at the Cubs ballpark, Wrigley Field, put up a sign saying Joe would always be welcome in the press box: "They knew that he would rather watch the Cubs play than go to the White House anyway."[142] José Cardenal, a Cubs outfielder, would smuggle Cuban cigars to Joe during the Cuban embargo, an act that demonstrates how close Joe was to the Cubs. Many people have told stories about how Joe loved watching the Cubs play on TV. His assistant, Pat Gessman, commented that when she called Joe, she would sometimes be greeted with, "Pat, I can't talk to you now, the

Cubs are playing."[143] Pat adds that Joe had season tickets to the Iowa Cubs (AAA farm team of the Cubs) for about 40 years. Typical of Joe, he did not own box seats but rather a block of reserved grandstand seats and would frequently let others, including Pat, use them. John Bucksbaum, who grew up around the General Growth offices before working there, would stop by Joe's office to "talk baseball." He found Joe knowledgeable about all of baseball but particularly well versed on the Cubs.[144] On more than one occasion, Joe took young John to Chicago for a ball game. Every year, Joe went with friends to Arizona during Spring Training season. John Chrystal and Tom Hutchison, another friend, would often accompany him, along with Chicago sportswriter Jim Enright.[145] Sometimes the Grinnell College Board of Trustees would organize their winter meeting in Phoenix to take advantage of Joe's presence as well as the Arizona warmth.[146]

Joe turned his passion for a Major League Baseball team into a successful effort to bring Minor League baseball to his city. What Joe cared about personally was almost always transformed into civic engagement, with his work often occurring behind the scenes and frequently through his personal mentoring of young men and women. Joe Rosenfield was, indeed, Des Moines' catalyst.

PART FOUR
JOE ROSENFIELD, TRUSTEE

THE COLLEGIATE SCENE

Before I narrate Joe Rosenfield's fifty-nine transformative years as a Grinnell College Trustee, it would be helpful to take a brief look at the landscape of America's liberal arts colleges and the locus of Grinnell within that landscape. We have become so accustomed to the thousands of liberal arts colleges that dot the American landscape that we usually fail to recognize how unique they are in the larger global context. The United States stands virtually alone in having created and fostered this species of higher education. These colleges are unique because they are financed privately, not publicly, and because almost all of them have ecclesiastical foundations. The citizens of other nations are stunned by the willingness of American citizenry to sustain this vast array of private colleges, allowing them to survive and in some cases flourish amid seemingly overwhelming challenges. Over time, there has been some blurring of the distinction between public and private education with the advent of publicly financed scholarship programs in private colleges, research grants for private institutions, and, on the other hand, the dramatic increase in private contributions to public universities and colleges. And yet, these two branches of American higher education continue to exist in quite distinct universes.

The private college phenomenon, in fact, pioneered higher education in America when Harvard College was established in the Massachusetts Bay Colony in 1636. Religion was at the heart of this creation as it was for virtually all of the colonial colleges. The colleges reflected the divide that split Protestantism in the home country, England. Radical dissent from the established Church of England produced the emigration that created the Massachusetts Bay Colony. Groups derisively called "Puritans" failed in their attempt to "purify" the Church of England from what they regarded as Roman Catholic remnant, so they determined to emigrate in pursuit of their own form of worship and polity. Those who settled in Massachusetts called themselves Congregationalists, and the more moderate settlers of the Middle Colonies, like New Jersey, were known as Presbyterians.

The "charter" five of colonial colleges reflected the Puritan/Anglican split common in England as well as America. Countering Harvard, the second American college, William and Mary, founded in 1693, was Anglican, mirroring the Virginia colony, which remained much closer to the English establishment than did dissenting Massachusetts. Yale, in the Puritan Connecticut colony, was founded by Congregationalists in 1701, making it the third of the colonial colleges. New Jersey, settled by less radical colonists called Presbyterians, created its own College of New Jersey in 1746. After two moves from its first home in Elizabeth, New Jersey, it settled in Princeton and changed its name to that of its new location. The Anglicans countered in 1754 with the fifth of the colonial institutions: King's College in New York City. Its name was changed to Columbia after the American Revolution made "King's" a hated anachronism, but the College retained its Anglican flavor in a city heavily populated with British loyalists. Brown College was established in Providence, Rhode Island in 1764 by a combination of Congregationalists and Baptists (another English dissenting church) as the first American college to admit students without religious distinctions. This innovation was consistent with the tolerance of Roger Williams, who, in 1637, founded Rhode Island as a breakaway from the religious restraints of Massachusetts Bay after he was expelled in 1636.

Following the end of the Revolutionary War in 1783, the United States became a nation and American churches sprinkled colleges across the rolling western frontier. New colleges included places like Williams (1793), Wesleyan (1831), Haverford (1833), Oberlin (1833), Grinnell (1846), Carleton (1866), Macalester (1874), Colorado College (1874), and Pomona (1887). Public universities soon followed, particularly after the Civil War when the 1862 Morrill Act created the land grant for universities focusing on agriculture and engineering instruction. By the time of the Morrill Act, the idea of public higher education was well established in the minds of much of the public; public universities thereafter became the norm for American higher education.

Iowa proved to be fertile ground for private colleges when the territory spearheaded trans-Mississippi settlement in the 1830s and 1840s. By that time, America had become a rich quilt of competing denominations sparked by at least two major religious revivals in the late-eighteenth and early-nineteenth centuries. Continuous European immigration also enhanced the Iowa quilt, as Catholics, Lutherans, Dutch Reformed, Quakers, Mormons, Brethren, Disciples of Christ, and as the more established Congregationalist, Presbyterians, and Methodists created colleges in the new state. Today, with its twenty-five independent colleges, Iowa has more private colleges per capita than every state except Vermont. This multiplicity is a tribute to the tenacity of the religious founders. Of course, many also owe their continuing survival to recent recognition by the state of Iowa that it is less expensive to provide substantial tuition grants to Iowa residents attending these colleges than it would be to create campuses to provide public education for the more than 30,000 students who collectively populate these twenty-five private institutions.

Over time, some of these colleges have drifted from their religious foundations, but the majority have retained their connections; in the case of the Catholic and Christian Reformed colleges, it remains very strong. Some, like Grinnell, which was founded by New England Congregationalists in the Harvard tradition, have almost completely severed the church connection. Today, Grinnell merely acknowledges a historical connection to its founding denomination.

GRINNELL COLLEGE

Before we begin to consider Joe's life-saving work for Grinnell, what follows is a brief history of the College, from its foundation to the beginning of World War II, when Joe first joined the Board of Trustees.

In the late 1830s, twelve Congregational graduates of Andover Theological Seminary, in Andover, Massachusetts, took a vow that they would go to the trans-Mississippi West, each to found a church and together a college. They acted in the tradition of the 1806 "Haystack Prayer Meeting" at Williams College, which is credited with establishing the American Protestant mission movement. It included foreign and domestic missions, and, in the case of the Andover graduates, the focus was domestic. This was also the time when the North and South were vying to populate the territories of the Louisiana Purchase with either free or slave-holding citizens. The Iowa Territory was a spearhead of free-soil settlers; and the Andover Congregationalists were dedicated to making the trans-Mississippi West free of slavery.

The "Iowa Band," as this group of eleven became known, established twelve Congregational churches on the western bank of the Mississippi River, and, in 1846, the year Iowa became a state, they combined to establish Iowa College (which would later be called Grinnell) in Davenport. This was the third college chartered in Iowa, following two Catholic institutions: Loras (1839) and Clarke (1843) in Iowa's oldest city, Dubuque. Doing so in 1854, Iowa College was the first to award a bachelor degree, in 1854.

Iowa College did not thrive in Davenport. Relations with the city were less than cordial and were exacerbated by the city's creation of two streets on the campus without adequate consultation with the College. Davenport, a river town, coveted the river's connection to the South, so an abolitionist college was not popular. By the mid 1850s, when Iowa College began looking for a new home, a new abolitionist colony, established on the prairie in 1854 by Josiah Bushnell Grinnell, was looking for a college to take up 100 acres the founder had set aside for a "university" when the town was platted.

J. B. Grinnell was a congregational minister from the East—New York via Washington, D.C. As he rode a Rock Island train in Illinois, looking for a potential site for an abolitionist colony, he encountered a Director of the Rock Island named Henry Farnam, who gave him the coordinates of a flagpole located at the expected intersection of his soon to be extended Rock Island and an as yet unconstructed north-south line. Grinnell found the flagpole, and it was there that he established his new colony in 1854, "modestly" naming it Grinnell.[1] J. B., an entrepreneur of the first order, not only set aside one hundred acres, but he also created a prospectus for his "university" complete with a non existent faculty and curriculum. The desire of the already established Congregational Iowa College to move was a gift to J. B., a Congregational pastor. So, in 1858, Iowa College moved to Grinnell; the move included only the charter and a wagon load of books and scientific instruments. The faculty remained in Davenport. The 1856 decision to admit women to a "Ladies Course" helped the struggling college to survive.

Little occurred at Iowa College in Grinnell until after the Civil War, which began in 1861, three years after the move. Thus, the story of Iowa College (which after 1909 became commonly known as "Grinnell"), continues as a post-Civil War Iowa phenomenon—though several students served during the war in Iowa regiments, with eleven perishing.

The nineteenth-century Iowa College was a profoundly religious place. By today's standards, it would be labeled Evangelical, embodying the Calvinist focus on the saving grace of Jesus Christ, who was crucified for our sins. The College's first President, George Magoun, was a deeply committed Congregational pastor whose passion was to replicate himself in order to produce a classically educated ministry for the frontier. Along with theology, classical languages, and mathematics were the curricular core. It was a demanding education.

The greatest physical challenge to the College in the nineteenth century was a devastating tornado that ripped through the campus just before commencement in June 1882. Though thirty-eight perished in the storm (the second largest loss of life in an Iowa tornado to date), only two students were among the dead. Many were away at Cornell College for a baseball game, which had been forbidden by the austere Magoun. All of the buildings were destroyed, but Magoun and J. B. Grinnell successfully plumbed the Congregational eastern roots to raise the necessary funds to begin rebuilding. None of the campus' extant buildings predates 1882.

The College revived, and along with the physical revival, its Evangelical, Christ-based theology shifted gradually but decisively to a new, socially active form of Christianity called "the social gospel." The new movement posed the question, "When faced with a challenging moral and social situation, what would Jesus do?" In other words, in this theology, the idea of "Jesus"—the man who taught and walked among the people—displaced the idea of "Christ"—who died for our sins on the cross. It was an ethical, outward-focused, activist kind of Christianity for social justice. Grinnell became a national leader of this movement with three people at the helm: George Gates, Congregational Minister and College President; George Herron, first Professor of Applied Christianity at Iowa College; and Edward Steiner, Herron's successor in that chair.

This environment of Christian social action blended with the innovative study of political science created by Professor Jesse Macy, who introduced students to practical analysis and participation in political action to create a generation of Grinnell graduates who became a core of President Franklin Roosevelt's New Deal in the 1930s. The New Deal was led by Roosevelt's "alter-ego" Harry Hopkins, a 1912 graduate, who enlisted Hallie Flanagan, class of 1911, Chester Davis, 1911, and Florence Kerr, 1912. The historical consensus is that the intellectual fabric of the New Deal was drawn from three collegiate institutions: Harvard, Columbia, and Grinnell.

Most outstanding liberal arts colleges have had long-tenured exceptional presidents, often in office in the first half of the twentieth century. Such was the case for Grinnell's John Hanson Thomas Main, who presided from 1906 until his death in office in 1931. He was Joe's College president, and he was the man who conceived of and built the dormitory system that became the College's architectural icon and the framework of social life for Joe and countless other Grinnellians. Main was enthralled by the Oxford/Cambridge model of residential life and did his best to replicate it on the Iowa prairie. The replication succeeded, though not entirely according to Main's model, and the cost of construction plunged the College into debt that was only deepened by the Depression of the 1930s. That debt persisted to greet Joe when he became a Trustee in late November 1941. This debt challenged Joe to pull the College out of looming bankruptcy and move it to solvency and, ultimately, robust health. Joe embraced that challenge and succeeded beyond his wildest ambitions.

JOE ROSENFIELD, TRUSTEE & SAM STEVENS, PRESIDENT

Joseph Frankel Rosenfield became "Joseph Frankel Rosenfield, Grinnell College Trustee" on November 29th, 1941, less than two weeks before the attack on Pearl Harbor. Samuel Stevens was the President of the College, having begun his term in September 1940. The College was still in the throes of the Great Depression, and Stevens greeted Joe at his first meeting with a speech in which he announced a $48,000 deficit in the previous year's operations. Stevens proceeded to wonder whether the Midwest could support a first-rate liberal arts college, explicitly stating that Grinnell might not be able to continue as a first-class liberal arts college since it was "run down." Stevens challenged the Board to be bold or the College would die: "There is no middle ground."[2]

This warning of dire financial straits left an indelible impression on the young Trustee and Des Moines civic leader, who had fallen in love with Grinnell when he was a student in the early 1920s. In a 1998 interview, just two years before his death, Joe said that if he had known about the condition of the College, "I might not have gone on the Board." Joe urged the Trustees to raise $10,000 to meet immediate needs: "The first meeting of the board I suggested that we get ten Trustees to give $1,000 apiece so we could ensure the College would open the next fall. I offered to put up $1,000, which was not a great struggle, but I couldn't get any of the other Trustees to go along."[3]

The financial stress on the College was longstanding. In 1932, Henry Conard, outstanding Professor of Biology, wrote to Frank Thone, a 1915 graduate:

> "There is increasing difficulty from year to year, which cannot go on much longer. But what can be done? The dormitories must be paid for! Of course, the Grinnell Foundation could be declared bankrupt, and the buildings sold for what they would bring—i.e. the debt repudiated, refinanced at reduced valuation, and begin over. But that would carry with it the ruin of the credit of Grinnell College. The Foundation is legally separated but not morally."[4]

It is easy to imagine how stressed a small, Midwestern liberal arts college would have been during the Depression. As just one example of the challenges, the previous President, John Nollen, and Treasurer, Louis Phelps, made an emergency trip to Chicago to ask to borrow enough money to make that month's payroll. They were met with rejection, but after immediately driving back to Grinnell and arriving at 3:00 a.m., they proceeded to Des Moines, where one of the banks made the necessary loan.[5] The College's enrollment had dropped, and in taking this loan, the College needed individual Trustees to guarantee the loan.

Joe Rosenfield was well regarded by his fellow Trustees, several of whom were from Des Moines. He was elected to the Executive Committee almost immediately and was soon elected Vice Chair of the Board. The Executive Committee met almost monthly in those days.[6]

In Joe's second biennial meeting, on May 29, 1942, the Board reacted to the heightened crisis of the advent of World War II. Stevens agonized that only three previous College Board meetings had occurred amid such a challenge: the founding meeting in 1846, the decision to move from Davenport in 1858, and the beginning of the Civil War.[7] Stevens was right. During the War, civilian enrollment dropped to as low as 328, in 1944. The College looked like it could fold.[8] It was Joe who, in December 1942, moved that the President go to Washington to secure a military officer training unit.[9] Stevens was successful in this mission, and an Army unit of 750 men arrived on campus in October 1943, with additional units added at various times, bringing the military training numbers up to 1,000. Officer training saved the College, but the Trustees had to make capital expenditures to build Cowles residence and dining hall and Darby Gymnasium, both of which were completed in 1942, to meet government specifications. To fund operating expenses, short-term borrowing continued, since the government only paid its bill at the end of each semester.

Joe's immediate influence on College finances is evident in the Trustee Minutes. Before his arrival, the endowment consisted almost exclusively of farms and dormitories, both of which were revenue producing in theory. However, many of the farms were not profitable, and the dormitories almost never returned a profit since it cost more to maintain them and serve student needs than room charges yielded. In the early 1940s, the recorded endowment was in the neighborhood of $2,000,000, but when the dormitories were subtracted, it was closer to $1,100,000.[10] In 1951, it was calculated that the dorms made up 60 percent of the endowment. Loose Hall had just been added at this time, and for most of the previous 40 years, the dormitories had been a drain on income.[11] Joe remembered that the productive endowment when he joined the Board was under $100,000.[12] His recollection indicates his clear-eyed assessment of the situation, and the Board Minutes for this period reveal that Joe and others were urging the College to sell farms and invest in securities. When Joe was appointed to the Finance Committee in May 1943, he immediately moved that the Board authorize the Finance Committee to buy and sell securities on its own.[13] This move allowed him to urge College financing in the direction that ultimately allowed him to build Grinnell's endowment into one of the largest of any liberal arts college in America.

Another enrollment crisis loomed well before the end of World War II. By the spring of 1944, it was becoming clear that the Allies would win the war. Since it took over two years to produce army officers from the collegiate training programs, the units were no longer needed. The military would be stuck with an excess of officers at the end of the war if the units continued training new officers. Army Chief of Staff George Marshall had persuaded President Roosevelt that he needed the men in army officer training units as soldiers for the forthcoming Normandy invasion.[14] In February 1944, Grinnell was notified that its army unit would be cancelled on June 3, 1944.[15] Joe immediately moved that the Board appoint a committee to raise $75,000 and that Sam Stevens go to Washington to determine if the army had further plans for Grinnell.[16] Sam found out that Washington did not have any future plans for Grinnell, and the army's departure left a big hole in the budget, subtracting $234, 529 of its $539, 403 revenue stream.[17] The Board met the crisis with large bank loans and a Rosenfield-directed effort to solicit $250,000 from the Trustees to match a $50,000 Cowles Foundation grant.[18]

The dramatic decline in enrollment in 1944–45 was soon reversed by the overwhelming tide of World War II veterans financed by the GI Bill. There were, of course, overcrowding problems in dorms, classrooms, and hastily secured government surplus barracks for married students. Sixty percent of the faculty were hired between 1946 and 1949[19] and the concern of the Trustees quickly shifted from too few students to accommodating too many. The influx of new faculty overwhelmed the housing market in a town with a population of no more than 5,000. In April 1947, the Trustee Executive Committee responded positively to Stevens' request to purchase 10 prefabricated homes with FHA loans. Some of those houses remain on Spring and West streets to this day. A few faculty members rented, while others purchased those homes.[20]

Grinnell College faced a variety of building needs, which were exacerbated by the dramatic growth in enrollment. The College planned and constructed Loose Hall for women in the immediate postwar years, and the Hall was completed in 1950. Loans—$350,000 from Equitable in particular—financed the $500,000 construction bill. In October 1949, the Board decided to construct Younker Hall for men, which was undertaken in the spring of 1950, with an estimated cost of $538,000. This construction again required significant borrowing. Younker opened in the fall of 1951. Joe was a major force in the efforts to arrange for Younker Trust money to be used for the new dormitory, even intervening with Ben Younker when he became discouraged about Stevens' negotiations over the Younker gift.[21] He also worked to gain Younker approval to put the dormitory ahead of a new student health center, which had been Rachel Younker's preference.

One other vital new construction need was a new science building. Anyone who remembers the old gothic structure of Blair Hall understands why a new science building was the highest priority of the Board, especially as science had attracted so much development and heightened importance during World War II. In October 1949, the Board decided to build a modern, rather than gothic building, and they knew the cost would be at least $832,000, by far the most expensive Grinnell College building to that point.[22] They hoped to start construction in the spring of 1950, but Stevens' fundraising had not progressed to a point where they could make the final decision to break ground. Joe began his four-year term as Board President, from June 1948 to June 1952.[23] Those years were among the most difficult in the College's history. The Board had been pressing the President over fundraising at each Executive Committee and Board meeting. The necessity for a new science building had been uppermost on the agenda since the end of the war. At the Annual Meeting in June, 1950, Sam Stevens reported that he had cash and pledges for $483,000, including $100,000 from the Marshall Field Foundation.[24] This particular gift was cultivated by an honorary degree to Marshall Field in 1946. Despite Stevens' assurances, the Field gift never materialized. The Trustees, of course, could not have known this at what turned out to be the crucial meeting on June 5, 1950. Even with the promised Field gift included, the amount raised was still only $483,000, and the estimated construction cost by this time was $832,000.[25] Stevens was feeling desperate as his fundraising efforts fell woefully short, and yet, by June of 1950, the College could not wait any longer before constructing new science facilities; Blair was badly outdated and postwar science was leaving Grinnell behind. The Board was somewhat reassured in 1947, when Oklahoma Oil man Fred Darby '95, gave the College perpetual rights to significant oil royalties. These rights soon were followed by a second royalty gift. Though he cautioned the College not to try to calculate the changing value of these gifts, Darby gave assurances that these wells would be productive for at least twenty years.[26] By June 1948, the College already had accumulated $650,000 from the first gift and $832,000 from the second gift.[27]

Fred Darby was, by a considerable margin, the wealthiest Grinnell Trustee, and he had great affection and loyalty for the College. Joe was his match in loyalty and affection, if not yet in resources. It was Joe who, convinced the College could no longer postpone the science building, forced the issue at the June 1950 Board Meeting. He stated that the College must begin the building despite the funding shortfall and that he, personally, would increase his pledge from $20,000 to $75,000 "so that some action can be taken." Darby spoke next, saying the Darby Fund would accumulate another $100,000, and then other Trustees indicated the extent to which they would increase their contributions. Stevens said that engineering drawings could be ready by September, so the Board voted to start the project immediately.[28]

There are several fateful elements to this meeting and its decision. One was the decisive financial and affirmative leadership that characterized Joe's contributions to Grinnell College. The other was Stevens' misleading information about the Marshall Field gift that encouraged the Trustee decision to build even though the structure was far from fully financed. In fact, because of their misplaced confidence in the Field grant, they did not know how great that distance really was. This misinformation would come back to haunt both the Board and Stevens, not to mention Joe, who had the responsibilities of Board Chair at this time.

By the time it was completed in 1952, the new science building grew to cost $1,000,000, considerably more than the anticipated $832,000. The postwar demand for new science facilities was ubiquitous, and between 1950 and 1960, American small colleges constructed 74 new science facilities. At $31.43 per square foot, Grinnell's was one of the most expensive.[29] Rudy Weitz, who replaced Joe as Board Chair in June 1952, was the general contractor for the science building, and he assured the Board that he would construct the building at cost. For its time, the building was a quality facility, but it left Grinnell with substantially increased debt.

That debt ushered in the crisis of the early 1950s that culminated in the departure of Sam Stevens in the summer of 1954. The College had to borrow regularly to meet operating expenses during the GI Bill days because the government, quite naturally, paid its bill only at the end of the semester when the veterans had demonstrated good standing. The Board took out short-term loans, which it repaid as soon as the government money arrived. In fact, there were three balanced budgets between 1946 to 1949, which were highly unusual exceptions to the regular successions of deficits.[30] By 1950, when most of the veterans had graduated, Grinnell returned to its normal run of deficits, this time with a vengeance.

There were two dramatic contextual challenges that plunged the College into crisis: the Korean War and the maturity of the slim crop of Depression babies. There simply were not nearly enough new college-age Americans to fill the beds left by the graduation of veterans. Korea then raised the specter of a massive draft of college-age men. To minimize the impact of the latter, the Board authorized Stevens in October 1950 to apply to the government for a Reserve Officer Training unit, a successful effort with the arrival of the Air Force ROTC in the fall of 1951.[31] Draft boards extended numerous college deferments, so fears of a massive draft similar to World War II were not realized. The Depression baby impact was bad enough, with enrollments dropping precipitously from 1,113 in 1949–50 to 856 in 1952–53, and they did not begin to recover until 1954–55 — and not significantly until after 1958.

Perhaps the only thing that ultimately saved Grinnell in these years was the death of Fred Darby in March 1953. His considerable estate was divided between his wife and the College, with the College receiving the larger share. This bequest consisted of extensive oil properties, which the College wisely decided to manage through the Poweshiek Oil Company rather than sell. Grinnell continues to receive significant Darby oil royalties today. The immediate benefit to the College was well over five million dollars spread over several years. This windfall provided the only realistic hope for survival in the early 1950s. I have said, on more than one occasion, that if ever the College would have died, it would have been while I was a student, from 1952–1956. After perusing the Trustee Minutes, I am more than ever convinced of this judgment. It really was on the basis of the near collapse and ultimate Darby lifeline that a platform was established for Joe to make his College "impregnable" through the building of its endowment.

At the April 1952 Executive Committee meeting in Des Moines, Treasurer Rupert Hawk, who had replaced long-time Treasurer Louis Phelps in June 1949, announced that the cash requirements for the next six months of operations would be $600,000 but the College was out of cash. Because of its constant bank borrowing, and because of frequent interfund borrowing, there was little flexibility in either direction. The College would need to borrow $300,000 to $325,000 in the next few days in order to operate until June. An immediate decision was made to borrow $325,000 to be repaid with the September 1952 tuition receipts.[32] At the very next Executive Committee meeting in May, Joe asked Stevens and Hawk to prepare a report on the endowment as a basis for deciding what might have to be liquidated for working capital purposes. He was referring to farms and city property.[33] At the June Board meeting, the Executive Committee was authorized to begin selling farms and city property. This must have been a bitter moment for Joe as the endowment architect, but, as he said, the College could not continue to meet its cash crisis with bank loans. In fact, the banks were becoming extremely reluctant to lend to Grinnell.[34] Stevens and Hawk presented the preliminary budget for 1952–53 at this meeting, which projected $1,458,500 income with $1,701,175 expenses, leaving a $242,675 deficit for the year. Joe, who was still Board Chair at that time, directed them to immediately cut expenses to produce a more reasonable deficit.[35]

The fall 1951 Board meeting provided an ominous backdrop to the angst of the following spring. In his customary opening speech to the Board, Stevens began by announcing a deficit of $200,000 for the current year, adding that he foresaw continuing deficits for the next three or four years. What the College needs, he said, is a $10,000,000 endowment—and the current endowment was at $3,000,000. He went on to lament how difficult it was to raise money in the current tax structure climate and lack of industry in Iowa. He predicted that there would be a shortage of students until the demographic turnaround, which would begin in 1954–55. The comprehensive fee should move from $1,300 to $1,400, but he pointed out the risk of an enrollment drop because the fee would then be the highest in Iowa. He darkened the mood even further by complaining about "this generation of students" whose poor character was the fault of families and societal conditions. Colleges like Grinnell had an almost impossible task, he complained, but "we struggle valiantly." "Unless we succeed," he said, "the hope of a good society must be indefinitely deferred . . .The indifference of students of college age to seriously disciplined social and academic responsibility is shocking." He closed by challenging the Trustees to share in these problems and the efforts to solve them.[36]

This outburst reflects a President at the end of his tether. Beset by the overwhelming challenge of the Depression babies, Korea, and economic inflation, Stevens faced a Board that expected him to raise money for operations and build a new science building, with gifts and tuition falling far short of the sums needed to accomplish both goals. Viewed against his successes in navigating World War II and its aftermath, it was almost more than a proud man could bear. He was looking for scapegoats, and he found them in the students and Trustees.

Sam Stevens took a more positive tack with the Board a year later, in November 1952, when he quoted one of Napoleon's generals at Austerlitz: "My right is falling back, my center has disintegrated, my left is faltering. I have given the order to attack." "Let us go forword," Stevens continued. "Let us be satisfied with no mean plans. Let us not be discouraged by temporary difficulties." He then proposed a $2,000,000 campaign, with $500,000 to be used over time to increase faculty and administrative salaries, $500,000 for the physical plant, and $500,000 for operating expense reserves, with the rest used to pay down debt. In his plan, the Trustees should organize this campaign and fund a significant portion of it.[37] It was, undoubtedly, a response to the fact that a month earlier, the banks had refused to lend any more to Grinnell, leaving interfund borrowing or fundraising as the only alternatives.[38]

In response, Joe, who had stepped down as Chair the previous June, offered a resolution "that the Trustees, at this time reaffirm their faith in the principles and objectives of Grinnell College as administered by Dr. S. N. Stevens." This resolution was met by one of the most injudicious presidential outbursts in the College's history. The minutes record of President Stevens that "he expressed himself as being somewhat bewildered at some of the opinions expressed as he said, 'You can't go forword and backward at the same time; you can't be positive and negative at once; you can't cross a chasm in two jumps.'" He added that it seems impossible to reduce the size of the operation and at the same time maintain the physical plant, improve faculty, and increase the size and standards of the student body. Grinnell will either be of high value, something of which the Trustees can be proud, or it will become nondescript, unattractive, and uninteresting. In his view, a reaffirmation of faith is not enough to get done what needs to be done. "Merely cutting the budget, increasing enrollment, and reducing faculty is not the answer. [He] personally would want something better than that for Grinnell."[39] The College cut more than forty faculty positions by 1955.[40]

Ever willing to raise money for Grinnell, Joe took up the challenge, suggesting that Grinnell embark on Stevens' $2,000,000 campaign. One can't help but wonder if this was the moment when Joe's faith in Sam Stevens began to plunge. The College had raised $1,000,000 in the Second Century Fund launched at the Centennial in 1946, but the new campaign never developed, as the ground began to crumble under President Stevens. Precarious as was his position, Stevens was back at it again at the spring Board meeting, saying, "It will be better for you to live a great college for 25 years than to live forever a mediocre institution."[41] Probably agreeing, Joe, as Chairman of the Finance Committee, suggested that money from the

Second Century Fund be used for operations, though that was not the intent of the Fund, and moved that Darby oil royalties, originally intended for endowment, be used for current operations.[42] He must have been hugely conflicted about this concession, as, after the crisis of the early 1950s had passed, he set out with renewed vigor to build and protect the endowment to the point where, as he often later said, "It would make the College impregnable."

Faculty opposition to Sam Stevens was building. Ferocity of the opposition is reflected in the Board minutes for the June 1953 meeting, where Stevens chided the Board for talking out of school with faculty and students. He said:

"This is one of the reasons why there has developed the conflict and tensions which has been observed.... It is impossible for the administrative officials of the College to carry water in a sieve. This is what we try to do when the policies we attempt to work from are not consistently interpreted by members of the Board who from time to time very properly talk to the faculty and students."[43]

This outburst was triggered by a visit from Homer Norton (Chair of the Faculty), Curtis Bradford (English), Grant Gale (Physics) and Jim Stauss (Economics) paid to several Trustees while Stevens was away from campus.[44]

By the end of 1953, Joe had turned against Sam Stevens completely. Joe's frustration is clear at the August 1953 meeting of the Executive Committee, where Stevens made a desperate appeal to increase faculty salaries. After laying out a thorough analysis of the state of Grinnell salaries, he then listed a succession of key faculty Grinnell could not stand to lose. Seeing this list, and considering the names that Stevens left out, it is obvious that Stevens had done a good job of building a strong faculty at Grinnell. Those he listed were: Fuller, Lovell, Klausner, Charlie Foster, Mendoza, Burma, Salinger, Dunner, Danforth, Apostle, Haner, Jensen, McKibben, Kuntz, Ellis, Crosley, Pfitsch, Knopf, Noble, Percas, Wall, Booth, Russell, Simone, Weston, Peterson, and Waters. Conspicuously absent were some leading faculty, most of whom were Stevens' opponents: Gale, Norton, Stauss, Kleinschmidt, Clapp, Bradford Ragsdale, and Robertson. All who had paid the spring visit to the Trustees were left off of Stevens' list of indispensable faculty. Stevens had even tried to fire Grant Gale in January 1954. What is most extraordinary about Stevens' performance is that he claimed all of the faculty on his list had received job offers at higher salaries from such institutions as Harvard, Yale, Princeton, Johns Hopkins, Chicago, Penn, Northwestern, Berkeley, Stanford, Oberlin, Amherst, Pomona, and "a host of others," and he asserted that none of those offers had been accepted. This was a "who's who" of American universities and colleges and *none* of these faculty had accepted those prestigious offers—and at higher salaries? Joe and the other Trustees must have recognized that Stevens had fabricated most, if not all, of this scenario.

Somewhat surprisingly, the Executive Committee, with Joe in the lead, responded positively to Stevens' plea, authorizing that $25,000 be added to the salary budget for the 1953–54 year, despite the College's desperate financial straits. With Joe leading the way, pledging $5,000 to increase the amount, and prompting Fred Maytag to follow suit, the total increase amounted to $35,000.[45] After this meeting, Joe reflected on what Stevens had said, realizing that the President's claim was an enormous fabrication and he had fallen for it. One thing Joe could not stand was dishonesty, and I suspect this incident overcame any lingering loyalty he had for Sam Stevens.

The denouement began on Friday, January 29, 1954 at a meeting that had planned to start with a session between the Board and the Faculty Committee on Educational Policy. The Trustee Minutes tell the story:

[The plan] had to be abandoned at the last moment because of the pressure of certain emergency matters. After convening in the Drawing Room of Main Hall, the Trustees went into executive session attended by themselves only, none of the officers of the administration or faculty representatives being present. The executive session lasted all day Friday, January 29th during which time matters of trustee policy were discussed, but no formal action of any kind was taken, according to the Information given the secretary (Rupert Hawk) for the purposes of noting it in the minutes of the meeting.

On Saturday, January 30, the minutes record: "Mr. Joseph Rosenfield wished to retire from the Board and that created a vacancy as to the chairmanship of the Finance Committee." In addition, the Board Chair, Rudolph Weitz, announced he would have to retire as President of the Board because his duties in Washington made it difficult to work closely with the College President. During a protracted lunch involving only Trustees, Weitz withdrew his resignation as Board President, but Joe's decision to resign held firm.[46]

This story ends with the next Board meeting, June 7, 1954, when Sam Stevens offered his resignation effective immediately. In response, the Board Minutes state:

"The point was raised that Mr. J. F. Rosenfield would reconsider his resignation from the Board. Mr. Welch, Chairman of the Trustee Committee on Trustees, made a motion seconded by Mr. Kirkpatrick and carried unanimously that Mr. J. F. Rosenfield be asked to reconsider his resignation from the Board and that he be invited to complete his unexpired term of the class of '59."

Not only did Joe return but also, he immediately was selected for the presidential search committee that resulted in the appointment of Howard Bowen.[47]

This is the story told by the Board Minutes, but there is, as one would expect, more to it; and that more is told in a memoir written by faculty icon Grant Gale, who was a close observer and participant in Sam Stevens' demise. According to Gale, Stevens actually forged Marshall Field's signature on the pledge of $100,000, reporting this pledge to the Trustee as a bona fide gift to the science building project. During construction, Trustees raised questions about the Field gift while Stevens offered excuses for the delay. Two Trustees then came to campus to see the pledge, which the president's secretary showed to them. It isn't clear whether the forgery was recognized at this point, but at a meeting in the Newton offices of Trustee Fred Maytag, which included Board Chair, Rudy Weitz, in early January 1954, Stevens admitted to the forgery, saying, "At least the building is built." This confession led to the day-long executive session of the Board on January 29th resulting in Stevens retention — albeit on a short leash — and Joe's resignation. Gale ends his account of Stevens' demise saying, "I'm glad I knew him. I'm glad he left. I wish for his sake and the college's that he had left earlier when he was still winning."[48]

Those words are a fair summation of the Stevens years.

The Minutes contain only the façade of the story. From their perspective, the Executive Session on January 29 discussed the fate of Stevens and concluded to retain him. Joe was so upset by the decision to retain Stevens—and we now know that his transgression was egregious—that he left the Board to which he had dedicated nearly unprecedented energies and resources for over twelve years. The fact that Sam Stevens did not respond well to whatever conditions had been laid down in January meant that, by the end of the spring semester, at the Board's invitation, he departed, and also, at the Board's invitation, Joe returned. The conclusion of this crisis was almost certainly the most fateful reversal of fortune in Grinnell College history. Where would the College be today had Stevens stayed and Joe remained permanently off the Board? I for one do not even wish to imagine it.

THE PARTNERSHIP OF JOE ROSENFIELD & HOWARD BOWEN

In the summer of 1955 the most productive Trustee/president partnership in Grinnell College history began with the appointment of Howard Rothman Bowen—the seventh president of the College. Bowen remained at Grinnell until July, 1964, when he moved to Iowa City to become President of the University of Iowa.

Howard R. Bowen was born in Spokane, Washington and did his undergraduate and graduate education at Washington State University (B.A. 1929; M.A. 1933). He received his Ph.D. in Economics from the University of Iowa in 1935, which he followed with further study of economics in England at Cambridge (1937) and the London School of Economics (1939). Bowen taught Economics at the University of Iowa from 1935 until 1942, when, during World War II, he became the Chief Economist for the Congressional Committee on Internal Revenue Taxation. Immediately following the war, he worked as an economist for Irving Trust. Then, in 1947, he became the Dean of the College of Commerce at the University of Illinois. At Illinois, during the McCarthy era, he was thought to be too Keynesian, which led to his resignation under pressure in 1952. He landed on his feet with a position in the Williams College Economics Department, where he remained until his appointment as Grinnell's seventh president in 1955. His wide experience and outstanding abilities made him one of the most important presidents in the College's history, especially as he formed a partnership with Joe, who had fully matured as a Trustee by the time Bowen arrived.

Joe's maturation was particularly evident during his six-month "retirement" from the Board as a result of his opposition to President Sam Stevens. Each Grinnell graduating class elects a Class Agent, who is responsible for collecting and passing along selected comments in the form of a Class Letter, which is published several times each year. The long-time 1925 class agent was Joe's best undergraduate friend, Bob Fell, who was famous for his lengthy class letters. In April 1954, in the middle of Joe's time as an ex and, presumably, disgruntled, Board member, he penned the following to his class. He commented that Fell had asked him to write to the class either humorously or seriously about the College's campaign for money:

While I usually prefer to attempt to be humorous rather than serious, I have been so intimately associated with the college and its terrific struggle for existence over the past ten or twelve years, that I find it impossible to treat the problem with much levity.

While a college cannot assume eminence with money alone, neither can it become a great institution without the generous financial support of its Alumni. Grinnell College has accumulated a huge deficit over the past several years because it chose to retain its reputation as a quality school, while at the same time risking possible bankruptcy. It cannot continue this policy forever. A large annual income from its alumni is imperative if the college is to continue its high standards.

I know it is difficult for one who has not been closely and directly connected with the financial operations of the college to realize this, but I can assure you that it is true...So, it is my hope that our class will continue to set an outstanding example for other classes in its generosity to the college. [49]

The subtext of Joe's disaffection from Sam Stevens is evident in the reference to accumulated deficits, but much more important is how this letter demonstrates Joe's undiminished love and concern for his College. No quarrel over a president's inadequacies could diminish Joe's undying commitment to Grinnell and his willingness to serve it.

When Stevens resigned in June 1954, Joe immediately returned to the Board and was appointed to the search committee that found Howard Bowen. The Treasurer, Rupert Hawk became Acting President in 1954–55. Hawk had helped hold the College together in the last years of Sam Stevens, and he proved to be the right choice to smooth the transition between the two presidents until the breath of fresh air that was Howard Bowen arrived in June 1955.

Joe was very active during the Hawk interim. He served as Board Vice President and chaired the Finance Committee and Committee on Trustees. He also served on the Presidential Search Committee. As Finance chair, he rode the whirlwind of borrowing that continued in 1954–55. In fact, in an April 8, 1955 special Board meeting, where President Elect Howard Bowen was introduced, Joe moved $300,000 of inter fund borrowing to meet cash needs.[50] In the previous December, the annual deficit had been estimated at $315,095 and farm income, the anchor of the endowment, offered little help.[51] At the June Board meeting, Bowen's first as president, the market value of the farms was reported at $650,000, with only $15,500 income having been derived during the previous year. The Board hoped the figure would rise to approximately $28,000 in 1955–56 with fewer maintenance expenses anticipated.[52] The gloom that greeted Howard Bowen at his first meeting deepened as Joe announced that balancing the budget was the greatest challenge Grinnell then faced; total deficit borrowing had reached $570,000 and total inter fund borrowing $575,000, all to meet current expenses—particularly payroll. Joe, as was typical, lightened the mood by announcing a personal gift to the College of Hotel Sherman stock. Nevertheless, few college presidencies could have begun more inauspiciously. Bowen faced a huge challenge, but Joe was determined to partner with him and to help him meet it. Fortunately, the Darby estate was contributed at this time as well, without which, even with Joe's determination, Grinnell might not have survived.[53]

Less pressing than the financial crisis, but still weighing heavily on the College, were issues of student quality and administrative inefficiency. Homer Norton remained as Dean of the College through the Hawk interim and into the early Bowen years. At the December 1954 Board meeting, Norton suggested that parents used small colleges as havens for "maladjusted children."[54] At the June 6, 1955 Board meeting, with Bowen in attendance, he described the lower third of the student body as "poorly prepared for college either academically or morally [but] they are easy to get and able to pay their way, but they are poison to a healthy academic community." Norton went on to say that the women tended to transfer after their sophomore year, seeking more vocational and social opportunities.[55] Bowen insisted the College use its newfound advantage to increase student quality before increasing enrollment; when, in fact, the demography and Grinnell's admissions began to improve it was in the Bowen era.

Rupert Hawk did a good job of counseling the Board during this most critical year. In December 1954, he said, with regard to the troubled end of the Stevens years, "Sometimes a little first-class forgetting is in order."[56] He then pointed out that he was trying to initiate a well-organized and regulated administration with procedures that were clearly understood. Hawk had previously served as Superintendent of Schools in Grinnell and, he said, there was too much of a cafeteria approach to administration. Stevens had, in Hawk's opinion, encouraged far too much to land on his desk. At the June 1955, Board meeting, Hawk pointed out that the College had become accustomed to flooding the president with far too many details and requests. Too many things that should be settled at a lower level were pushed up to the President.[57] Hawk's analysis provided important intelligence for a talented administrator such as Howard Bowen at his first Board meeting.

Sam Stevens had been an "imperial" president, a style that worked to Grinnell's advantage during the crises of World War II and its aftermath. With plunging male enrollment during the War, only quick action to secure a military officer training unit could have guaranteed institutional survival. Then, the rapid build-up of faculty, staff, and facilities immediately after the war required decisive and unified leadership, which Stevens supplied in abundance. However, the high quality sixty-percent of the faculty hired, often directly by Stevens, between 1946 and 1949 would not accept Stevens' imperialism, nor, it turns out, did the Trustees—Joe in particular. The combination of presidential imperialism, faculty rebellion, poor fundraising, and lack of honesty ended the Stevens regime. Dignified and reserved, Stevens' replacement brought extensive experience and understanding to the Grinnell presidency. Bowen was an expert in the economics of higher education. He published several books on the subject in his post-Grinnell years. Equally important was his broad vision of American higher education. To read the Trustee Minutes of the Stevens and then the Bowen years is to witness the transformation of Grinnell from a regional, somewhat parochial institution to a national college with a clear sense of belonging on a much larger stage. This transformation was driven by Bowen in partnership with Joe and his Trustee colleagues. The change would be achieved through major grants— particularly from the Ford Foundation—careful management and expenditure, excellent faculty recruiting, outstanding new buildings, and significantly improved student quality and numbers drawn from an increasingly national base. Joe's role, besides offering his unwavering support to Bowen, was to build the endowment, which he achieved by selling farms and using the income for astute purchases of securities. The crucial role of the Darby estate in supplying a financial buffer as the College strove to regain its footing cannot be overemphasized.

    The dismal picture Norton gave Bowen at his first meeting in June 1955 was trumped by a gloomier scenario in the November Board meeting. Bob Kinsey wanted everyone in the room to be aware of the dire shape of Grinnell's financial meltdown. Kinsey began by stating that the College must immediately borrow $425,000 from the banks, adding that it must borrow an additional $200,000 on July 1 to get Grinnell through the summer until September tuitions arrived. In September tuition payments would arrive, but $475,000 of that would be returned immediately to the banks, leaving a balance of $75,000 in revenue for the vast cost of operating the College for a semester. The College would have to turn around and borrow another $500,000 to get to June 1, 1956 and then another $200,000 to get through the summer. All together, these moves would produce a $700,000 debt to the banks. Kinsey closed by projecting that by September 1956 Grinnell would have an unmanageable deficit.[58]

Bowen and Joe addressed this problem with intense fundraising, endowment development, and efficient management with such success that, by the end of the Bowen years in 1964, the only persistent borrowing was for the annual summer operating funds to bridge the gap between spring and fall tuition payments. The College was not completely out of the financial woods at this time, but the situation was no longer critical, and the endowment had nearly doubled from $4,900,000 in 1955 to $9,900,000 in 1965.[59] By todays standard of a $1,800,000,000 endowment figure, that amount may not seem impressive, but these were 1955–1965 dollars, and the endowment had been almost non-existent when Joe joined the Board in 1941. The steady growth of Grinnell's endowment from the time Joe joined the Board to the end of the Bowen years is a testimony of Joe's abilities and his vow "to make Grinnell impregnable." The financial shambles recorded thus far in Grinnell history crystallize how a person who loved Grinnell as did Joe, and who possessed the talents he had, could convert that love into action and dedicate himself to building Grinnell's endowment, first for survival and then for greatness.

Where Sam Stevens had not been a particularly effective fundraiser, Howard Bowen was brilliant at it, an attribute calculated to warm Joe's heart. The Trustees staved off the disaster Bob Kinsey had outlined by liquidating some of the Darby securities while Joe, with his reverence for securities, must have "bit his tongue" when he moved the sale. Here again we can see how the Darby estate allowed the College to continue to navigate its debts and operate while Bowen and the Trustees gradually stabilized the ship. At this point, the Darby estate was valued at $3,683,000, but a lot of that was in the potential for future oil and gas revenues. To the eternal credit of the Trustees, they decided to retain the wells for their future revenues rather than seeking an immediate bonanza in selling them.[60] Those wells have continued to provide revenue for Grinnell, as much as a million dollars per year, which is far exceeding the initial estimates of the value of the Darby estate.[61]

As early as the fall of 1957, the Trustee Minutes reflect hopes for a balanced budget; they also announce a jump in yearly enrollment from 866 to 938. That increase might have been even larger, but Bowen courageously insisted that the College should opt for quality over quantity as demographics and reputation slowly turned in Grinnell's favor. "If the quality increases, the numbers will follow," Bowen told the Board, pointing out that some of the enrollment increase was already due to improved retention.[62]

The Board Minutes during the Bowen years reflect a transformed fundraising environment in many ways—none more dramatically than the appearance of major grants from significant national foundations, such as Ford and Sloan, as well as the advent of National Science Foundation (NSF) grants. On February 4, 1956, Grinnell received a large challenge grant from the Ford Foundation to increase faculty salaries and improve facilities.[63] Bowen urged the Board to accept the ambitious challenge to raise $2,460,000 to meet a Ford $1,000,000 grant.[64] Never before had the College accepted such a campaign challenge, and it met that challenge successfully by June of 1959.[65] Joe gave a lead gift and chaired the effort to solicit almost $1,000,000 from the Board.[66] The campaign funded the building of Burling Library and the Fine Arts Center, both boldly designed by Howard Bowen's favorite architect, Walter Netsch, and his firm, Skidmore, Owens, and Merrill (SOM) of Chicago. The Burling design initially called for four glass curtain walls, but Trustee objections converted the east and west walls to masonry.[67] The naming of the library for Edward Burling (1890), senior partner of the famous Washington DC law firm Covington and Burling—specialists in federal agency law— was well merited due to his impressive campaign gift of $700,000, which was earmarked for the library.[68]

The Ford Foundation definitely favored Grinnell during the Bowen years; Grinnell received two more Ford grants, with the second coming prior to the successful completion of the first Ford challenge. In November, 1956, Bowen told the Trustees that Ford wished to award a grant to Grinnell for a Social Science project in three areas: 1. the teaching of the Principles of Economics; 2. education within the liberal arts setting for careers in business; and 3. for recruiting and educating promising young people for service in underdeveloped foreign areas. The grant would support the hiring of two economists, one historian, and one political scientist. The Board responded positively to this opportunity, courageously adding that the prospect of future growth should allow the College to incorporate these positions into the budget when grant funds ran out.[69]

In February 1961, Bowen told the Board about a third invitation from the Ford Foundation. Twenty-four colleges were invited to apply for a 2:1 match for a grant that would be apportioned one-third for endowment and two-thirds for operations. The Board immediately encouraged the College to apply for $2,500,000, entailing a $5,000,000 match.[70] Grinnell was Ford's choice for the Midwest, with a grant of $2,000,000 and a match of $4,000,000 to be completed by June 30, 1964.[71] At the next Board meeting in October 1961, Paul Younger, of the consultants Martz and Lundy, asked Joe to speak to his colleagues about the importance of this campaign. Joe said "that this was the most important financial effort in the history of the college and, in his opinion, will require exceptional giving by a relatively few trustees and others." With the June 30, 1964 matching deadline, he added, donors will have to be thinking of giving sums even greater than they can deduct for income tax purposes."[72] The fact that Joe was asked to make this speech reflects his maturation into the position that he would hold until his death: leading donor and the catalyst that shaped most major Board decisions.

This campaign occupied Bowen and Joe for the next three years and its successful conclusion by the end of 1963 was a major reason Bowen left Grinnell to accept the presidency of the University of Iowa in July 1964.

Though preeminent, Ford was not the only major foundation granting money to Grinnell College. In February 1963, Bowen announced to the Board that Grinnell was one of ten colleges chosen for a major National Science Foundation matching program; Grinnell had just received a Rockefeller Foundation grant for a planned addition to the science building.[73] Anyone familiar with college fundraising could see that Bowen was an unusually effective advocate for presenting Grinnell's needs and plans to national foundations. For a fortunate few colleges and universities, foundations are mainstays of fundraising, especially for capital projects; Bowen was a master of the art of presentation, which contributed materially to the average giving of $2,000,000 per year from 1961 to 1964.[74] Through the Bowen and Rosenfield partnership, Grinnell had found a prominent place on the national foundations' map.

Howard Bowen's fundraising prowess, which Joe ably supported, is visible in the physical transformation of the Grinnell campus from the deteriorating nineteenth-century structures of the crisis years to the striking glass and concrete of Skidmore, Owens, and Merrill's Burling Library, Fine Arts Building and Forum, and the somewhat less successful SOM Norris residence hall. Because of the dramatic nature of the SOM architectural style, the Bowen buildings not only beautified the campus but also added to the eclectic trend in Grinnell campus architecture. One cannot deny that these structures, along with so much that happened under Bowen, brought Grinnell firmly into the national collegiate environment.

Many of the Trustees were not happy either with the SOM style or the persistent cost overruns, but when the objectors prevailed with the selection of the firm of Loeb, Schlosser, and Bennett of Chicago for the estimated $1,000,000 science addition, the cost overruns continued; in this case, the cost went as much as $275,000 over budget.[75]

The College also built a new, prairie style presidential home for Howard and Lois Bowen. The Trustees felt that the elegant Georgian home that had served generations of Grinnell presidents would be more appropriate as a guest house; it had frequently served that function even while the presidents were in residence. Bowen was quite apprehensive about the idea of the College spending institutional funds for a new presidents' home. He suggested an available 8th avenue house that would serve nicely for much less than the cost of a new home. Over Bowen's objections, the Trustees were determined to spend $100,000, which turned out to be $150,000, on the new home. They did, however, agree with Bowen's concern that they should raise the money rather than draw it from other sources the College needed for various operating expenses.[76]

A hallmark of the Trustee Minutes for the Bowen years is the prevalence of Joe's motions in support of financial and building matters. Joe chaired the Finance Committee in these years, so it was natural that he should make such motions, but it also is clear that he was of one mind with Bowen's successful efforts to revitalize the College. Such motions are in stark contrast to the role Joe would play under successive presidents Leggett, Turner, Drake, Ferguson, and Osgood. In those administrations, Joe was the ever increasingly dominant force on the Board, but that role is less evident in the Minutes, especially after the Leggett years, though virtually nothing of importance was decided by the Trustees without Joe's initiative or, at very least, his imprimatur. Joe was, quite simply, the catalyst that shaped Board reactions and decisions, so that matters would often be decided quite precipitously, even in the absence of prior discussion. The Board trusted Joe and his devotedly sound judgment implicitly. I personally watched this phenomenon transpire during my Trusteeship in the Leggett and Turner years as well as in my own twelve years as Grinnell's president. Joe worked frequently behind the scenes, detected neither by most of his fellow Trustees nor the Board Minutes. The decision to purchase a commercial television station in the late 1970s is a prime example of his covert work. The Board decided on the spot to invest eleven million dollars in a Dayton, Ohio, ABC network station after an extensive presentation from Joe and Warren Buffett, who had colluded before the meeting. Though this type of investment was completely unorthodox for a college, the moment had to be seized before another offer was made. The Board took the great risk because it had complete trust in Joe (and Warren). The station had more than quintupled in value by the time it was sold in the mid 1980s.[77]

Another sign of Joe's colossal Board stature is how easily he played this role on a Board studded with stars such as Warren Buffett, Steve Jobs, and Bob Noyce.

Bowen recognized this, writing in 1988:

Anyone connected with Grinnell will tell you that Joe Rosenfield is an authentically great man. As such, he chose to concentrate his talents and energies and resources on development of a great liberal arts college in his native state. I have served at different times on the boards of nine different colleges and on corporate boards as well, and I have never met a trustee or director who comes close to equaling the record of Joe Rosenfield.[78]

Bowen himself was known for his fundraising prowess and brought scholarly experience to Grinnell. In contrast to Sam Stevens, he tolerated and even fostered active faculty engagement in college policy. As a result, the quality of both the faculty and the curriculum flourished in the late 1950s and early 1960s. A major step was in the development of a successful new curriculum, which the College adopted in June 1959. It featured two highly successful required

General Education courses: Humanities and Historical Studies. The former featured sequential semesters of Greek and Latin literature in translation, while the latter focused on great European texts and historical developments with a combination of large group lectures and small group discussions. Courses from the Humanities sequence have survived in the current Grinnell curriculum.[79] The introduction of a Junior Liberal Arts Examination in 1961, while carefully planned, was much less successful. Another feature of the Bowen years was the expansion and division of the modern language department into separate French, German, Spanish, and Russian departments. The Economics Department was, unsurprisingly, revitalized by Bowen with three additional faculty positions, two initially supported by a Ford Grant and one by the College. Today, the College's Economic Department is one of the top five Economics Departments nationally in the percentage of graduates who earn PH.D's.

Faculty tenure was regularized by the adoption of the standards of the American Association of University Professors (AAUP) in 1957.[80] Faculty salaries, with the help of grants from Ford, Lilly, Sloan, Danforth, and others increased steadily in these years so that, by Bowen's last year, they reached the top level of the colleges in the Associated Colleges of the Midwest (ACM), of which Grinnell became a charter member in 1958. The group included Carleton, St Olaf, Lawrence, Beloit, Ripon, Knox, Monmouth, Cornell, Coe, and Grinnell. Grinnell also inaugurated the Heath Visiting Professor Program in October 1959; this program brought such international luminaries as Arnold Toynbee and Sir Dennis Brogan to teach at the College for a year or a semester.

Sometime after he left Grinnell, Howard Bowen told Professor Don Smith of the History Department that the one encouraging thing he found when he arrived at Grinnell was the number of superb teachers. Bowen added to their number and found the funds to reward the core group more adequately. Not all faculty remained at Grinnell, but Bowen once told me he took pride in the number of outstanding universities that sought them. To insure against undue losses, endowed professorial chairs were revived in 1961, with fourteen outstanding faculty named to chairs in the natural sciences, humanities, and social studies.[81]

The humanities and social studies curricula remained closed to non-western canon literature throughout the Bowen years. While that canon was thoroughly explored, there was little expansion into East Asia, Latin America, Africa, the Middle East, or even Eastern Europe. Those areas only arrived in the curriculum in the seventies and eighties, often as a the result of urging from students. Grinnell was not unique in this regard; one of the more positive outcomes of the student revolution was a long overdue extension of the curriculum into non-western regions.

By 1961, in yet another sign of Grinnell's transformation through the partnership between Joe and Howard Bowen, Bowen had begun to present the Trustees with a new comparison group of colleges. Colleges seek comparison groups for analytical and promotional reasons. The new group Bowen introduced was Swarthmore, Reed, Bryn Mawr, Haverford, Amherst, Williams, Wesleyan, Carleton, Wellesley, and Oberlin. Some, though not all, of those colleges were a "stretch" for Grinnell, but aspiration is part of the "comparable college" process.[82] Connected with this process was the decision to drop Elementary Education from the curriculum in February 1963. It was deemed no longer appropriate for Grinnell.[83] This move resulted from the notion that colleges like Grinnell don't engage in elementary education, a decision that acknowledged "snob appeal" as well as a misaligned curriculum.

The slowly emerging decision to distance Grinnell from its Congregational Church founders (now the United Church of Christ) was another result of the College's newfound sense of comparison among the nation's elite liberal arts colleges. In the summer of 1963, the Iowa Congregational state offices, which had long been located on campus, moved to Des Moines, capping the slow distancing between Grinnell and the church.[84] The colleges in the new comparison group in which Grinnell now saw itself, were non-sectarian, and Grinnell wished to position itself in that company. In fact, it had been many years since the church relationship was deemed important, so "non-sectarian" was, in fact, an accurate description of Grinnell College. Today, Grinnell remains historically connected to the United Church of Christ (UCC) but is not church-related in any other way.

Bowen and the Trustees were acutely aware of Grinnell's relative isolation "in the corn fields of Iowa." In the fall of 1960, the College created a full-time position for an "events booking agent," which was filled by the talented Georgia Dentel. Grinnell was noted for the outstanding speakers and performers who came to campus so that students, faculty, and the community could enjoy a rich cultural life on campus. Bowen's first major effort was a special Convocation in October 1957 on "American Culture at Mid-Century," which featured such headliners as alumnus Joseph Nye Welch of Army McCarthy Hearings fame, Dean James Pike of the Cathedral of St. John the Divine, Will Pollard, Director of Oak Ridge Laboratories, Sociologist David Riesman ("The Lonely Crowd"), James Sweeney, Director of the Guggenheim Foundation, and Edward R. Murrow, Director of CBS News. There was a fundraising dimension to this cultural phenomenon, as the Symposium was timed to kick-off the first Ford Grant match.

With elevated sights and stronger finances, Howard Bowen's Grinnell, with Joe and the Trustees with him at the helm, stretched into the world. A dramatic example of this stretching was the early 1960s Grinnell Travel Fellowships; the Fellowships sent several recent graduates to developing countries such as India, Ceylon, Malawi and Turkey, as well as European countries such as Greece, for a year at the College's expense. The funds, in part, came from a residual endowment that was left over when Grinnell abandoned its China program amid the Depression of the 1930s.[85]

The Grinnell revival in the Bowen years also extended to intercollegiate athletics, an area dear to Joe, who claimed never to have missed an athletic contest during his student days. Football and basketball won conference championships, which was unusual for Grinnell; track, cross country, and swimming continued in their winning ways. The intercollegiate athletic success was not accidental, as special efforts were made to recruit outstanding scholar athletes; indeed, several of those outstanding athletes went on to serve on the Grinnell Board of Trustees, including Jim Lowry, Ron Sandler, Dennis Homerin, and Randy Morgan. John Hartung, another scholar athlete, became the Executive Director of the Iowa Association of Colleges and Universities in the 1980s and early 1990s.

The almost ten-year partnership of Howard Bowen and Joe Rosenfield was one of the most important eras in Grinnell College history. During this decade, Grinnell grew from a good but struggling regional college into one of the premier national liberal arts colleges. With the help of the timely "maturity" of the Darby estate and major grants and gifts, Bowen was able to stabilize finances and reconstruct the campus. Bowen's leadership significantly strengthened the already good academic program he inherited upon arrival in 1955. Joe's focus on building the endowment began to show results in the Bowen years, particularly with the assistance of the second Ford Grant, though the really dramatic gains did not begin until the 1970s.[86]

In Howard Bowen, Joe Rosenfield found a President (he was even on the search committee) who shared his love and care for Grinnell—one who possessed the competence Joe so admired, particularly in financial and fundraising acumen. Howard was a great academic leader as well. The only obvious weakness evident in the Trustee Minutes was Bowen's inability to deal effectively with student unrest. Until that unrest began to invade the campus, it is clear that Bowen had dealt unerringly with the Board and with the College as a whole. As a result, Grinnell was transformed from a college with an uncertain future into a leading American collegiate institution, all in the span of a single decade.

ENDOWMENT GROWTH & STUDENT UNREST

On review of the Trustee Minutes, Grinnell students appear only by numbers and only in names in the earlier years when the annual graduations list were appended. The focus changes, however, in Howard Bowen's last years as Grinnell's president. He served on the cusp of the student revolution of the late 1960s and beyond. The administration took the first revolutionary step by ending the outdated practice of freshman hazing in 1960 after Bowen failed to convince the students to drop it of their own accord.[87] The students agitated to eradicate parietal rules, such as closing hours for women, no drinking on campus, restrictions on student cars, and limitations on dorm visitation by the opposite sex. Bowen's response to these demands was to challenge the students, saying he would not negotiate with them until their behavior improved. Incidents, such as drunkenness at the traditional men's Christmas Boer's Head dinner, were on the increase, and the faculty and administration, as well as the parents, were greatly disturbed. Bowen received several letters from parents pleading with him to preserve women's hours and the drinking rule.

The February 1963 Board meeting, a harbinger of the future, was particularly focused on student issues. The discussion began with Bowen commenting on the overcrowding of the dormitories and asking the question, "Should off-campus housing be continued?" The Trustees had no advice, though, at a later date, they would agree with an administrative plan to bring all students back to campus residence and build a new dorm to eliminate overcrowding. Bowen then speculated that student unrest over social rules might be due to increased academic pressure. Furthermore, he said, student misconduct had increased and was hurting the College's reputation. There had been a significant decline in applications in 1963 compared to 1962 (828/985). When the student government had asked him to liberalize the drinking rule, he replied that the students should first become more responsible before any rule change would be discussed. There was an immediate backlash, and, Bowen confessed, he did not handle the situation very well. In a discussion with the Trustees, he agreed that lightening the drinking rule might create a better environment than the current categorical prohibition, but he could not bring himself to make that change without the quid pro quo of improved student conduct. The Trustees declined to give much advice on the matter; they saw these issues as the purview of the administration, but the time soon would come when vast swaths of Trustee meetings were consumed by student demands.[88]

The College and the Board had no idea what was coming; Howard Bowen certainly did not see it. At the next Board meeting in June 1963, Bowen commented with some relief that he had discovered what was happening at Grinnell was not unique; Oberlin, Carleton, Lake Forest, Swarthmore, Vassar, and Radcliff, among others, faced similar problems. There seemed to be, said Howard, changing student attitudes toward sex mores and adult authority as students sought greater autonomy. In response, he had bowed to the surge of student activism by appointing a Faculty Committee on Student Affairs, which had recommended: 1) elimination of closing hours and bed checks for women; 2) cars for seniors who were not on financial aid; 3) women in men's dormitory lounges for a short time after dinner; 4) more explicit rules on sexual contact.[89]

The Board minutes for this period do not reveal Joe's attitudes toward the coming student revolution; the protracted discussions were recorded only in generalities without attribution. I sat through countless Trustee meetings with Joe at the height of the student revolution of the 1970s and early 1980s, and of all the Trustees, he seemed to be the most understanding of student attitudes, often commenting, "Aw, they're students and they're young and they'll change, but let's listen to them now." Joe understood college students instinctively because of his inveterate sense of humor and his own lively undergraduate experience as "line-a-day Rosenfield."[90]

Symbolic of the coming revolution and the slowly dawning recognition of both administration and Trustees was the issue of "the dorm that never was." At the February 1963, Trustee meeting, Bowen said the dorms were overcrowded by fifty or sixty students and that all students living in town rentals should be drawn back to campus to fulfill Grinnell's mission as a residential College.[91] The following October, Bowen recommended the Trustees approve the construction of a 100-bed men's dormitory to be financed by a loan that would be paid off by student fees.[92] At the March 1964 meeting of the Board, the decision was made to locate the new dorm on MacEachron Field.[93] In November, 1964, in the absence of Howard Bowen, who was on a Carnegie Foundation presidential leave, Dean James Stauss, the Acting President, recommended the dorm plans be revised because the demand for women's housing took precedence over the need for more men's beds. The Trustees then instructed Stauss to begin planning for a 150-bed women's dormitory to be located west of Loose Hall.[94] Discussion of the new women's dorm continued into 1968, well after Howard Bowen's departure, but it was never built. Looking back, it is clear why the dorm plans were abandoned. Grinnell soon moved to coeducational dormitories, so either a new men's or women's dormitory would be an anachronism, but even as late as October 1967, plans for the new women's dorm were crystallizing with an estimated cost of $4,175,000 from SOM, the architects. Joe reported that the Finance Committee, after protracted discussion, had decided not "to recommend either way on a new residence hall, but to put the question to the full Board of Trustees for consideration of the financial risks involved." Bowen's successor, Glenn Leggett, recommended that the residence hall be constructed and won a unanimous vote to proceed.[95]

A January meeting in 1968 reported that the plans for the new dorm were complete and construction could soon begin, but by the May meeting, the momentum had dissipated. John Norris, reporting for the Buildings and Grounds Committee, advised that there was a serious question about the need for the building because of "possible changing concepts of residential living, and the ability of the town to provide housing capacity for students, and the response of students to the new changes in the residential system."[96]

Coed dorms had effectively arrived and were instituted in the fall of 1968, putting an end to discussions for a new dormitory. The revolution in campus residential living also coincided with a strong desire for upper class students to have the option of living in apartments and rooms in town. In effect, despite all the Trustee planning, the students made the dormitory decision themselves. Try as they would over several years, the Trustees were never able to implement the decision to build the dorm. The students, not the Trustees, ultimately made the decision. "The dorm that never was" stands as an early and dramatic symbol of the student revolution that swept over Grinnell and all of higher education in the 1970s and 1980s. No longer would the Trustees, administration, and faculty be able to act without responding to student pressure; Grinnell College was particularly revolutionary in this regard.

From the first of November 1963 until March 1, 1964, Howard and Lois Bowen were on a college presidents' global study tour sponsored by the Carnegie Foundation. At a mid-March Executive Committee meeting, Bowen announced that he was leaving Grinnell at the end of June to take the presidency of the University of Iowa.[97] It is unclear precisely when Bowen had made this decision, but it was clearly unfolding during his absence from campus. It does not stretch the sources to judge that the pressures created by student unrest in his later years as president had much to do with Bowen's decision. Bowen told me as early as 1961 that he did not believe a President should serve one institution for more than ten years.[98] That said, it remains clear that Howard Bowen was disturbed by student misbehavior and demands for changes in time-honored social rules. Doubtless, student unrest hastened his decision to leave Grinnell. Howard Bowen confessed: "They and I were no longer working from the same assumptions. I was no longer their parent and they were no longer my children. I thought what they were asking for was wrong."[99] He was met with similar student agitation and demands at the University of Iowa, though the President was more heavily buffered by subordinate administrators at Iowa than at Grinnell.

Even though the student unrest that is so evident at the end of the Bowen presidency exploded on Leggett, as it did on virtually every college campus in 1970s America, the spectacular gains of the Bowen years were sustained in the late 1960s and early 1970s during the presidency of Glenn Leggett. I was Dean of the College at a sister institution, Colorado College, in this period, and the convulsions caused by the Vietnam War tore that campus apart, as they did, even more dramatically, at Grinnell College. Grinnell students demonstrated over many other issues not obviously related to Vietnam, but the war was the fuel. Looking back on that time, we know it was a war that deeply split our society and a war that, because of the draft lottery, many college students, though profoundly opposed to it, would be obliged to fight and perhaps even die fighting. It is easy to understand how anguished the students were over it and how readily they equated administrators and Trustees with the "establishment" that had brought them the Vietnam War. Passions were so intense that many students wrote off the "establishment" as almost entirely corrupt, and they wanted no part of the society it controlled. This transposition prompted students to disagree with much of what the College represented. This is not to say that Grinnell College and all other colleges did not need to change, but the intensity of protest was certainly increased by the Vietnam War. The war created a dismal situation for Grinnell, but Joe navigated it with compassion, understanding, and dignity, as did Glenn Leggett.

Glenn Leggett became Grinnell's eighth President on September 1, 1965, though he and his family did not arrive on campus until September 15. He came from the University of Washington, where he had served as Provost from 1963 to 1965. He had been at Washington since 1958, first as Assistant to the President and then

Vice Provost before he advanced to Provost in 1963. A 1940 graduate of Middlebury College, Leggett earned his MA and PhD in English from Ohio State University. He was an Instructor in English at MIT from 1942 to 1944 before he served in the United States Navy from 1944 to 1946. After the war, he taught English at Ohio State, while also finishing his graduate study there. In 1952 he moved to the University of Washington as Associate Professor of English before shifting to administration.

Grinnell College in the Leggett years underwent an almost bewildering array of changes; these resulted from almost constant student agitation and disruption reaching deeply into Trustee concern and actions. This was also the time when the College established a new curriculum, eliminating requirements. The College also struggled to assimilate the presence of significant numbers of students of color (mostly African American). It also faced the paradox of a rapidly growing endowment but static and then declining enrollment, which created financial pressure that led to cuts in the number of faculty and administration.

As challenging as the late 1960s and early 1970s were for Grinnell College, it was a good era for Joe; this was when he first met and became a lifelong friend of Warren Buffett, who has said on several occasions that Joe was the most important person in his life next to his father.[100] As Warren told business reporter Jason Zweig in 2000, "Joe is an extraordinarily generous and smart man. I'd never wanted to replace my real father—but if after Dad's death I could have adopted Joe as my father, I would have."[101] This friendship was destined to transform the fortunes of Grinnell College.

Joe and Warren were introduced in 1967 by an Omaha couple, Dick and Betty Hiller. Betty had been married to Joe's cousin Robert Lubetkin.[102] Warren described this occasion in an interview conducted in his office on June 5, 2014:

> *They were good friends of ours and were talking one time, and they said, "you know, there's a guy in Des Moines that you should know, you'd like him and he'd like you too;" and they arranged a trip over there. We just went for dinner ... and naturally everybody hit it off with Joe ...*

and I just thought he was fabulous. And I think it wasn't too long after that he invited us to the big celebration at Grinnell when Martin Luther King was there. It was a big deal and we had a terrific time there. We just made a point of seeing more and more of him as the years went by.

For his part, Joe said about his meeting with Warren Buffett, "I could see what a fine mind he had and I was immediately attracted to him."[103] One reason for the Hiller's insistence that Warren and Joe should connect is that Warren had just bought a department store in Baltimore, a purchase that gave the two men another common interest.[104]

The Grinnell "celebration" Buffett mentions was a symposium kicking off a major fundraising campaign. It was held on October 26–27, 1967. Besides King, it featured Fred Friendly, President of CBS News; communications theorist Marshall McLuhan; molecular biologist and double Nobel laureate Linus Pauling; semanticist S.I. Hayakawa; painter Robert Rauschenberg; anthropologists Loren Eisley and Ashley Montague; newsmen Richard Rovere and Peter Hackes (a Grinnell graduate); musician Louis Armstrong; and journalist Willie Morris.

Drawing Warren Buffett to such an outstanding Grinnell event was Joe's way of luring him onto the Board of Trustees—a task which he accomplished in January 1968. Warren was so taken with King's speech that, years later, he acquired a personal copy and sent it to "all kinds of people" because "it was one of the greatest speeches I had ever heard."[105]

According to Fred Little, acquiring the essential members and building the endowment were Joe's two Board passions; in drawing Warren Buffett to the Grinnell Board, he hit the jackpot on both goals.[106] Buffett has said that agreeing to join the Grinnell Board was "one hundred percent Joe ... it was one hundred percent the reason I went on the Board, there is no question about that."[107] On another occasion, Warren told me he really did not have much reason to care about Grinnell, but Joe asked him to serve Grinnell as a Board member and "I would do anything for Joe."[108]

Joe moved quickly to involve his new friend. He relinquished the chairmanship of the Finance Committee in favor of Buffett at a special meeting held at the Marriott Hotel in Chicago on January 18, 1970.[109]

This move was a stroke of genius; Buffett became deeply involved with Grinnell finances for several years, acquainting himself with the College's fiscal needs, as well as its operations. During those years, he was active on the Board and committed to strengthening the College despite his initial disinterest. In June 1973, he became Vice Chairman of the Board.[110]

"Disinterest" in no way captures Warren Buffett's commitment to partnering with Joe to build Grinnell's endowment. It was a challenge that fascinated him, and he was totally enthralled by Joe's commitment:

I mean Joe got me working on [the endowment] and he cared ... far, far, more about the performance of the Grinnell endowment than he did about his own net worth; and you know that is very rare when you get a Trustee who feels that way. And that enthusiasm and passion, it couldn't help but spill over. So he asked me to help on it and kind of assured me that if the two of us came up with something, he would ram it through one way or another. And, of course, there was nobody more fun to work with than Joe, so we got started.[111]

When asked if anyone else on the Board had influenced their investment decisions, Warren answered emphatically, "No." When questioned about whether he and Joe disagreed about investments, he added:

I don't think we ever disagreed. He thought he was one hundred percent on anything I came up with and I was certainly one hundred percent for anything he came up with. And, of course, when he came up with it, he used to make these risk-free deals, where if it went down, he would take a loss. I mean, it doesn't have to be a very good idea to get my approval on something like that where you take a loss and the College takes the gain. So, we would talk fairly often at night and it was always about the College and particularly the endowment and that if he had an idea I was for it, and if I had an idea, he was for it ... Our idea of a perfect investment committee was Joe, me, and Helen Keller.[112]

With Buffett's arrival, the Board minutes reflect a much more aggressive investment philosophy. At Warren's first meeting,

Joe presented a policy for a new "aggressive investment fund." Stockbroker, Don Wilson, Joe's 1925 Grinnell classmate and fellow Board member, was asked to suggest currently held stocks that could be shifted into the aggressive growth category. Eventually, this fund was set at $500,000.[113] Another manifestation was the November 1969 decision to accept the recommendation of the annual audit to finally remove the dormitories from the endowment, a practice that long had prevailed in higher education. Dormitories produce revenue, so it is tempting to enhance the endowment by including them, even though dorm expenses usually exceed revenues, which they did at Grinnell.[114]

Another aggressive move Joe and Warren made was deciding to embark on a gift annuity and deferred giving program. In November 1972, Buffett moved to establish a gift annuity program, and a year and a half later, the College hired Dick Jenkins to administer a full-blown deferred giving program.[115] It was not cutting edge, but with Joe and Warren driving the process, Grinnell moved into an area that has brought many large gifts to the College. Joe moved and Warren seconded approval of the administration's recommendation that a campus pub be established, breaking the historic covenant that no alcoholic beverages would be officially served on the Grinnell College campus. Joe and Warren shared broadly liberal instincts.

Joe and Warren also proposed the most famous investment of the new era: the November 1975 purchase of a network television station, WDTN, in Dayton, Ohio. Buffett called Joe to tell him that AVCO was selling stations in Cincinnati and Dayton. Warren, as a board member of the *Washington Post*, could not buy either of them because, in so doing, he would hit the *Post's* federal limit of five stations (the *Post* already had four.) Buffet said if such a purchase would have been good for him, it also would be good for the College. The Cincinnati station was quickly snapped up, but the Dayton station remained when the Board met in June 1975. Warren gave the Board with an hour and half seminar on why the purchase of WDTN for $12.9 million was a great opportunity. The price was two and one-half times revenue at a time when most TV stations were selling for three to four times revenue.[116] Immediately following his pitch, the Board voted to invest $2,000,000 of College equity and borrow the rest of the money. The bulk of the discussion involved how to structure station management in a way that created a firewall between the station and the students, who, it was feared, would agitate to influence broadcast policy. That problem was solved in the creation of a separate board, chaired by Trustee Gardiner Dutton '53.[117]

Though Warren Buffett still ruminates about what might have been had the more profitable Cincinnati station been available, the College nevertheless made a huge profit when the station was sold in the early 1980s for $49,000,000, a 281 percent profit over a time when the stock market went up ninety percent.[118] Added to that profit was the cash flow, which, using 1977 as an example, amounted to $1,700,000, much of which went to retiring debt.[119]

For a college to purchase a network TV station was unprecedented; the move called national attention to Grinnell while underlining the commitment of the Board to unique investment opportunities. That commitment came only out of implicit trust in Joe Rosenfield and Warren Buffett. Joe did not trust committees to make key investment decisions, admitting that he and Warren "just bulled things through."[120] The most dramatic aspect of that trust goes against the generally accepted wisdom, then and now, that boards usually do badly if they do their own investing. Grinnell was unique not only because of the trust placed in two Board members but also in the fact that this trust led to spectacular investment success. This investment success colored many actions in an era when the Board often acted on instinct and trust rather than carefully articulated procedures. That was the Board I served on and later served under, and I believe that successful "instinct" was possible only because the Board revered and trusted Joe Rosenfield completely. He was the very matrix of the Board.

Before the Rosenfield/Buffett partnership, the endowment was beginning to prosper, but the gains were not extraordinary. In 1965, the endowment registered at $10,400,000, having grown by $2,500,000 over the preceding five years. By 1970, the dormitories had been subtracted from the endowment and were never again to compromise the calculation. From 1970 to 1975, the Grinnell endowment gained $17,500,000, closing at $28,200,000, and by 1980, it was $43,700,000 — a $15,500,000 growth in five years. The really dramatic upward spiral began in the early 1980s with a gain for the decade of $143,837,000 to close at $287,537,000. The magic of Joe and Warren continued even more spectacularly in the 1990s, but that is a story for another section.[121]

With Joe at the helm, the College saw continuing unprecedented endowment growth, perhaps fulfilling what Joe told Gardiner Dutton when he joined the Board in 1970: "Our job is to make this institution financially impregnable."[122] Warren Buffett once said of Joe's investment acumen: "Joe is a triumph of rationality over convention."[123] One of the ways Joe applied his rationality was to invest in the ventures of young men in whom he sensed unusual qualities of character, innovation, and intelligence. This pattern fueled his decision to enlist another Grinnell Trustee Sam Rosenthal to join him in backing a young Grinnell alumnus and fellow Trustee Bob Noyce '49 when Noyce decided to turn his invention of the microchip into a new company called Intel. Joe and Sam each contributed $100,000 and the College's endowment contributed another $100,000, amounting to 10 percent of Intel's initial capital. Joe and Sam told the Board, "If it goes down it is our loss and if it goes up it's the College's gain, absolutely."[124] This is a classic example of how Joe cared more about the College's interests than his own. Grinnell made $14,000,000, a 4,583 percent profit, from Joe's and Sam's venture capital. The only down side is that, in the 1980s, the College sold its Intel shares because Bob Noyce believed too much of the College's endowment was vulnerable to Intel's fortunes; this move forsook billions of dollars had the College retained its Intel investment.[125]

Warren Buffett tells another interesting story about the "triumph of rationality over convention":

One time we set up a position where we would either long AT&T and short warrants or long the warrants and short AT&T, I don't remember which, but we did get a kick out of having a college that had a short position; that we were breaking new ground. Harvard had been around for a few hundred years and they had never had a short position; so Joe got a special kick out of it and we made money out of it. It was sort of a limited amount of money we would make, but it was a sure thing basically. And we went ahead and set up a short account. Not sure the trustees ever heard of

> *that one. [Joe] just enjoyed making money so much that it was just fun to work with him on it. He was like a little kid almost if we came up with something.*[126]

The relationship between Joe and Warren depended in part on their mutually shared wicked sense of humor, well-illustrated by this story regarding two deals Buffett proposed:

> *I put some money in and told him "you'll probably lose your money in this" and Joe said, "Warren, you kept your word." He said, "the money was gone before the check cleared." And then, we had something called the Community Bank here in Omaha, which was supposed to be black controlled, but I was to raise half the money [from] the white community and then we would, if it was a success ...sell our stock to other black citizens at our cost. But they were to raise half the money and we raised half the money; and I wrote Joe [I think the letter was three pages long] about this deal. I said, "Joe if this works you'll get bought out and get your money back." And he wrote me a long letter back and said, "I'm enclosing my check for $25,000." He said, "Warren, I've known you for ten years or whatever it has been" and he says, "On this deal, you told me if everything works, I'll break even." And he said, "after ten years, I now understand this is the best deal I'm ever going to see from you."*[127]

This story also reveals Joe's and Warren's shared concerns over social and economic injustice, particularly regarding African Americans. They also shared a deep commitment to Planned Parenthood, for which Joe was by far the strongest financial supporter in Iowa. Warren said:

> *[Joe] called me one day and said, "Warren, your fondest wish has come true." And I said, "What's that Joe?" and he said, "I put you in my Will." That was kind of unexpected, so it was just kind of touching, but he says, "You belong in my Will." . . . So I said, "Tell me more." He said, "Well, I've been giving Planned Parenthood a buy with $25,000 a year and I put you in there to succeed me." He was always joking about that.*[128]

Occasionally, one meets a human being who seems to stretch the normal boundaries of character and ability. Joe Rosenfield and Warren

Buffett are such rare individuals, so it is of particular importance to appreciate what Warren says about Joe as a person: "There was nobody more fun to work with than Joe. " Saying that the big thing about Joe "was his generosity of spirit," Warren continued:

> *I remember one time we were walking along some place, maybe it was Chicago, and there was some guy hitting people up for money, and the odds are about 98% he was a phony or something like that, and Joe gave him a couple of bucks ...I said, "Joe, he's a con artist, he's got it written all over him; there's 2% chance he isn't." He says, "I don't need it, maybe he does." ...He still believed in this other man. It was impressive.*[129]

Further enlarging on Joe's generosity of spirit, Warren said:

> *I never heard him make any remark the whole time I knew him that was unkind or that didn't make sense. There's some people who are very bright and some who say a lot of dumb things and then there's others that just don't. Everything he says makes sense. That was certainly true with Joe.*[130]

In Joe's later years, he and Warren would spend the Christmas holidays together at Warren's California home. In describing those occasions, Warren also commented on Joe's love for and connection with all generations:

> *He would spend every Christmas with us out in Laguna. He connected with all generations...he'd connect with children, he'd connect with grandchildren. I mean everybody loved him and it was this incredible generous spirit obviously and he was fun to talk with. I mean the guy had a fantastic sense of humor. I'll tell you a few of the things [and] I'm sure you have a hundred illustrations of it: he was very, very smart. We could talk politics; we could talk sports; we could talk business; we could talk family; any subject he was fun to talk to. And my kids thought he was fun to talk to...He would stay with us a couple of weeks, year after year. We put in a special chair so he could go up the steps and all, and we did not want to have Christmas without him. And I never really saw any aspects of his behavior or*

personality or anything in any way that would turn people off. He just embraced humanity.[131]

Their relationship was one of the most important in both Joe's and Warren's lives. Warren is one of the most respected and famous citizens of the United States and, for that matter, the world. Warren Buffett's love and admiration for Joe Rosenfield knows no bounds; he offers the definitive insight into who Joe was:

"I would say, I found his life as admirable as any I've seen. I mean in terms of combination it happened to fit me too because, in a sense, it was business knowledge, political knowledge and actions that fit in, with all presented in a way that was enormously both educational and entertaining; both, at the same time ...He had a story that fit every situation."[132]

Apparently his "line-a-day Rosenfield" ways continued in his adult years. In a 1998 interview, two years before he died, Joe summarized his effort to build Grinnell's endowment. Thinking back on his partnership with Warren Buffett, Joe reflected:

We did get [the endowment] started and then from there on, year after year somehow we kept the college open and kept increasing the endowment bit by bit. We got Warrren Buffett on the board as a trustee. Warren didn't give the college personally a lot of money, but he put us in some deals with stocks and so forth that gradually built our endowment up and as we went along, the stock market went along with us and today we have an endowment that is the envy of most liberal arts colleges in the country. I spent ...a good part of my time as a member of the board raising money for the college so we could have group of professors and buildings ...that we need for a college like Grinnell.[133]

Both Joe and Warren moved relatively easily with changing times—an example of their adaptability being when Joe moved and Warren seconded that a college pub be established. This required not only changing college practice but also suspending a civic code restricting the availability of intoxicating beverages on the campus. It is not at all surprising that these two men teamed to drive a progressive decision amid a somewhat contentious Board discussion about a breach both with history and social convention.[134]

This action provides a bridge to a discussion of the various strata of student activism during the late 1960s and early 1970s, the years Glenn Leggett confronted and managed with grace. He was probably better suited to this Grinnell era than Howard Bowen would have been, especially when confronted with the decision to close the College two weeks before graduation in the spring of 1970. The deaths of four students at the hands of the Ohio National Guard at Kent State, as well as the bombing of targets in Cambodia, prompted faculty and administration to conclude that it no longer was safe to hold students on campus. Classes, which had become tangential to student concerns, were cancelled, and the College officially closed two weeks before graduation. Ironically, Grinnell's lone Nobel laureate, chemist Tom Cech, was a member of the "non-graduating" class of 1970.

It was Joe who made the motion in the annual Board meeting on May 31/June 1, 1970 to give Trustee approval to the emergency decision of the administration and faculty to close the College; in this motion, Joe showed once again that he, more than most Trustees, understood the changing student and college culture. Joe resonated with young adults and their changing lives.

A letter he sent to a fellow 1920s alum, E.A. Norelius, shines with Joe's instinctive understanding of student culture in the Vietnam era:

Now for the situation of the College. I would be foolish to say that student behavior is perfect or that the Administration and the Trustees haven't made mistakes in judgment. I know that there are a small number of students (very, very small) who are out to destroy our basic society and the College along with it. But I am equally certain that the overwhelming majority of students are bright, dedicated young people who are genuinely concerned with the fabric of our society and the seemingly unsolvable problems rampant in our country today. I get to the College several times a year and have a chance to talk to lots of them—and at length. I constantly compare them with the students who were in school during our day. We were a decent enough lot and I think that the education we received at Grinnell helped us to become better citizens as the years rolled by. But how many of us had the slightest concern about ending war, assisting the poor and underprivileged, giving the black minorities a decent chance at a normal existence? The students of today are concerned with these problems, and if this concern occasionally results in intemperate or hasty conduct, I think we, as old and imperfect alumni should not cast the first stone.[135]

The College's closing in the spring of 1970 is crucial for understanding the rise of student agitation and protest that first challenged the College in the concluding Bowen years of the early 1960s. We have already seen some of the steps along the way to rebellion, such as the saga of the "dormitory that never was." Another indication of ingenious student initiative was a call to the state Fire Marshall, Wilbur Johnson, to "blow the whistle" on the long-standing practice of locking women into their dormitories at 10:00 p.m., a clear violation of the Iowa Fire Safety Code. Henry Willhelm, activist, made the call. It was League Board President Karen Lauterbach who tipped Willhelm off. She had been looking into the College's deficient fire safety practices on South Campus. A week after this call, the practice, which had endured since the dormitories were constructed in WWI, was dropped.[136] Other steps on the path to the unprecedented student revolution were early administration and Trustee discussions about when it might be advisable to call police onto campus.[137] The May 1968 arrival of activities of the Students for a Democratic Society (SDS) and the infamous "Playboy Incident," when several women students disrobed at a public session headlined by Hugh Hefner's lieutenant in February 1969 (leading to charges of indecent exposure), are indications of heightened radicalism.[138] Enterprising students, who by this time included newspaper "stringers," made sure the *New York Times* and others got the "Playboy story," making Grinnell nationally notorious for radical demonstrations. The Trustees then voted to support the administrative and faculty decision to close Grinnell's Air Force ROTC unit in 1972 when the current participants had graduated.[139] In response to that decision, as well as the pattern of student demonstrations, the FBI sent agents to campus to interrogate students in the fall of 1969.[140] Soon after, the Iowa Attorney General, Richard Turner also called for investigation of student activism at Grinnell.

Leading up to the decision to close the College in May 1970, students occupied the ROTC building. They broke a window, the only act of violence on the campus in these years, prompting the Trustees to consider moving the ROTC administrative quarters to a more central campus location.[141]

Shaken by the closing of the College, the Trustees decided in November 1970 to schedule periodic open meetings with students, inaugurating a pattern that would prevail into the 1980s.[142] Such meetings were leaps and bounds away from the days when the students appeared in Trustee Minutes only as numbers. Increasing student access prompted a complaint two years later from the Chair of the Faculty, Phillip Kintner, that the students had more contact with the Board than did the faculty.[143]

One of the long lasting positive results of these years was an entirely new curriculum, developed, ironically, in the fall of the fateful 1970 year and instituted in the fall of 1971. Students argued against curricula structured around all-college distribution requirement. Students also included grading systems in their criticisms, often asking for faculty written assessments in lieu of grades. Grinnell decided not to make significant alterations in the standard grading system, but it did move radically in the direction of a "no requirements" curriculum, or, as it is described today, an "individually advised" curriculum. The curriculum of 1970 remains at present-day Grinnell, making it one of only two or three colleges and universities in the nation at which curricular reform driven by the student revolution has remained. The reason for this longevity is most certainly the Freshman Tutorial (today labeled the First Year Tutorial) that was a key feature of the new curriculum. The Tutorial is the one course required of all students; it introduces them to Grinnell during their first semester on campus. Tutorials are limited to twelve or thirteen students and the instructor also serves as the students' academic adviser until they declare a major by the spring of their sophomore year. The close student/advisor relationship is critical to the success of the individually advised curriculum as the advisors, who receive considerable training from the College, often are quite directive in their advising during the freshman year. The result is that most Grinnell students take calculus and foreign language even though these subjects are not required. The faculty has consistently supported the individually advised curriculum, partly because they would rather teach volunteers than conscripts. Periodic transcript analyses have revealed that the vast majority of Grinnell students take a curriculum that appears as though the students in fact had distribution requirements.

It helped that the highly respected Physics Professor Beryl Clotfelter was the architect of the no-requirements curriculum and that he was ably assisted by a committee of the most respected faculty from a wide variety of academic disciplines. The Freshman Tutorial was the brainchild of History Professor Allan Jones and two students, Barry Zigas (now an affordable housing administrator in Washington DC) and student body President Andrew Loewi (later a Grinnell Trustee). The fact that students were key to the Tutorial proposal underscores the importance of the student revolution in creating a curriculum that has served Grinnell College for almost fifty years. Never in College history have students contributed so much to curricular reform and seldom in College history has a curriculum endured for almost half a century with every prospect of continuing indefinitely. It has become a Grinnell hallmark.[144]

Flushed with their curricular success, students began to push for a larger role in faculty personnel decisions in the spring of 1974. They wanted a voice in the hiring process as well as decisions about retention and tenure of faculty.

Students seized the initiative by creating a booklet that evaluated faculty based on student classroom experiences.[145] This initiative met faculty resistance, but by the late 1970s, student departmental "educational policy committees" were incorporated by the faculty into the hiring and retention process. It surprised no one that in February 1977, student body President Ruth Montgomery advised the Board that students should be part of all decisions that directly affected them.[146] While this recommendation was unsuccessful, students persisted in their efforts to control or at least participate in decisions that had significant relevance to their lives.

A consistent theme in campus life and a preoccupation of the Board was the drive toward a more multicultural Grinnell, especially to increase the presence of African Americans on campus. This was an issue near to Joe's heart, and he made it his business to enlist African Americans to the Board of Trustees as well as to the student body, faculty, and staff. As Fred Little said, Joe's focus outside the endowment was building the quality of the Board. That certainly meant adding African Americans, including Chicago business consultant, Jim Lowry '61, Dr. Randall Morgan (father of a Grinnell graduate), and Spellman College President Donald Stewart '59. They were added to the Board in the late 1960s and early 1970s. Successful recruiting of African American students unsurprisingly led to activism in an effort to awaken the College to their presence and needs; activism was spearheaded by a new and enduring organization, Concerned Black Students (CBS). The Trustee minutes are replete with references to activities of and meetings with CBS, beginning with the fall of 1968 when CBS successfully persuaded Grinnell to create a Martin Luther King Scholarship Fund specifically for black students.[147] This success, of course, did not by any means muffle CBS pressure. The students were back six months later at the March 15, 1969, Board meeting expressing concerns over admissions policy, financial aid needs, difficult town relations, failure to recruit black faculty, and need for an African American Studies Program.[148] Student pressure was intense enough to produce a special Board meeting in Chicago at the Newberry Library the following May to discuss the characteristics and concerns of the College's African American students. The Board considered the impact of a recently received grant from the Rockefeller Foundation to increase the number of black students admitted to the College. In that regard, the grant was a success; Grinnell had many more African American students than ever before, pushing the enrollment above seventy. However, the rush to elevate numbers had brought many students for whom Grinnell was a steep adjustment both socially and academically. The Newberry discussion focused on the need for more institutional support, as well as the possibility of the need to adjust admission standards. It was estimated that an annual infusion of $235,000 over ten years from 1969–70 to 1978–79 would be required to make up for the conclusion of Rockefeller Foundation support if

Grinnell's commitment to African American students were to be sustained. CBS students demanded that the College maintain a fifteen percent enrollment of black students; Dean Jim Stauss contended that such a policy would bankrupt Grinnell. The seriousness of the situation was underscored by near-violent CBS demonstrations in the months leading up to the May 1969 special Board meeting.[149]

At the regular meeting on campus less than a month later, the Board learned that the faculty had indeed established an African American Studies Program. The Board responded positively by making the commitment to sustain scholarships for black students once the Rockefeller grant ended.[150] On the other hand, the Board backed the administration in refusing to sanction the request for a blacks-only dormitory; rather, it held to a commitment to integration. It did however approve the request for clusters of black students to live together, sanctioning this arrangement in Younker Hall so long as white students were not excluded.[151] My nephew, who was a resident of Younker in the early 1970s, found it a somewhat tricky environment for white students to navigate, even those who were socially liberal.

In April 1972, 12 percent of Grinnell's financial aid went to black students, who made up 5 percent of the student body. This occasioned a query from former President Howard Bowen, who had recently joined the Board; he wondered about Grinnell's tendency to define minority almost exclusively as "black." "What about Hispanics and Native Americans?" he asked. Despite Bowen's challenge, the College tended to focus primarily on African Americans for several years to come. This focus certainly did not "solve" the problem of providing a comfortable environment for students of color, though many minority graduates from this era went on to distinguished careers in medicine, law, business, and government. One black student named Al Wheat became a member of the U.S. Congress; another, current Trustee Henry Wingate '69, became the first black federal judge in the state of Mississippi. Wingate's college roommate, John Garang, went home to Africa after earning a PhD from Iowa State, to lead the southern forces in the Sudanese Civil War. Graduates of those years told me repeatedly during my Grinnell Presidency that while they did not particularly enjoy their student days, they were eternally grateful to the College for the quality of their education, which helped them to achieve subsequent success in their careers.[152]

Though many of his colleagues on the Board were deeply committed to making Grinnell into a springboard for successful black students, Joe led the way. His commitment, sound advice, and monetary gifts were crucial to the limited success of the College, and they were crucial to the collegial conscience that drove Grinnell to keep striving to become truly multicultural—a difficult task among the "corn ields of Iowa."

One final thrust of student activism in the 1970s was the demand for divestment of Grinnell's stocks from companies engaged in South African business. The first mention of "corporate responsibility" in the Trustee minutes was in April 1973, when Trustee John Price, '60, successfully moved that the College should be mindful of its ethical responsibility to vote its shares.[153] The issue of ethical responsibility did not boil over until November 1977, shortly after the 1976 massacre of black students in Johannesburg's Soweto Township. This act propelled strenuous worldwide protests over South African apartheid and brought this issue center stage on college campuses nationwide. The story begins with the November 1977 Board meeting when the Finance Committee, on which Joe sat, proposed new investment guidelines: 1. The list of investments should be made public; 2. The College should take no position on political issues; and 3. The Chair of the Board, College Treasurer, and Finance Committee should monitor Grinnell's proxies. In addition, a resolution was passed stating that the College has an ethical responsibility to exercise its rights as a shareholder to influence corporate policy and that a set of guidelines should be developed to advise the Finance Committee in administering this new policy.[154]

The divestment issue persisted at Grinnell until Nelson Mandela was released from prison in February 1990. The Board finally agreed to a selective divestment policy in the late 1980s, but Joe, while sympathetic to the students concerns, never could bring himself to be comfortable with divestment. For the Trustees, maximizing the endowment was a sacred principle and, besides, no one was sure whether divestment would help or hurt black South Africans. Above all, Joe was concerned about the precedent of divestment. He said: "Today South Africa, tomorrow liquor and cigarettes. There's no end to 'ethical' investment."[155] To Joe and most of the Trustees, the fiduciary responsibility to maximize the endowment was the Board's premier obligation to Grinnell College.

The principal physical addition to the campus in the 1970s was the Physical Education Complex (PEC). It was the brainchild of long-time Athletic Director John Pfitsch, and he introduced the project to the Board of Trustees in November 1966.[156] Pfitsch told the Board about a meeting he had with a federal official who was also a Grinnell alum. Federal loans for facilities were available for an attractive interest rate, but the application deadline was January 31, 1967, less than three months hence. The Board immediately instructed the administration to apply for the loan which was later secured. At a January 9, 1967, Executive Committee meeting, Joe made the critical motion to have plans for the PEC drawn up by Skidmore, Owens, and Merrill in time to qualify for the government loan, pledging the endowment as collateral.[157] At the Executive Committee meeting on March 12, 1968, Joe moved that PEC construction begin as soon as possible and that, ironically, construction of the new residence hall (that never was) be deferred "pending further study."[158] Joe, who loved athletics, was right on both counts: The PEC would be a huge addition to the campus and the residence hall no longer would be needed in light of changing student residential patterns.

The PEC was completed and in use by the fall of 1971 at a cost of $2.2 million, but the government loan, though quite favorable, remained part of a troubling plant funds deficit for several years (at that time it reached $2,325,825, despite the federal loan of $943,000).[159]

Grinnell's north and south campus dormitory complex stands for many as the icon of the College. Built during World War I, at a cost that saddled the College with significant debt for several decades, they stood as the very soul of Grinnell's commitment to on-campus residence and communal life. We have seen a glimpse of that commitment in the story of Joe's student days; those dorms were critical elements of the Grinnell experience for generations of students. President John Hanson Thomas Main's vision was of Oxford/Cambridge-style quadrangle living, though Grinnell organized by floors rather than staircases. Each dorm houses fifty to sixty students in manageable communal clusters, and for years, the men remained in their dorm for all four years, allowing them to identify as, for example, a "Langan Man" almost as much as a Grinnellian.

By the end of the 1960s, the historic pattern of dormitory living was revolutionized by coeducational living. The College's decision was precipitated by a blatant defiance of campus rules by top student leaders, the Council of House Presidents of the male dorms in the spring of 1967, who collectively spent all night in the women's dormitories.[160] After several years of agitation, the dramatic change to coed dorms soon followed this defiant act, exerting fresh pressures on the physical space, particularly on bathrooms. The limit of one bathroom per floor along with room-by-room rather than floor-by-floor coed living led to the coeducational bathrooms for which Grinnell became notorious in the early 1970s. The inconvenience of the bathrooms called for some dormitory renovation; in addition, women in particular increasingly objected to the dilapidated state of the erstwhile men's dorms. Men are harder on buildings than are women; many women who lived in the formerly men's halls objected to downtrodden spaces whose conditions most men had overlooked. When buildings became coed, their conditions tended to stabilize whereas the all-male dorms that persisted in the early days of coed living continued to deteriorate.[161]

The Trustees acknowledged the problem without hesitation, since the majority were alums who had lived their four years in these same buildings. They knew the dormitories were very well constructed and were hallmarks of the campus. Therefore, they never really considered starting over with new buildings. The April 1967 meeting of the Executive Committee determined that the seventeen dormitories should be renovated, not replaced, and Joe made the motion to provide $27,000 for a study.[162] A subsequent Board meeting decided that campus planner Dick Dober should conduct the study of what needed to be done and what it would cost. Dober made his report at the February 1977 Board meeting, concluding that at least $3.9 million would be required to bring the dormitories up to an excellent standard, with a further recommendation that Mears Cottage—though not currently in residential service due to its frame construction from the late nineteenth century—should be retained and renovated. The Mears issue was set aside; many on the Board thought that it should be demolished, while the faculty and students were adamant that it should be retained and were working to place it on the National Register of Historic Places.[163]

In June 1977, the Trustees voted to embark on a complete dormitory renovation project, with North Campus Clark Hall and South Campus James Hall as the pilots. The budget was set at $5,500,000 million, with an estimate of $1,000,000 for Mears should it be retained and renovated.[164] By June 1979, Norris, the 1960s dorm, was added to the project; a fourth floor was added, and bricking over most of the Air Force Academy-like, all-glass exterior walls was decided as well, adding $900,000 to the dormitory project.[165] Chicago architect Ben Weese was hired the previous June to assess Grinnell's remaining nineteenth-century buildings, Mears and Goodnow, for possible renovation.[166]

The dormitory renovation project was quite successful in its effort to enhance high-quality living space for students. Almost certainly, this success would not have been possible without Joe's generosity. It is not easy to raise money for renovations, and it is particularly difficult to raise funds for dormitories, but Joe, who had absolutely loved dormitory life at Grinnell, was determined to retain that life as the anchor of the Grinnell experience he so cherished. He also wanted to prevent dangerous elevation of the plant funds deficit created by construction of the Physical Education Complex. In the end, he gave as much as $12,000,000 to the dormitory project.[167]

Though finances were definitely improving in the '60's and '70's, expenditures often overwhelmed revenue, so that summer borrowing between tuition payments continued, as did calls for year-end philanthropy to balance the budget. In some years, Joe would call Wally Walker, who oversaw the budget, to ask about the balance as year-end approached. He was told frequently that the College would be tens of thousands of dollars shy of balancing, and Joe would most often fill the gap so Grinnell could report a balanced budget. Having a balanced budget was particularly important when soliciting funds from foundations and industry. Once, Joe said to go ahead and show the $40,000-plus deficit to see if the alums would step forword to fill the gap. When they didn't, Joe resumed his practice of filling the gap.[168]

At Warren Buffett's first meeting as Chair of the Finance Committee in March 1970, he stimulated a question about the constantly increasing necessity for gifts to balance the budget; Joe added a caution against invading the endowment to finance current operations. Both were particularly concerned with the plant funds deficit, which had exceeded $1.6 million.[169] Joe and Warren fueled an era of budget austerity throughout the 1970s. Consequently, the following October, Dean Wally Walker reported that the faculty was responding well to position cuts, made largely through attrition, which by the spring of 1971 had amounted to 5 percent of the previous faculty size.[170] In 1970–71 there were 109.6 faculty and in 1971–72 that had been reduced to 100.8, causing the ratio of students to faculty to rise from 9.56 to 1 to 12.38 to 1.[171] This change revealed that, once again, it was Joe who, in partnership with Warren Buffett, influenced important aspects of college policy—finances in particular.

Grinnell embarked on two capital campaigns in the late 1960s and late 1970s. The first, designated the AIM Campaign, was officially launched in January 1968 and built on the spectacular October 1967 Symposium featuring Martin Luther King, Jr.—the event Joe had used to lure Warren onto the Board of Trustees. Bob Noyce was the National Chair of the Campaign, and his goal was to raise $10,000,000 over five years. The designated Trustee portion was $3,000,000, and the campaign was declared a success after seven years in June 1975.[172] Encouraged by this success and the need to raise funds to renovate the dormitories, Burling Library and Goodnow Hall, the Trustees immediately began to plan for another campaign, hiring consultants Martz and Lundy. At the February 1976 Board meeting, Martz and Lundy reported that another campaign was feasible.[173] In June 1977, the Board decided on a new campaign with an $18,000,000 goal, which included a total of $7,000,000 for capital needs. Trustee Fred Little was named the National Chairman.[174] The capital needs portion of the campaign grew as the projects materialized;[175] early fundraising succeeded due to the generosity of the Trustees, who gave over $6,000,000 by early 1978.[176]

The second campaign began under a new Grinnell President, A. Richard Turner, who assumed the position in January 1975. Glenn Leggett had given advance notice that his resignation would be effective January 1, 1975.[177] Thus, the decision in June 1975 to embark on the second campaign of the 1970s was made under the new President. The campaign was not complete when Dick Turner resigned in the spring of 1979, so it was finished in a series of fundraising efforts for capital projects, including the dormitories and a major renovation and extension of Burling Library under Turner's successor, myself.

In Dick Turner, the Trustees found the most eminent scholar in the history of the Grinnell Presidency. Turner was one of the best art historians of his generation; he collaborated on the monumental *The Art of Florence*. The Dean of Renaissance Art History, H.W. Jansen, conceived the project, but it was far from complete when he died in 1982. Turner and his two collaborators published *The Art of Florence* in 1988 after Turner had left Grinnell for New York University, where he served as Director of the Institute of Fine Arts and later Dean of Arts and Sciences before his retirement in 2000. In 1993, Dick Turner published a landmark study of Leonardo da Vinci, under the title *Inventing Leonardo*. Turner's career prior to his Grinnell presidency was as Professor of Art History and Dean of the College at Middlebury, which followed teaching positions at Michigan and Princeton.

Dick Turner was a proactive leader who was determined to leave his stamp on Grinnell. There is a letter among the minutes for a November 1974 Executive Session of the Board indicating that the faculty members of the search committee favored Executive Vice President Waldo Walker, and they considered Dick Turner only "provisionally acceptable." When the Trustees chose Turner, some of the faculty felt as though their desires and judgment had been overridden.

As a result, many faculty members were, from the beginning, inclined to oppose Turner's initiatives. He was the sort of President who advanced initiatives quite early in his tenure. He proposed a number of innovations through a white paper, holding two conferences on campus with invited alumni, parents, and friends of the College to discuss the white paper in November 1976.[178] Due to their initial inclinations, Turner could never get the faculty to seriously discuss the white paper, so, practically speaking, it was dead on arrival.[179]

Turner also believed Grinnell's financial and intellectual future was threatened by an overly tenured faculty. The Board was sympathetic to his concern and adopted a tenure quota policy in June 1976, whereby the total of tenured faculty was not to exceed two thirds and no department was to be fully tenured.[180] At that time, the tenured faculty percentage was 56.[181] The subsequent Trustee minutes reveal a high degree of faculty angst over this new policy manifest in meeting after meeting.

In February 1977, under pressure to eliminate administrative positions, Turner announced the decision to cut three positions. A campus uproar ensued because all three positions were held by women. After months of protests, which including alumni, over the elimination of the position that had successfully booked national talent to appear at Grinnell, two of the women were restored and the Affirmative Action Officer position was established.[182]

The white paper, faculty tenure quotas, and proposed administrative cuts made for a tumultuous Presidential tenure, and Dick Turner ultimately decided to return to an academic position in a more congenial environment at New York University's Institute of Fine Arts in 1979.

The '60's and '70's held the most crucial period of Joe Rosenfield's contributions to Grinnell. In those years, he met Warren Buffett and together they established the pattern that would build Grinnell's endowment into one of the largest of any small college in America. Joe had served Grinnell as a Trustee for 39 years when the 1980s arrived, and he had another 20 years of service awaiting him. As those years unfolded, his appearance in the Trustees minutes receded, but his activities on Grinnell's behalf as the "sage of Grand Avenue" never dimmed.

THE ELDER STATESMAN

The last twenty of Joe Rosenfield's fifty-nine-year Trusteeship of Grinnell College held three of the seven Presidents with whom he worked: myself, Pamela Ferguson, and Russell Osgood. I served from August 1979 to July 1991 and was the only alumnus President of Grinnell College; I graduated in 1956 at the end of Howard Bowen's initial year. After earning Fulbright and Rhodes Scholarships for study in Paris and Oxford, successively, I received my PhD in Church History from the University of Chicago. I taught in the History Department at Colorado College (CC) for fifteen years before coming to Grinnell. I also served as Dean of the College at CC for six years, overseeing a calendar shift in 1970 from the standard semester to a one-course-at-a-time schedule. After twelve years as Grinnell's President, I returned to teach History, following two years of service with my wife, Sue, as Peace Corps Volunteers in Lesotho, southern Africa.

I was succeeded by Pamela Ferguson, who served from August 1991 until February of 1998, and Dean Charlie Duke was chosen as Acting President for the remainder of the 1977–1978 academic year. A brilliant mathematician, Pamela Ferguson earned her PhD from the University of Chicago following graduation from Wellesley. She taught at Northwestern before moving to Miami University, where she served as Associate Provost and Dean of the Graduate School before becoming Grinnell's eleventh President. She, too, remained at Grinnell after leaving the Presidency; she served as a successful Professor of Mathematics until her untimely death in 2004.

Russell K. Osgood assumed the Grinnell Presidency in July 1998, serving until the summer of 2010, well after Joe's death in 2000. He earned a JD at Yale Law School in 1974 following his undergraduate degree at Yale. After several years in private practice as a tax lawyer in Boston, specializing in compensation and employee benefits, he became an Associate Professor of Law at Boston University, joining the Cornell University Law Faculty two years later in 1980. In 1988, he became Dean of the Cornell Law School, serving for ten years before moving to the Grinnell Presidency; his twelve-year term was highlighted by the campus' dramatic physical transformation. After leaving the Grinnell Presidency in 2010, Osgood has taught at the Washington University (St. Louis) School of Law.

Over the two decades from 1979 to 2000 Joe Rosenfield's dream to make Grinnell College impregnable came to fruition. In those years, the endowment grew from $43,700,000 to $862,487,000—and it continued to grow in the twenty-first century, reaching $1,787,775,000 in 2015 after a succession of bull markets.[183] The best description of how Joe and Warren orchestrated this growth is in an article by Jason Zweig in *Money* magazine, published in May 2000, just before Joe's death in June. The article, "The Best Investor You've Never Heard Of," sensitively details the partnership of Joe and Warren, while analyzing their matching investment philosophies: "Joe is a triumph of rationality over convention," said Buffett, and he could just as well have been describing himself. If there is any single descriptor that encapsulates the investment success of Warren and Joe and, equally, the success of the Grinnell College endowment, it is this: "the triumph of rationality over convention."

"Rationality" led to a policy of investing in few securities, while selling even fewer. In more than twenty years, the Rosenfield/Buffett partnership made just over half dozen investments. In fact, when Joe died in 2000, Grinnell held fewer than twenty different stocks and mutual funds, and ten of those stocks were with the Sequoia Fund. Many colleges had more investment managers than Grinnell had investments. The first of the most significant investments of the partnership was when Joe bought $5,252 worth of Berkshire Hathaway stock for Grinnell just after meeting Warren in 1967. When those securities were sold between 1989 and 1992, they were worth $3.7 million, and neither Joe nor Warren could remember why they decided to sell.[184]

The narrative of this partnership includes the Intel venture capital decision, previously mentioned. Joe had great faith in young Bob Noyce '49, which extended to Noyce's partners Gordon Moore and Andy Grove; Joe's faith in Noyce led to the decision to provide ten percent of the startup capitalization of Intel. Joe contributed $100,000, which was matched by fellow Trustee Sam Rosenthal, a successful Chicago lawyer. One hundred thousand dollars came from the College's endowment, adding up to $300,000 of the $3,000,000 required to capitalize the computer chip startup. Both Joe's and Sam Rosehthal's investments were made on behalf of the College; they would take the losses while the College would benefit from the gains, and the gains turned out to be massive. Three years after Intel went public in 1971, the Grinnell endowment had doubled to $27,000,000, an increase largely due to the appreciation of Intel stock. In the same period, the market lost 40 percent. Bob Noyce, as a Grinnell graduate and dedicated Trustee, was unusually sensitive to the high degree of endowment dependence on Intel stock and he urged Joe to sell all or most it, which the Trustees did from 1974 to 1980. The College's initial $300,000 investment had turned into $14,000,000, a profit of

4,583 percent. As spectacular as was this profit, Jason Zweig estimates that the College lost several billion dollars through the premature sale of its Intel stock.[185]

The most well-known of the Rosenfield/Buffett investments was the 1976 purchase of WDTN Television station in Dayton, Ohio. Though not the most profitable of the partnership's investments, it was, nevertheless, virtually unique among colleges and universities, none of which had dabbled in network TV. We have seen that Warren Buffett was frustrated that the more valuable AVCO station in Cincinnati had been snapped up. Still, a $12.9 million investment in the Dayton station became $49 million in 1991, a 281 percent profit from the sale, not to mention the substantial annual cash flow during the years the College owned the station.

In 1978, Warren suggested and Joe quickly agreed that the College should invest in the Sequoia Fund, and the College took a $10,000,000 position. By 1997, the Sequoia Fund had swelled to two thirds of the Grinnell endowment, $600,000,000. At the time, it was the largest investment ever made by a single investor in a mutual fund. From 1977 to 1997, Sequoia outperformed 94 percent of all diversified stock funds and beat the S&P 500 by 2.7 percent annually.[186]

The final major move of the "partnership," at Warren's suggestion, was a significant investment in 1990 of Freddie Mac, adding $130,000,000 to the Grinnell endowment before it was sold in 2000—well before the Freddie Mac debacle of 2008.[187]

As one takes survey of this succession of remarkable investments, it is virtually certain that few, if any, would have been made by the typical Trustee investment committee. Warren said that he and Joe did not consult the Grinnell Investment Committee as they talked weekly or biweekly about Grinnell's investments. Furthermore, he and Joe never disagreed about their investment philosophy.[188] Their philosophy was grounded in research, brilliant intellect, and ironclad patience and discipline. For example, in 1990, just after Grinnell purchased Freddie Mac, the stock dropped 27 percent, which gave a major blow to the Grinnell endowment, but Joe and Warren did not waver. They had suggested only a few investments based on their assessment of long-term value; those stocks must therefore be held to reap their long-term value, and that is exactly what Joe and Warren did. Warren said, "Joe invests without emotion."[189]

All of this presupposed excellent knowledge of the businesses behind the investments. For a long time, Warren refused to invest in technology because he did not understand it. Joe agreed with him about the importance of exceptional understanding of the value and the management of the few businesses in which the College would invest. Everyone makes comments about Joe's intelligence, and Jim Hoak of Heritage Communication emphasized that Joe's elevated understanding of the communications business led to his investment in Hoak's business, Heritage Communications.[190] Joe's wisdom about communications translated in the Grinnell context to the purchase of WDTN TV in 1976.

At the conclusion of the story about Joe's experience with his first President, Sam Stevens, I stated that the firing of Stevens in June 1954 and the consequent return of Joe to the Board of Trustees was *the* pivotal moment in Grinnell College history. That assertion should be self-evident at this point, since none of what has been previously described would have been possible without Joe. He built Grinnell's financial foundation, most obviously in the partnership with Warren Buffett but also in earlier years as he painstakingly began to build a small endowment into a useful one. He accomplished this growth by offering excellent advice to shift from farms to securities, constantly urging focus on the endowment, willingness to create a venture capital fund and, finally, a steady flow of substantial gifts, to the endowment and operations. He quite literally saved his impoverished College from collapse.

The renewal of the Rosenfield/Bowen partnership did so much to raise Grinnell College to national prominence in the 1960s. Howard Bowen, who had become a Trustee in the early 1970s, frequently commented on the power of compound interest.[191] As finances stabilized and endowment grew in the 1980s, Bowen, with Joe's backing, proposed setting aside $1,000,000 of the College's endowment to compound over one hundred years. It was not to be touched unless the College faced a financial crisis. His suggestion, titled "The Howard Bowen Continuity Fund" (February 1982), further advised that every ten years there should be a similar set-aside from the endowment.[192]

Howard's fixation on compound interest was not Joe's fixation, but Joe was open to a variety of approaches to endowment building, and he very much liked finally being in a position to wall off portions of the endowment from the constant drain of college operations.

A significant dimension of the story of Joe's love affair with Grinnell College was the College's struggle to maintain academic and communal excellence in the face of near overwhelming financial challenges. The last two decades of the twentieth century coincided with Joe's last two decades of a life, which spanned the twentieth century. Those decades were years of declining health for Joe but ascending health for the College. In those years of growing prosperity based on spectacular endowment growth, what was happening on the campus?

Most notably, the pattern of annual borrowing ended in the 1970s, the last of which were short-term loans to tide the College over the summers between the tuition payments of January and September. In the 1980s and 1990s, when the College did borrow, it did so for specific capital projects; but more often than not, these projects were funded by grants, capital campaigns, and other forms of fundraising. In fact, in 1997, Grinnell received a AAA rating from both Moodys and Standard and Poors, inaugurating a steady stream of AAA ratings, quite unusual for a collegiate institution and, for Grinnell, a stark contrast with its debt-ridden past.[193]

Enrollment stabilized during these decades at 1,250 to 1,300 students, topping out at 1,322 in 1993. Enrollment by 2018 had grown to over 1,650. Though there was an applications crisis in the early 1980s, in which applications barely exceeded 1,100 for entering classes of over 350, applications grew steadily to 2,000 by the end of the decade. Financial aid grew rapidly, and by 1985, over seventy percent of the student body was on scholarship. The College worked hard to limit student debt, so financial aid packages featured a high proportion of grant to loan. For example, a comparative study of the classes of 1984 and 1989 revealed 52 percent of the class of 1989 graduated with no debt in comparison with the class of 1984's 27 percent. At the other end of the scale, 2 percent of the class of 1989 had high debt ($10,000–$12,499), while 17 percent of the class of 1984 had been saddled with high debt.[194] The policy of a high grant to loan ratio continued at Grinnell into the twenty-first century. Today, Grinnell graduates carry the lowest student debt of any college or university in the state of Iowa.[195]

Grinnell became a charter member of the Associated Colleges of the Midwest in 1958, a consortium of outstanding Midwestern liberal arts colleges including Carleton and St. Olaf in Minnesota, Knox, Monmouth, and Lake Forest in Illinois, Lawrence, Beloit, and Ripon in Wisconsin, and Cornell, and Coe in Iowa. In the 1980s and 1990s, Grinnell often had the highest student retention in the Consortium, usually graduating over 80 percent of entering students. Faculty salaries also rose to equal the highest level in the Consortium by the late 1980s.[196]

In the 1980s, the weekly news magazine *US News and World Report* inaugurated an annual rating of colleges and universities, divided into various categories, according to their student selectivity. Grinnell was and continues to be rated as a "Highly Selective College." Throughout the 1980s, the College was consistently ranked in the top ten of Highly Selective Colleges, and in 1988 it rose as high as eighth. The rating criteria frequently changed, and in the 1990s, with new and far more extensive criteria, Grinnell slipped into the teens, but in another, newer category, "Best Buy," Grinnell frequently ranked number one.[197]

The rising endowment was a tide that lifted Grinnell to expanding excellence. The endowment also contributed substantially to dramatic physical changes on campus, particularly after Joe's death in 2000. Joe fought hard against using endowment income to fund capital projects. I was well aware of Joe's tenacity on this point. He would only very reluctantly agree to use several thousand dollars of endowment proceeds when a project fell short of funding goals. Joe's stature and identification with the endowment was such that his wishes controlled Board action on such matters.

After Joe's death in 2000, the Board increasingly agreed to use endowment income as a major element in funding capital projects, in part because the endowment had grown so large that nonprofit spending guidelines forced a level of annual endowment expenditure that rose substantially beyond an appropriate level of support for annual operations. This was a huge shift from the historic patterns of Grinnell College finance.

As often happens, "the rich get richer." Knowledge of Grinnell's endowment success, along with obvious growing excellence and national presence, led to a succession of significant foundation grants in the 1980s and 1990s. Some of these, such as one from Kresge, were for capital projects, but the majority were for academic programs and equipment. Grinnell received at least four grants from the Pew Foundation, three from the Mellon Foundation, and at least five separate grants from the Joyce Foundation. Individual faculty, as well as the College more generally, earned a series of National Science Foundation (NSF) grants, and the Hewlett Foundation gave a grant on its own and another in partnership with the Mellon Foundation. The Sloan Foundation awarded several grants to the Sciences, and the Cowles Foundation created a flourishing Chinese Studies Program. The College received one Howard Hughes Foundation grant and an extremely interesting Ford Foundation Grant, given to Grinnell and the University of Iowa to encourage faculty interaction between a small private college and a large state university. This idea was the brainchild of Rawlings of Iowa and me in my presidency at Grinnell, an unusual example of a grant inspired from the campus rather than determined by foundation agendas.[198]

During the long lean years, the fabric of Grinnell's campus had deteriorated. With rising prosperity, the Trustees and administration made dramatic progress in renovating existing buildings and constructing much needed new facilities. The comprehensive dormitory renovation project undertaken in the 1970s was completed in the early 1980s; in 1985, the former dormitory and oldest campus building, Mears Cottage, was completely renovated to become the College's Admission and Financial Aid office. The long-standing President's residence, now guest house, Grinnell House, was renovated in 1982. The most extensive expansion and renovation of the 1980s was that of Burling Library, which was substantially financed, as it had been in its initial construction, by Edward Burling (1890)—by his estate in this case. The results were enshrined by *Rolling Stone* magazine, which labeled Burling the "comfiest library in America."[199] This 1983–1984 project was followed quickly by construction of the Gale Observatory, which was completed in 1984. Intel founder and Grinnell Trustee Bob Noyce organized the fundraising and contributed to this project substantially in honor of his Grinnell mentor, Grant Gale, who had introduced him to solid-state physics, which started him on a path that would lead to his invention of the integrated circuit on a silicon chip.[200]

Constructed amid the conflict over Sam Stevens, one thing that can be said for the science building of 1951 is that it happily accepts additions without compromising its bland architecture. A Physics wing was constructed in the 1960s, and in 1987, a second addition was built on the east side to accommodate the Mathematics and Psychology departments. Ten years later, the building was significantly expanded again with a wing that curved completely around the south and west sides of the building. Finally, in 2007, the Biology wing on the north side was replaced completely to include a spectacular two-story glass façade of the new science library.

In 1990, the Alumni Recitation Hall (ARH) was completely renovated through the genius of Ben Weese, who was also the architect for the Burling and Mears renovations.

While the 1980s mostly focused on restoring existing campus buildings, the College added one more new building besides the Gale Observatory.

For several years, students had justly complained about the College's inadequate social space. They convinced me of their need when I was serving as President, and I decided to let the students use their power of persuasion with the Trustees. They were so successful in meeting with the Board in the late 1980s that Trustee Jack Harris '39 and his wife, Lucile '40, made a large challenge gift that led to the construction of the Harris Center—completed in 1991. Joe also made a substantial contribution to the project. Designed by a Cedar Rapids architect named Herb Stone, Harris Center contains a cinema, concert/dance hall, offices, and a small recreation space.[201]

One of the last significant renovations of the '80s and '90s was an upgrade and new wing on Steiner Hall, which finally created appropriate space for the Education Department while improving the offices and classrooms for Philosophy and Religious Studies. The Steiner renovation was completed in 1992, while a long delayed renovation of the College's other nineteenth-century building, Goodnow, was completed in 1995 as a symbol of the College's sesquicentennial.[202]

When the College was able to pay its debt to previous financial neglect following the 1980s, it was free to turn to much-needed new construction. Of course, it should be stated that throughout the almost interminable years of debt and financial stringency the College made the right decision to put its emphasis on the academic program and student financial aid; as a result of that choice, the most important measures of quality and access were much stronger than Grinnell's straitened financial circumstances signaled.

When the $22.5 million addition to the science building was completed in 1997, adding an extensive wrap-around section to an already twice enlarged building, the entire complex was named for Bob Noyce, who had died suddenly in 1990. The previous name for the science building in honor of Howard and Lois Bowen was given instead to a section of the building.

The other major construction of the 1990s was a large extension of the Fine Arts building, which added a new concert hall and practice space along with an art studio wing surrounding an art gallery in the middle of the expansive addition. This project was finished as the twentieth century expired. It was named for Kay and Matthew Bucksbaum, who were such a large part of Joe's life and whose General Growth offices Joe occupied for his last quarter century of life.

Grinnell continued to build in the first years of the new century, most notably the Rosenfield Campus Center, which was completed in 2006.

Modesty, as we have seen, was Joe's hallmark, and he consistently refused to accept a Grinnell College building named in his honor. In fact, Jason Zweig's article in *Money* commented on the absence of a Grinnell building named for Joe. Russell Osgood was finally able to persuade Joe to allow the projected campus center to be named for him. In part, I'm sure Joe agreed because he realized he would not live long enough to have to see his name on a building, and he probably recognized that his estate would pay a significant share of the cost. The May 2002 Board minutes announce that Joe's estate had left Grinnell $30,323,952 and that $25,000,000 would be earmarked for the funding of the new campus center.[203]

Building continued unabated in the first decade of the twenty-first century, including four new dormitories to accommodate a student body that had risen to 1,650; a new Admission/Financial

Aid/Registrar's building named for Rosenfield friend and fellow Trustee John Chrystal (2002), and a magnificent new field house with a two hundred meter running track, fifty-meter pool, large gymnasium, and auxiliary gymnasium named for Trustee Charles Bear '39 (2006–2010). With inflation and the expanded ambitions of the College, the costs of building these facilities made the sum spent on earlier buildings seem paltry. While the post-WWII science building had reached the unheard of figure of $1,000,000 in 1951, the most recent buildings cost upward of $50,000,000. The College raised significant funds for these projects, to be sure, but none of the projects would have been possible without contributions from the endowment that Joe so lovingly created. In fact, the size of the endowment created fundraising challenges because most of the alumni who were old enough to seriously consider making major donations were products of the years of the College's impoverishment; it was hard for them to be convinced that the now wealthy College needed their money. Grinnell alums are generous, but they are discerning. They desire to leave their money in places where it will accomplish the most good. Thus, the College's development office engaged and continues to engage in a prolonged struggle to make its case to an alumni body that has a hard time adjusting to Grinnell's spectacular endowment growth.

The academic program of the College, as well as its ethos, was, as might be expected, significantly enriched by the increasing financial wellbeing of the last two decades of the twentieth century. At the beginning of those decades, the College established the Joseph and Dannie Rosenfield Program in Human Rights and International Relations, with faculty icon Joseph Wall '40, who was lured back to Grinnell from the State University of New York at Albany, named its director in 1980. This program has endured as one of the most stellar features of the College; the program sponsors two or three major symposia each year, as well as major visiting speakers. Before the opening of the Rosenfield Center in 2006, the Rosenfield program was the primary vessel for carrying the Rosenfield name on campus.

Another vehicle, was the Rosenfield Chair in Social Studies, established in 1984 through Joe's million dollar gift to recognize a promising young scholar, Daniel Kaiser of the History Department.[204]

In the fall of 1983, Joe gave a similar gift to establish a chair in Women's Studies, naming it the "Noun Chair," for his sister Louise.[205] Typical of Joe, he led the way in a Trustee program to establish a series of new endowed chairs to draw donors to support one of the largest college expenditures: faculty salaries. In 1985, fellow Trustee Patricia Papper endowed a chair in international economics in honor of her father, Sidney Meyer, which drew Jack Mutti, an outstanding established scholar, to Grinnell.[206] In the same year, Don Wilson, who was Joe's 1925 classmate and a fellow Trustee, endowed the Wilson Chair in Enterprise and Leadership to draw distinguished business leaders to campus. In 1989, the Trustees established a chair in Religious Studies to recognize the tenth anniversary of my presidency. The capstone of the 1980s initiative for endowed chairs came at the beginning of the next decade, when the Henry Luce Foundation funded a chair in Nations and the Global Environment, to be held by the outstanding scholar and teacher David Campbell, who was recruited to Grinnell in 1990.[207]

Though not quite the equivalent of faculty chairs, Trustee Jack Harris ('39) and his wife, Lucile, gave $800,000 to endow a young scholars' faculty leave program. Newly minted faculty frequently arrive on campus with most of the research and some of the writing for books in the form of doctoral dissertations, but they are overwhelmed by the teaching demands of Grinnell, especially at the beginning when they must design and teach a number of new courses. With their feet on the ground and good pre-tenure reviews, the opportunity for a year's leave following their third year at Grinnell is a godsend for young faculty. The Harris Fellowship has sponsored two junior faculty each year since 1985.[208]

Though, as a Trustee, I unsuccessfully argued against the tenure quota policy, when I became president, I set out to abandon the policy. My argument to the Trustees was that a policy of limiting the total faculty to sixty-six percent on tenure, with no fully tenured department, was far too arbitrary and that a fair and stringent tenure policy could and would be administered without those restrictions.[209] In fact, before my arrival, the first time a department could be fully tenured, it was. This was the case for the Physics Department, and it immediately created an exception to the policy. In May 1980, the Trustees agreed to abandon the tenure quota policy and charged the administration with sustaining high standards for tenure.[210] The following year, two faculty members who had been recommended for tenure on split votes were denied by the administration. This event precipitated a campus crisis and demonstrations. In the aftermath, however, faculty members adopted new procedures to strengthen the review process well before the sixth year when a faculty member faces the final review. As a result, there has been instated a much more effective policy whereby the third, not the sixth year, has become the primary gateway to tenure. It is much easier to deny a colleague after three years, when he or she is still a relative beginner, than after six years, when he or she has become an integral part of the institutional fabric.[211]

A sidebar to the tenure issue was the federal mandate raising the standard retirement age from sixty-five to seventy. The legislation, which was passed in October 1981, required a shift in retirement policy, which was instituted in July 1982.[212] As a result, tenured faculty could normally hold their positions for an additional five years, which compounded the danger of an overly tenured and aging faculty. In anticipation of this change, Grinnell Executive Vice President Waldo Walker developed an early retirement program, which he first presented to the Board in May 1980.[213] Over the years, the plan has been updated, allowing tenured faculty to move to Senior Faculty Status as early as age sixty-two and, in any event, at age 70. Senior Faculty are paid 55 percent of their final salary, and with the other 45 percent of a full professor's salary, and the College can hire a replacement at a beginning assistant professor's salary. If a faculty member assumes Senior Faculty status, he or she agrees to retire at age 70. Why is such a commitment necessary? The legality of forcing retirement at age 70 is questionable, and since teaching is relatively "sedentary," it would be perfectly possible to continue teaching into one's eighties, which usually would not be a good thing either for the students or faculty.

As we have seen, Grinnell, along with many colleges and universities in the 1970s, opened its curriculum significantly by dropping all distribution requirements. Originally labeled a "no requirements curriculum," it now is called "individually advised." The point here is that this curriculum has endured; Brown University and Grinnell College are now the only two major collegiate institutions to have retained the radical departure of the 1970s well into the twenty-first century. Maintenance of the "Indiviually Advised Curriculum" did not go unchallenged; in 1982, Professor Morris Parslow was commissioned to lead a major effort to examine the curriculum with the option of suggesting major changes. In May 1984, Parslow suggested significant changes for a more tightly structured curriculum. Faced with this more structured curriculum, the faculty voted two to one against it. The majority were fundamentally satisfied that the vast bulk of students graduated with a well-balanced set of liberal arts courses, and in the process, the students had the benefit of being volunteers, not conscripts.[214] While the curriculum lacked structure, the advising system, on the other hand, is quite structured; it begins with the advising relationship with the First Year Tutorial professor. Student choices are heavily influenced by extensive faculty advice. These factors weighed heavily with the faculty as they voted on the Parslow proposal; it was in no way inconsequential that many of those voting had, in fact, been undergraduates in the 1960s and '70s who had clamored for the removal of requirements. They were, as we might say, true believers.[215]

In the mid 1980s, Grinnell faculty began to push hard for a reduction in the standard teaching load of three courses each semester. Leading liberal arts colleges, such as Bowdoin, Swarthmore, Carleton, and Oberlin, had made the change to a 3/2 load, in which faculty teach three courses in one semester and two in the other. The Grinnell faculty had grown more "professional," which is to say they expected to do significant research and writing while engaged in a demanding teaching schedule. Grinnell has always been a college in which teaching comes first, but as the quality of the faculty improved, more and more of those recruited to Grinnell thought of themselves not only as teachers but also as scholars intent on making significant contributions to their fields. To their credit, the Trustees recognized this shift and agreed with my recommendation in February 1987 that a 3/2 teaching load become the standard for Grinnell faculty. This change was instituted in the fall of 1988.[216] The Trustees were savvy enough to wonder when they would be faced with a request for a 2/2 load, but that has not so far occurred.

When I announced the Board's decision to the faculty, I speculated that the greatest impact of this change was more likely to be felt in the classroom than in the rate of faculty publication. To be sure, the latter has grown, but it also is clear that moving to a 3/2 load significantly enhanced teaching and learning. Faculty now had the time to introduce fresh elements to their courses in their two-course semesters and, in good conscience, could not therefore refrain from including them in their three-course semesters. In reality, the 3/2 load inspired the faculty to work even harder as teachers, which was not exactly the result most of them had in mind when they pushed for the reduced course load.[217]

The accumulation of important physical upgrades to the campus, significant increases in applications and concomitant greater selectivity, and, perhaps most important, improved faculty salaries and overall quality—all driven by vastly improved finances anchored to the growing endowment—produced a much stronger Grinnell College in the late twentieth and early twenty-first centuries. This was clearly evident in 1990 when African American student, David White, won a Rhodes Scholarship and Julia Janisch won an equally prestigious Marshall Scholarship. Three students, Janisch, Steven Pickle, and Jake Kosak, were awarded highly competitive Watson Fellowships, the most for any single year in College's history. This was also the year that 1970 graduate, Tom Cech, won the Nobel Prize in Chemistry—becoming Grinnell's first and, so far, only, Nobel Laureate. Also in 1990, Bob Noyce was awarded the Draper Prize in Engineering for his contributions to the betterment of the human condition through his invention of the integrated circuit on a silicon chip. All of these awards topped a previous bonanza in 1982, when Grinnell graduates were awarded two of the thirty total national Marshall Scholarships.

As Joe's work to grow the endowment began to have a significant impact on the College, another validation of the Grinnell experience in the 1980s was a National College Experience Study, conducted in 1988 and published in 1989. The study determined Grinnell was a college that provided excellent experiences to its students. Paradoxically, it concluded the good experience was, in part, because of the College's relatively remote location, which the study claimed stimulated the College to work extra hard to provide programs for its students. These programs were made possible by the College's strong financial resources, which allowed it to create an affordable environment. The College has a clear vision of itself, said the study, and its students' commitments to service and justice are a major element to the ethos of Grinnell. Student initiative is highly valued, and the small size of the residence halls (each housing around 50 students) encourages this initiative in an interactive community. The College Experience Study also found unusually high varsity athletic participation; varsity athletic programs involved 40 percent of the student body in a remarkably balanced approach to athletic competition. The study concludes "that highly selective colleges could learn much from Grinnell."[218]

Both Joe Rosenfield and Warren Buffett were concerned that the administration and faculty were not creative enough in their response to the endowment's dramatic increase. Their concern was well placed, as institutions too often don't "think outside the box"; they tend to seek more of the same if the "same" has been working. I plead guilty to this charge and thank Joe and Warren for their constant pressure to be more creative.[219]

Joe and Warren had a strategy that led to the creation of a Venture Fund in 1983 which called for the faculty to apply for institutional grants (funded by the endowment) to create "unique and unusual opportunities to benefit the College, which also should stand out as being Grinnellian."[220] In the Trustees' estimation, this initiative was only mildly successful. Nevertheless, they were encouraged enough to repeat the experiment in October 1998, setting aside $5.7 million from the endowment for a "Fund for Excellence." It invited faculty to seek grants for creative new projects.[221] One salient result of the Fund for Excellence was the Grinnell Corps, which funded recent graduates for a year of teaching or serving in one of six places: Nanjing, China; St. Rodrigue, Lesotho; the Desert Research Station in Namibia; Thailand; New Orleans; or Grinnell. Two years later, the Fund for Excellence ended, but the Trustees were satisfied that it had materially strengthened the College program.

The history of the Venture Fund and the Fund for Excellence illustrates a tension that was building between the Trustees and the faculty/administration over whether those charged with the work of the College lived up to the promise of Grinnell; the promise created by the successful Trustee effort to build the endowment. This conflict came to a head in 1993–1998, when the Trustees pushed the Chairman of the Faculty, Economics Professor Jack Mutti, and others to oblige the faculty to produce metrics that would demonstrate to the Trustees that the faculty and the academic work of the College were improving from year to year in order to justify annual salary increases. From the faculty perspective, they had been assigned an impossible task; teaching and learning cannot be accurately encapsulated in "metrics." Some of the Trustees regarded the faculty perspective as a lame excuse that covered both a lack of objectivity and the absence of sufficient effort. We don't know for sure what Joe's reaction to this initiative was, other than the fact that he played no visible role; he probably had something to do with the discouragement of the two newly appointed Trustees who led the "metrics" effort. They were, to a degree, his protégés. Both resigned after only five or six years on the Board, and it is not surprising that the easing of the pressure on the faculty coincided with their resignations.[222]

Strong financial underpinnings allowed the College to expand its curriculum. Though there was no language requirement at Grinnell, the foreign language departments were exceptionally strong. Even the classical languages, Greek and Latin, were robust, defying the downward trend in most colleges and universities. A one million dollar grant from the Cowles Foundation, following a seed grant of $100,000, established the Cowles-Kruidenier Chinese Studies Program in 1985. Chinese Language became a major and was strengthened by cooperation with Nanjing University in China, beginning in 1989. Japanese language studies were added in the 1990s.[223]

Grinnell College does not have an education major, though it does offer teacher certification. Because it was so difficult for a student to combine education courses, practice teaching with a major, and also consider off-campus study, which engages the majority of students, few Grinnellians could choose to enter public school teaching. This problem was alleviated by the creation of a ninth semester option, whereby practice teaching and some education courses were reserved for the semester after graduation. To make this option feasible, the College offers a forgivable loan for the ninth semester's tuition. If the student enters the teaching profession within three years of being certified, the College forgives the loan.[224] This option has significantly elevated the number of Grinnell students who enter a career in public school teaching, though the number still is small compared to what prevailed until the 1960s.

Though Joe and Warren remained skeptical about the faculty's and administration's ability to take full advantage of the opportunities afforded by increasing prosperity, there is no doubt that the academic program and the faculty who shaped it grew steadily in quality in the last two decades of the twentieth century. Nothing more loudly proclaimed this growth than the development of widespread undergraduate research—long a feature of the natural sciences. The Mentored Advanced Project Program (MAP) flourished in the 1990s and beyond, with strong institutional backing. Students in all of the academic disciplines did MAP's in the summer or during the academic year; teaching a MAP became a part of a faculty member's compensated teaching load. The 1990s also witnessed a significant increase in the number of interdisciplinary courses and interdisciplinary majors, such as Biochemistry, and interdisciplinary concentrations, such as Gender and Women's Studies, Neuroscience, Global Development Studies, Policy Studies, Technology Studies, and Environmental Studies.[225]

Grinnell celebrated its sesquicentennial in 1996. The College was the third collegiate institution founded in the Trans Mississippi West and the first to grant a degree. Joe was the Honorary Chair of the celebration, and Political Science Professor Wayne Moyer chaired the campus planning committee. The Sesquicentennial provided the focus for a $75,000,000 capital campaign, which was successfully completed in June 1999 upon reaching $86,300,000.[226] Major additions to the Fine Arts Building, now named the Bucksbaum Center for the Fine Arts, and the largest of the additions to the Noyce Science Center were the major accomplishments of the Sesquicentennial Campaign led by Pamela Ferguson.

Compared to the late 1960s and all of the 1970s, which were the most profound years of student revolution and tumult thus far, Grinnell students seem mostly absent from the College's story of the 1980s and 1990s. Though not as aggressive as they were at the height of the revolution, students nevertheless acted decisively to influence and even shape college policy in the 1980s. The students were in no way silent and complacent after the 1970s. I remember my introduction to the president's office in August 1979 featured information about a "red phone" that I could use to reach the outside world should students occupy the building and cut the phone lines.

There is one somewhat unique example of Joe being on the "wrong side" of a major Trustee decision in the 1980s: after ten years of refusal, the Trustees finally began to divest stocks in corporations doing business in South Africa. The South African apartheid regime had become the pariah of the world. Whereas colonial independence and racial justice was the overwhelming trend after World War II, South Africa lurched in the opposite direction with the victory of the National Party in the 1948 election. As the apartheid government became increasingly ruthless—with the Sharpeville massacre of 1960 and, especially, the Soweto riots and deaths of 1976 and beyond—world opinion turned dramatically against South Africa. It was Soweto in particular that projected anti-apartheid efforts onto the world stage and demanded the attention of Grinnell College. Stringent international sanctions in sports, travel, and business isolated South Africa, and a salient way an institution such as Grinnell could participate in these sanctions was through divesting South African tainted stocks from its portfolio and adding boycotts against the products of the divested corporations. From 1976 until the release of Nelson Mandela from prison in February 1990, South African divestment was the major student issue at Grinnell. As college issues go, it had an exceptionally long shelf-life.[227]

Joe consistently opposed "ethical" divestment from the portfolio he had so lovingly built. He would say:

South Africa today, nuclear energy, cigarettes, and liquor tomorrow. There is no end to ethical divestment.

It is our business as trustees to maximize the endowment, not to create arbitrary limits.

Besides, how do you determine what is ethical? Corporations do many things and often ethics is in the eye of the beholder. What should we do about mutual funds?[228]

Joe's opposition, and that of many of the Trustees, was gradually overwhelmed by constant and effective student pressure, especially after conditions spiraled out of control in South Africa in 1986 creating a state of emergency as the government suspended most civil liberties in that tragic country.

The Trustee Minutes from the late 1970s to 1990 chronicle mounting student pressure year-by-year and, often, meeting-by-meeting. In September 1979, the Trustees created an Investor Responsibility Committee largely to deal with South Africa.[229] In October 1981, that committee identified 18 corporations doing business in South Africa, suggesting it might be possible to do selective divestment.[230] In May 1982, a large number of students who had been demonstrating outside invaded the Board meeting and demanded that Grinnell subscribe to the principles developed in 1977 by Rev. Leon Sullivan of Philadelphia. These principles provided information about what corporations were doing in South Africa, along with recommendations for divestment. The students further demanded that the College cease all activities that supported apartheid and that student members be placed as voters on the Trustee Investor Responsibility Committee. The students asked for a response at the next Trustee meeting, and the Trustees agreed.[231]

At the next meeting in November 1982, the Trustees compromised by agreeing the Investor Responsibility Committee would meet with students at each meeting, but it did not place students on the committee as they had demanded in May. The Board also agreed that the students could vote on the College's shares at stockholder meetings.[232] It was in this period also that the Trustees had an entirely admirable and intelligent response to conditions in South Africa: "We're not very good at divestment; we're good at education. Let's educate black South Africans at our expense."[233] There was already a program sponsored by Harvard

University to bring black South African students to US colleges. Grinnell received more of these students than any US college or university—in many years accepting four—and by the late '80s, there was a steady presence of twelve or more graduation-bound, black South African students at Grinnell. They were initially fearful of retribution if they became involved in the student anti-apartheid movement. They soon learned, however, that there would be no retribution, so they quite naturally became leaders of the student efforts, which considerably raised the temperature of the movement. I remember a Trustee meeting in the mid 1980s when, after deciding once again not to divest, the Trustees said, "George, go outside and tell them that we are not divesting." I was met by tears of anguish from the South African students in the crowd gathered outside.

Allowing students to vote the College's stocks and even travel to stockholder meetings soon paled as students realized how difficult it was to get to the meetings while, in any case, seeing their proxies ignored.[234] They felt that the Board had given them a hollow victory in order to avoid the real issue of divestment. Under renewed and unrelenting student pressure for divestment, the Board voted in May 1985 to consider selective divestment. It took ten years, but the students had finally broken through Board defenses. A committee of five (three Trustees and two students) was established to consider divestment recommendations, using the Sullivan Principles as a guideline. The Board resolution contained one important caveat: divestment must not have "undue effect on the portfolio."[235] It was further resolved that the College would not purchase goods from a divested business. In the end, the Board was most comfortable with the last clause of its resolution, which called for increasing the number of South African scholarships from two to four annually.

A year later, with the impact of the recent State of Emergency in South Africa on their minds, the Trustees engaged in a protracted debate about divestment. Some Trustees had visited South Africa and argued that sanctions on one hand hurt blacks most of all and on the other that even though they would suffer more than the whites, blacks wanted sanctions as the only effective way to bring the apartheid regime to its knees. Some Trustees said that divestment was a clumsy weapon, and, after all, Grinnell was much more effective as the national leader in educating black South Africans. In fact, the Trustees had added a fifth scholarship funded by Grinnell at Marshalltown Community College.[236]

This discussion was stimulated by a recommendation from the Students to End Apartheid that shares in Exxon, Ford, PNC Financial, US Steel, and IBM be divested. The Board preliminarily voted only to divest Ford. But as the question of the boycott of Ford vehicles was confronted, the Trustees backed off because their divestment would hurt the local Ford dealership. Finally, the Board decided to review the divestment policy at the fall 1986 meeting, including a previous decision to divest MGM/United Artists. John Price, who chaired the committee of Trustees and students making divestment recommendations, was instructed to inform the students that divestment of Ford was a possibility but that students should know that an increasing number of Trustees were changing their minds about divestment.[237] Joe's concerns, along with those of several of his colleagues, were beginning to sway the Board.

At the fall 1986 meeting, the Board made no decisions regarding divestment. Rather, new procedures were set in place to structure and slow the process. Decisions should be made only at the May meeting, and recommendations should be sent to the Trustee Investor Responsibility Committee at least eight weeks before the full Board met. Also, the College president and the Board Finance Committee should review all recommendations to determine if they would have an adverse effect on the College. It was also noted that the Alumni Association had recommended a policy of selective divestment.[238]

Following these new guidelines, the Board voted to divest Tenneco, Chevron, and Texaco at its May 1987 meeting.[239] Unsatisfied with these moves, the Students to End Apartheid presented a twenty-four-page proposal at the May 1988 Trustee Meeting. Their proposal called for much more aggressive divestment and repudiated the Sullivan Principles, deeming them too conservative; they suggested that a new set of guidelines by the more radical Investor Responsibility Research Center be adopted. The Board quite naturally said it could not give a response to this document at that meeting; they would address it at their October meeting. They also agreed to examine the suggested new guidelines.[240]

A group of Trustees and students met in Des Moines before the October meeting with nothing resolved, particularly regarding the student recommendation that there be total divestment over the next five years.[241]

In the end, the conflict between the students and the Trustees was resolved by dramatic events in South Africa. It is no exaggeration to say that the entire world was stunned by the release of Nelson Mandela in February 1990 at the hands of the newly organized apartheid government under the presidency of F.W. De Klerk. Discussions about South Africa continued at Grinnell, but all passion was drained from them. Finally, on the eve of the April 1994 democratic elections in South Africa, the Students to End Apartheid disbanded.[242]

Focus on the controversy over South African investments is an important element in the story of the 1980s because it was *the* student issue of the decade and because it is unique as the lone significant issue where Joe's influence was not decisive. The Board knew Joe opposed divestment, but constant student pressure and events in South Africa weighed more heavily than Joe's influence, and Joe accepted this with good grace.[243]

Much more could be written about student life in the 1980s and 1990s, but South African divestment surpassed all other student concerns. It was the aspect of student life that most involved Joe directly.

A few other events that merit mention were: the shift in the student drinking age from 19 to 21, the growing percentages of international students and students of color, curbing the debt of graduates, and increasing recognition of gay rights.

The most successful alcohol rules and practices at Grinnell, in my opinion, occurred during the relatively brief time when the legal drinking age was 19. Under this law, most students, except freshmen, were of legal age. As a result, the College created a campus pub at which drinking was an entirely comfortable social experience with little excess. Joe was the Trustee who moved support of the administration's recommendation for a campus pub. Faculty and students frequently met in the campus pub over a beer on Friday afternoons. But all of that changed in 1986 with a federal mandate that any state that did not raise the drinking age to 21 would lose its highway appropriations. The result was a national shift to the elevated drinking age, which was followed by a reversion to a "publess" campus at Grinnell and the spread of illicit drinking. Monitors at official campus parties still attempt to confine drinking to the few students who have turned 21. The new rule stimulated, rather than diminishing, unhealthy alcohol consumption—an issue that has continued in the present.[244]

In the 1980s, Grinnell made a concerted effort to attract more international students, resulting in a steady increase throughout the decade that reached ten percent of the student body by 1989.[245] This growth continued through the 1990s and into the twenty-first century, reaching a striking 20 percent in 2016. International students add richness to the classroom and exciting variety to campus life; their presence helps open the eyes of US students to the world they inhabit. The strenuous efforts to enroll students of color began to pay dividends in the 1980s, reaching 16 percent in 1990.[246] That growth also continued in the 1990s and the twenty-first century, reaching 25 percent of all Grinnell students in 2016. Grinnell College now looks much more like the nation at large.[247] The College was also successful in achieving its essential goal to curb student debt, which was made possibly only by Grinnell's growing endowment.

It is tempting to dwell on the next college issue because it was such a challenging part of my penultimate presidential year. It involved a freshman student who wanted to marry her non-student lesbian lover and be allowed under college policy to move out of the dormitories as a married student. Marriage was just about the only way a student would be permitted to live outside of college residences in his or her first two years. This policy was part of Grinnell's efforts to build strong campus communities through the residential system. Had this request been granted, Dean of Students Tom Crady and his staff feared a deluge of requests from heterosexual students who also would want to be permitted to live together off campus in their first two years, claiming "they were just as married as those lesbians." The College catalog stated that the College did not discriminate according to gender or "affectional" preference, which meant if the College continued the practice of allowing married heterosexual students to live off campus in their first two years, it should extend the same privilege to married gay and lesbian couples. If it did allow students to do so, not only would it be faced with the aforementioned heterosexual requests, it would have been the first institution in the State of Iowa to recognize a lesbian marriage.

The administration decided to withdraw the marriage privilege of heterosexual students in order to be even-handed in its decision not to allow the freshman who made the request to move off campus as a married student, even though the College chaplain, Dennis Haas, had performed a marriage ceremony for the couple. The campus erupted in demonstrations, which were well covered by Des Moines newspapers and television stations; the demonstrations led to rumors that Grinnell had a majority of homosexual students. Ever inventive, the students tied up the calendars of the Provost, Deans, and President with meetings over the issue and staged "same sex kiss-ins" when the President and Provost addressed assembled prospective students and parents. Students festooned their 1989 commencement gowns with pink triangles in solidarity with gay and lesbian students.[248]

Though challenging at the time, I look back on this event with admiration for Grinnell students and their manifest support for their gay and lesbian brothers and sisters. It was a time of sensitive and growing awareness of gay rights, with the campus joining hands to express solidarity as human beings.

Until his death on June 7, 2000, Joe Rosenfield was the heart of the Grinnell College Board of Trustees. From 1997 on, Joe was wheelchair bound and unable to attend Board meetings. However, as his "godson," Fred Little, said, "Joe ran Grinnell from his apartment on Grand Avenue."[249] This assertion is all the more striking as one looks at the roster of luminaries who made up the late-twentieth-century Grinnell College Board of Trustees. At least two of the Trustees are now regarded as American icons: Warren

Buffett and Steve Jobs. Bob Noyce runs them a close second in fame and importance, not to mention Howard Bowen, who was widely regarded as one of the most important educators in the country. Bob Burnett, who chaired the Grinnell Board for six years in the 1980s, was the CEO of Meredith Corporation, and Joe's classmate, John Norris, was a long time CEO of Lennox Furnace. Don Stewart '59 was a past president of Spelman College and then President of the College Board, administrators of the SAT examination. Katherine Mohrman '67 became President of Colorado College and John Price '60 was a major figure in the Nixon White House. Somewhat less famous Trustees were equally strong and effective: business consultant Jim Lowry '61; Time Magazine Group Vice President Charles Bear '39; Chicago Tribune lawyer Dennis Homerin '65; bank CEO John Chrystal; conglomerate business owner Alf Johnson '53; Business rehabilitator and Stanford Law Professor, Bill Lazier '53; Lennox Vice President, Dick Booth '54; investor Gardiner Dutton '53; lawyer Elizabeth Kruidenier; business executive Fred Maytag; construction CEO Ted Lovejoy '28; and lawyer Fred Little '54. As President of the College, I usually felt as though I was run over by a steamroller at every Board meeting; I was often left with multiple items to attend to, many that had not been part of the agenda. Board meetings with this group sparkled with creativity and spontaneity. If a president desired a predictable and controllable Board, he or she should not have been at Grinnell in these yeasty years. This Board would not be contained by rules or consistent obedience to procedure, and it all worked brilliantly because of Joe Rosenfield. *Everyone* knew Joe always put Grinnell College's interests above his own and that he devoted full measure to the College. Joe was, moreover, strikingly effective in advancing Grinnell's interests, and he understood the College so instinctively that trust in and devotion to Joe was universal. My anticipation when I joined the Board of Trustees in 1970, when I would finally meet and work with the legendary Joe Rosenfield, was fully rewarded as I watched Joe subtly guide his colleagues with brilliantly timed comments, stunning investment results, abiding concern for his colleagues and their judgment, a firm grasp of college goals and culture, and love for students—all leavened by his unique, Rosenfield humor.

Recognition of Joe's extraordinary Trusteeship was not confined to Grinnell. He was recognized with the Distinguished Service Award in Trusteeship by the Association of Governing Boards, the preeminent Trusteeship professional organization, at their annual meeting in March 1988 in Washington DC. A delegation of Trustees traveled to DC to hear Joe lauded "for his exemplary initiatives with respect to the college endowment and for his dedication to the liberal arts ...[His] efforts have shaped Grinnell into the first-rate institution it is today."[250] His colleagues would have added, "No trustee in America has done more for his or her college than Joe Rosenfield has done for Grinnell." Joe's response was typically self-deprecating and humorous; he counseled that his job now "was to keep George Drake and his bandits from raiding the endowment."[251]

Joe had done so much and his presence loomed so large that a crisis was imminent as his declining health and age signaled the impending end of the more than half-century Rosenfield era. How was the Board to adjust to Joe's absence? That problem particularly engaged Board Chair Bill Lazier in the 1990s. Bill was a planner and an advanced thinker, which his profession of rescuing failed business amply demonstrated. The solution gradually adopted in the 1990s and accelerated in the twenty-first century following Joe's death was to regularize procedure and accept a new degree of disciplined decision making. As the new century advanced, analysis and decisions came to rely increasing on what we today call "metrics," which is to say that the Board has become reliant on extensive research and data to shape its decisions. The Grinnell Board has come to look a lot more like most good college boards after decades of being an outlier under the aegis of Joe Rosenfield.

The last manifestation of Joe in the Board Minutes is in May 2002, when his final bequest to Grinnell was announced to his erstwhile colleagues. As of May 10, 2002, his will left the College $30,323,952: "Having declined in the past, Joe consented one week before he passed away to have a facility named in his honor; NOW, THEREFORE, BE IT RESOLVED BY THE TRUSTEES OF GRINNELL COLLEGE: 1. The Trustees of Grinnell College direct the appropriate College officers to allocate not less that $25 million of Joe's bequest, trusts and term endowments ('suspense funds') to the new Campus Center, sited at the heart of Grinnell College and bearing Joe's name." This was to be the "Joe Rosenfield Center." It was dedicated in 2006 and cost considerably more than the $25 million provided by Joe's estate.[252]

We owe a profound thanks to Joe—as well as to President Russell Osgood who persuaded him—who finally allowed his name to be attached to a major campus building. It would have been a tragedy beyond bearing had Joe's name gradually disappeared from the collective campus conscience. Joe Rosenfield and Grinnell College were and are truly synonymous.

EPILOGUE & OBITUARY

EPILOGUE

When Joe Rosenfield died in 2000, Grinnell's endowment had reached an extraordinary $862,487,000. Following the Rosenfield/Buffett investment philosophy and riding bull markets early in the new century, it reached c.$1,800,000 billion in the summer of 2016. Some may ask, has Grinnell College made appropriate use of its good fortune? Warren Buffett posed that question at his famous annual Berkshire Hathaway stockholders' meeting in Omaha in April 2016. Warren had not been involved with Grinnell since Joe's death, and he had not even met President Raynard Kington, who became Grinnell's President in 2010. At the stockholders meeting, which, as usual, lasted about five hours, Warren happened to mention that he had become a Trustee "of a small college" in 1968 when the endowment was about $10,000,000. Without dwelling on his role, he said the endowment had grown to well over a billion dollars, and he wondered what the College had accomplished with its good fortune. He also wondered if enrollment had increased. He raised these questions amid a discussion of the increasing costs of higher education and the national dialogue about value versus cost.

Warren underestimated the degree of interest the press would have in this offhand statement, and he did not believe that the College would be identified. But, as almost anything Buffett says publicly becomes national news, within a few days Bloomberg News had contacted the Grinnell Communications Department for a reaction. In response, President Kington wrote a letter to Warren Buffett that alluded to Grinnell's accomplishments with the endowment and asked if he and I (President Emeritus Drake) could meet with him. Ever generous and fair, Warren agreed to a meeting, which took place in

May 2016. President Kington provided a detailed analysis of what the endowment Joe and Warren built means to Grinnell today. The data clearly impressed Warren, leaving him much more satisfied that his work for Grinnell had led to significant improvements in the College he had first joined as a Trustee in 1968.

The highlights of President Kington's presentation illuminate what the endowment has meant to the Grinnell in the present. Warren wondered at the Berkshire Hathaway meeting whether the College's enrollment had increased over the 1150 it was when he joined the Board; Grinnell had, in fact, grown to 1665 students in 2016, a 69 percent increase. This growth would not have been possible without the significant enhancement of program and facilities provided by the endowment. Equally important, the overall quality of students had improved significantly.

Of particular interest to Warren were the statistics about access and student debt. Grinnell College is one of only forty higher education institutions nationwide that has a need-blind admission policy. This means students are admitted without regard to need, and once admitted, their costs in excess of what the family can provide are covered by the College through scholarships and loans. Grinnell is 39th among these 40 institutions in its percentage of "full-pay" students. Its need-blind policy is close to being the most generous of any US college or university. In the 2015–2016 academic year, 24 percent of Grinnell's students were Pell Grant eligible, meaning they and their families could provide almost none of the cost of their education; in fact, 28 percent of the student body received financial aid that covered 100 percent of tuition. Grinnell compares itself to sixteen highly selective colleges: Amherst, Bowdoin, Carleton, Colorado College, Davidson, Kenyon, Macalester, Oberlin, Pomona, Reed, Smith, St. Olaf, Swarthmore, Vassar, Washington & Lee, and Williams. Among this "who's who" of the nation's best liberal arts colleges, Grinnell receives the least in tuition payments. Tuition payments amounted to a total of $25,500,000 million at Grinnell in 2014; in contrast, the median total of tuition received by this group of colleges was $46,600,000 million, a $16,300,000 million gap. In fact, at Grinnell, endowment income covered 54.1 percent of expenses in the 2014 fiscal year, and that percentage has been climbing.

Furthermore, Grinnell's students leave with unusually low debt because financial aid packages are high on grants and low on loans. Grinnell students graduate with the least debt of any of the graduates of Iowa colleges and universities and one of the lowest debts in the US. The average student debt for the class of 2014 was $15,982, whereas the composite average debt of Iowa College and University graduates was nearly twice as much, at $29,730. All of these impressive statistics are the result of the endowment Joe and Warren built.

Grinnell College's exceptional financial aid has been a "gate-opener," making it one of the most accessible colleges in America. The *US News and World Report's* 2016 ranking of colleges and universities listed Grinnell along with Amherst and Vassar as the most economically diverse of the top 25 highly selective colleges. Grinnell ranked ninth of the top 25 highly selective colleges in its percentage of domestic students of color at 22 percent of the student body—a definite accomplishment for a school in the middle of the Iowa cornfields. Grinnell led all the other Midwestern colleges, including Oberlin, Kenyon, Carleton, Macalester, and St. Olaf. Moreover, being exceptionally economically diverse has not appreciably affected graduation rates: 86 percent of the top income quartile have graduated by age 24, while 84 percent of the lowest income quartile have graduated by age 24—a difference of only 2 percentage points. This minimal difference is unusual. National statistics show the average gap between graduation rates of the top and lowest income quartiles is almost 40 percentage points. A further indicator of the parity of opportunity and accomplishment at Grinnell is that 55.28 percent of Pell Grant students take advantage of the coveted opportunity to study abroad, while 55.47 percent of the non-Pell Grant students take this opportunity. Clearly, the opportunity for Grinnell students to study abroad does not depend on family wealth.[1]

The "moral" of the story illustrated by this cascade of statistics is that Grinnell's endowment, and the use made of it, has created an institution of exceptional quality that is the most accessible of all of its peer institutions. At the conclusion of Kington's and my meeting with him, Warren Buffett advised that the College's was an impressive story that should be told more broadly. This epilogue is one attempt to do so. But more importantly, this epilogue is a seal on the extraordinary contributions of Joe Rosenfield with Warren Buffett's help not only for Grinnell but for higher education more generally. Because of what Joe did, and the spirit in which he did it, Grinnell College demonstrates that quality and access can go hand-in-hand.

OBITUARY

Joe Rosenfield's obituary appeared in the *Des Monies Register* on June 8, 2000. I quote it in full:

Memorial services for Joseph Rosenfield, 96, a Des Moines businessman and philanthropist, who died of heart failure Wednesday at Iowa Methodist Medical Center, will be held at a later date at Grinnell. The body was cremated and burial of the cremains will be at Woodland Cemetery in Des Moines.

Mr. Rosenfield was born in Des Moines and had lived here most of his life. He was a trustee of Grinnell College from 1941 until his death and served as director of companies including Younkers, Equitable Life Insurance Co., Bankers Trust Co., Northern Natural Gas Co. and Northwestern Bell Telephone Co. He was a board member of Iowa Methodist Medical Center, Living History Farms, Des Moines United Way and Natural Heritage Foundation, and a member of Temple B'nai Jeshurun.

A sister, Louise Noun of Des Moines survives.

Memorial contributions may be made to Grinnell College, Planned Parenthood of Iowa or Chrysalis Foundation.

It is no longer than the other obituaries that appeared on that day. There was nothing special in the notice about his passing. There would be only one memorial service held for him later that summer at Grinnell College. Joe died on June 7, 2000 of congestive heart failure. The simple obituary does little to expound Joe's extraordinary stature in Des Moines and central Iowa.

Apart from the catalog of some of Joe's boards, the most arresting fact in this obituary is Joe's longevity. Just as he had lived it, Joe left this life without fanfare.

Joe's last years were difficult. What Louise Noun observed of her brother's decline was a major reason why she decided to take her life when her own declining health became unsupportable. Pat Gessman, who frequently came to Joe's apartment to help with his affairs, particularly to write his checks, said that though Joe was in severe physical decline, his mind was sharp, as was his sense of humor. Joe would tell her that Bankers Trust was the only one that would know his signature because of his weak hand.[2] Jill June blamed the acceleration of Joe's decline on a recent knee surgery. In her opinion, "the doctors should have left him alone." His weight declined so noticeably after his surgery that "his suits fit him more loosely than before."[3] Of course, most who reach Joe's exalted age show severe signs of decline. But regardless of his frailty, Joe had enriched those years as few before or after him.

I have collected testimonials from a wide variety of those who knew Joe. They well remind us of the richness of the man who left us in June of 2000:

> First of all, from Joe himself (as reported by former Meredith CEO and fellow Grinnell Trustee Bob Burnett): Bob asked Joe the secret of his business success and Joe responded: *"Make sure the other guy gets a better deal than you do."*[4]
>
> Billionaire investor, Warren Buffett: *"My feelings for Joe come pretty close to worship . . . My Dad was number one in my life, but if I were to adopt another father, I would adopt Joe and my kids would adopt him as a grandfather." "Joe was a someone who made everyone around them a better person."*[5]
>
> Des Moines business and civic leader, Bill Knapp: *"[Joe was] probably respected more than anyone else I've ever known in Des Moines."*[6]

Retired Planned Parenthood CEO, Jill June: *"Joe walked the talk."*[7]

Des Moines business leader and Grinnell Trustee Connie Wimer: *"I have never known anyone say a bad word about Joe Rosenfield and that's kind of unusual."*[8]

Des Moines businessman and civic leader Dick Leavitt: *"Joe was a towering human being . . . [but] if there was an ego, I never saw it."*[9]

General Growth executive, Stanley Richards: *"He was just such a pure gentleman and such an honest individual that nobody ever questioned his motives."* And again, *"His record toward human rights could not have been stronger."*[10]

Des Moines businessman and sponsor of this biography, Jim Cownie: *"I always wanted to spend more time with him and learn from him. I just loved every minute I could be around the guy . . . So, when he died, I just felt [this biography] was unfinished business."*[11]

Joe's "godson," lawyer, and fellow Grinnell Trustee, Fred Little: *"He was drop-dead honest . . . Most people would go out of their way to facilitate the continuance of their name. Joe used to go out of his way just the opposite."*[12]

Former Grinnell College Vice-President for Development, Tom Marshall: *"He was not someone who was dominant because of his leadership; he was dominant because he was Joe Rosenfield."*[13]

Des Moines Register feature writer, Wendell Cochran, speaking to his editor, Michael Gartner, about one of his frustrations in researching a profile of Joe: *"I couldn't get anyone who had anything negative to say about Joe Rosenfield."*[14]

Des Moines business leader, Fred Hubbell: *"All people that knew him respected him."*[15]

Former Younkers CEO, Bill Friedman: *"Joe was accessible. He would meet with almost anyone who wanted to talk to him."*[16]

Former democratic United States Senator, John Culver: *"Wisdom was Joe's hallmark."*[17]

I will claim special privilege as the author to end with my statement on a videotaped tribute to Joe; which, of course reveals that I had a distinct bias when I undertook this project.

George Drake: "Joe was one of the great human beings to walk this earth and that greatness was manifested in a lot of ways; and maybe the core . . . was a set of ethical values. I mean [he was] an absolutely straight person, an honest person and a sincere person."

APPENDIX I JOE ROSENFIELD'S BOARDS

Unsurprisingly for a man of his prominence and talents, Joe served on a large number of governing board and agency leadership positions.

BOARDS:

1. Younkers
2. Grinnell College
3. General Growth
4. Equitable Life
5. Bankers Trust
6. Northern Natural Gas
7. Northwestern Bell Telephone
8. Iowa Power and Light
9. National By-Products
10. Iowa Methodist Hospital
11. Hospital Services of Iowa *(Founder)*
12. Blue Cross Hospital Services
13. Living History Farms
14. Munsingwear
15. Wilkie House
16. University of Iowa Law School Foundation
17. The Des Moines Jewish Federation
18. Executive Committee of the Des Moines Chamber of Commerce

AGENCIES:

1. Des Moines Enterprises President *(subset of the Chamber of Commerce focused on bringing professional baseball to Des Moines).*
2. Governor's Economic Growth Council of Iowa
3. The Greater Des Moines Committee *(Economic Development)*
4. Chair of several Des Moines United Campaigns

A NOTE ON SOURCES

This book is based on a variety of sources. The Frankel Legacy section relies heavily on *Journey to Autonomy*, the autobiography of Joe's sister, Louise Noun. The Rosenfield and Frankel Papers at the Jewish Historical Society of the Des Moines Jewish Federation were also indispensable to that section, supplemented by several interviews. The "Des Moines Catalyst" chapter was drawn primarily from interviews, supplemented by material from biographies of Des Moines business leaders. The Younker archives at the Iowa Historical Society of Des Moines are the spine of the "Younkers" section; and the section on Joe Rosenfield's education and fifty-nine year Trusteeship at Grinnell rest mainly of the archives at Burling Library, Grinnell College, supplemented by interviews and the author's memory.

BOOKS

Burns, James MacGregor. *Roosevelt: Soldier of Freedom 1940–1944*. New York: Open Road, Kindle.

Friedricks, William B. *The Real Deal: The Life of Bill Knapp*. Des Moines: Business Publications Corporation Inc., 2013.

Friedrichs, William B. *In For the Long Haul: The Life of John Ruan*. Iowa City: The University of Iowa Press, 2003.

Ingram, Vicki. *Younkers: The Friendly Store*. Charleston SC: The History Press, 2016.

Noun, Louise. *Journey to Autonomy: A Memoir*. Ames, IA: Iowa State University Press, 1990.

Wall, Bea. This information is drawn from the manuscript of a continuation of Joseph Wall's history of Grinnell College in the Nineteenth Century by his widow, Bea. Bea's manuscript is being edited by Terry Bissen. The particular reference is on page 107 of the manuscript.

NEWSPAPERS

The Des Moines Register
The Des Moines Tribune
The Cedar Rapids Gazette

ARCHIVAL COLLECTIONS

Grinnell College Archives, Burling Library. Board of Trustees Minutes.

Grinnell College Archives, Burling Library. Board of Trustees, Executive Committee Minutes.

Grinnell College Archives, Burling Library. *The Cyclone*.

Grinnell College Archives, Burling Library. *The Malteaser*.

Grinnell College Archives, Burling Library. *The Bulletin* (College Catalog).

Grinnell College Archives, Burling Library. "Class Letters for the Class of 1925."

Grinnell College Archives, Burling Library. Grant Gale Papers.

Grinnell College Archives, Burling Library. Joseph Rosenfield Papers.

Iowa Jewish Historical Archives, Waukee Iowa. The Rosenfield and Frankel Papers and a December 30, 1998 Interview with Joseph Rosenfield for the Des Moines History Project.

State Historical Society of Iowa, Des Moines. Younkers Inc. Archives.

I am indebted to former Grinnell College Chemistry Professor, Gene Wubbels for providing me with a 1950s NSF study, "Research and Teaching in the Liberal Arts Colleges." This study details the postwar construction of science facilities in leading liberal arts colleges, including costs per square foot.

INTERVIEWS AND CORRESPONDENCE WITH AUTHOR; AND VIDEO INTERVIEWS WITH AND ABOUT JOE ROSENFIELD.

Batesol, Jon. Interview by author, Des Moines, Iowa, 23 May 2014.

Buck, David. Video-taped "Tribute" to the life of Joe Rosenfield prepared following his death featuring interviews with Joe and several who knew him, 2000.

Bucksbaum, John. Interview by author, Chicago, Illinois, 3 December 2014.

Bucksbaum, Kay. Interview by author, Chicago, Illinois, 3 December 2014.

Buffett, Warren. Interview by author, Omaha, Nebraska, 5 June, 2014.

Burnett, Robert. Interview by author, West Des Moines, Iowa, 8 October, 2014.

Clay, David. Interview by author, Grinnell, Iowa, 20 November, 2014.

Cownie, James. Interview with author, Des Moines, Iowa, 8 October, 2014.

Cownie, James. Telephone conversation with author, 9 March, 2018.

Culver, John. Telephone conversation with author, 7 June, 2017.

Friedman, William. Interview by author, Des Moines, Iowa, 23 May, 2014.

Gartner, Michael. Interview by author, Des Moines, Iowa, 11 November, 2014.

Gessman, Pat. Interview by author, Chicago, Illinois, 3 December, 2014.

Green, Christopher. Interview by author, Des Moines, Iowa, 19 November, 2014.

Harkin, Thomas. Telephone conversation with author, 9 October, 2017.

Henderson, Stacy. Interview by author, Marble, Colorado, 28 July, 2014.

Hoak, James. Interview by author, Dallas, Texas, 17 March, 2016.

Hubbell, Fred. Interview with author, Des Moines, Iowa, 8 October, 2014.

June, Jill. Interview by author, Ankeny, Iowa, 17 December, 2014.

Knapp, William. Interview by author, West Des Moines, Iowa, 4 February, 2014.

Leavitt, Richard, Interview by author, West Des Moines, Iowa, 23 May, 2014.

Little, Fred. Interview by author, San Francisco, California, 17–18 March, 2016.

Marshall, Thomas. Interview by author, Grinnell, Iowa, 8 January, 2015.

Miller, Thomas. Interview by author, Des Moines, Iowa, 2 May, 2016.

Musser, Robert. Interview by author, Grinnell, Iowa, 9 October 2014.

Richards, Stanley. Interview by author, Des Moines, Iowa, 10 June, 2014.

Rosenfield, Joseph. Videotaped interview by the author and Professor Joseph Wall, Grinnell, Iowa, 26 November, 1990.

Rosenfield, Joseph. Videotaped interview conducted by Fred Little and Angela Voos, Des Moines, Iowa, 14 May, 1998.

Steinger, Elaine. Telephone conversation with author, 20 January, 2017.

Walker, Waldo. Interview by the author, Grinnell, Iowa, 5 June, 2014.

Wimer, Connie. Interview by author, Des Moines, Iowa, 10 June, 2014.

I am indebted to Grinnell College Emeritus History Professor, Daniel Kaiser, who found this letter in the Smithsonian Institution Archives, Washington, DC.

GRINNELL COLLEGE TRUSTEE MINUTES

Grinnell College Archives, Burling Library. Board of Trustees Minutes, November 29, 1941.

Board of Trustees Minutes, May 29, 1942.

Board of Trustee Minutes, December 12, 1942.

Board of Trustees Minutes. May 21, 1943.

Board of Trustee Minutes, January 8, 1944.

Grinnell College Archives, Burling Library. Board of Trustees Executive Committee Minutes, February 10, 1944.

Executive Committee Minutes, April 1, 1944.

Board of Trustee Minutes, May 26, 1945.

Executive Committee Minutes, June 16, 1945.

Executive Council Minutes, April 24, 1947.

Board of Trustees Minutes, December 12, 1947.

Board of Trustees Minutes, June 4, 1948.

Board of Trustee Minutes, June 2, 1949.

Board of Trustees Minutes, October 29, 1949.

Board of Trustees Minutes, June 5, 1950.

Board of Trustees Minutes, October 28, 1950.

Board of Trustees Minutes, June 4, 1951.

Board of Trustees Minutes, November 3, 1951.

Executive Committee Minutes, April 22, 1952.

Executive Committee Minutes, May 27, 1952.

Board of Trustee Minutes, June 9, 1952.

Executive Committee Minutes, October 15, 1952.

Board of Trustee Minutes, November 11, 1952.

Board of Trustees Minutes, May 21, 1953.

Board of Trustees Minutes, June 8, 1953.

Executive Committee Minutes. August 5, 1953.

Board of Trustees Minutes, January 29, 1954.

Board of Trustees Minutes, June 7, 1954.

THE AUTHOR AS A SOURCE

From 1970 until 1991, I, the author, interacted with Joe Rosenfield in the context of Grinnell College while I served as a Trustee from 1970 until 1979 and as President of the College from 1979 to 1991. Joe was a Trustee and friend throughout those years.

NOTES

INTRODUCTION:
[1] Recollections of then President Glenn Leggett, and trustee and Joe Rosenfield's friend, Kay Bucksbaum. Captured on a video tribute, "Joe Rosenfield '25," produced by David Buck, 2000.

PART I:
JOE ROSENFIELD AT GRINNELL: 1921-1925
[1] Grinnell College Archives, Burling Library. *The Scarlet and Black*, May 24, 1924.
[2] *Scarlet and Black, February 28, 1923.*
[3] Interview with Kay Bucksbaum, December 2, 2014.
[4] Grinnell College Archives, Burling Library. The Bulletin.
[5] The Bulletin.
[6] Grinnell College Archives, Burling Library. The Cyclone.
[7] Interview with Bob Musser, October 9, 2014.

JOE'S COLLEGE DAYS
[8] The Bulletin.
[9] Grinnell College Archives, Burling Library. Trustee Minutes, 1951-1952.
[10] The Bulletin.
[1] The author's recollection.
[2] Scarlet and Black, March 21, 1923.
[3] Scarlet and Black, 1921-1925.
[4] Scarlet and Black, October 11, 1922.
[5] Scarlet and Black, 1921-1925.
[6] Scarlet and Black, November 1, 1924.
[7] Bea Wall and Terry Bissen, Manuscript of a forthcoming history of

GRINNELL COLLEGE IN THE TWENTIETH CENTURY.
[8] Scarlet and Black, May 3, 1924.
[9] Scarlet and Black, September 27, 1924.
[20] Scarlet and Black, 1921-1922.
[21] Scarlet and Black, April 4, 1925.
[22] Scarlet and Black, October 10, 1922.
[23] Scarlet and Black, October 25, 1922/Scarlet and Black, 1922-1924.
[24] Scarlet and Black, April 9, 1924.
[25] Scarlet and Black, March 28, 1925.
[26] Scarlet and Black, April 15, 1925.
[27] Scarlet and Black, May 5, 1925.

JOE AS A STUDENT
[28] Scarlet and Black, November 5, 1924.
[29] Scarlet and Black, November 19, 1924.
[30] Scarlet and Black, November 22, 1924.
[3] Scarlet and Black, November 19, 1924.
[32] Scarlet and Black, April 22, 1925.
[33] Scarlet and Black, November 12, 1924.
[34] Scarlet and Black, December 3, 1924.
[35] Scarlet and Black, November 19, 1924.
[36] Scarlet and Black, April 22, 1925.
[37] Scarlet and Black, January 14, 1925.
[38] Scarlet and Black, January 21, 1925.
[39] Scarlet and Black, April 15, 1925.
[40] Scarlet and Black, April 22, 1925.
[4] Scarlet and Black, April 27, 1925.
[42] Scarlet and Black, April 22, 1925.
[43] Scarlet and Black, April 27, 1925.
[44] Scarlet and Black, May 20, 1925.
[45] Scarlet and Black, May 27, 1925.
[46] Scarlet and Black, April 28, 1923.
[47] Scarlet and Black, April 28, 1923.
[48] Scarlet and Black, May 12, 1923.

IMPORTANT COLLEGE ISSUES, 1921-1925
A SECRET FRATERNITY
[49] Scarlet and Black, April 26, 1922.
[50] Scarlet and Black, May 3, 1922.
[51] Scarlet and Black, May 3,1922.
[52] Scarlet and Black, April 28, 1922.
[53] The 1923 Cyclone, p. 220.

THE ORACLE
[54] Scarlet and Black, January 9, 1923.
[55] Scarlet and Black, November 8, 1924.

LITERARY SOCIETIES
[56] Scarlet and Black, October 22, 1924.
[57] Scarlet and Black, October 25, 1924.
[58] Scarlet and Black, October 29, 1924.
[59] Grinnell College archives, Burling Library, The Malteaser, November, 1924, p.ll.
[60] Scarlet and Black, November 1, 1924.
[61] Scarlet and Black, November 8, 1924.
[62] Scarlet and Black, November 22, 1924.
[63] Scarlet and Black, February 28, 1925.
[64] Scarlet and Black, April 25, 1925.

STUDENT GOVERNMENT
[65] Scarlet and Black, March 21, 1925.
[66] Scarlet and Black, May 4, 1924.
[67] Scarlet and Black, March 19, 1924.
[68] Scarlet and Black, April 30, 1924.
[69] Scarlet and Black, April 22, 1925.

CONCLUSION
[70] Fred Little. Interview by author, San Francisco California, 17 /18 March, 2016.

Warren Buffett. Interview by author, Omaha, Nebraska, 5 June, 2014.

PART 2:
THE FRANKEL LEGACY

[1] Iowa Jewish Historical Archives, Waukee, Iowa. The Rosenfield and Frankel Papers, 1998 Interview with Joseph Rosenfield for the Des Moines History Project.

[2] Kay Bucksbaum. Interview by author, Chicago, Illinois, 3 December, 2014.

[3] Iowa Jewish Archives, Waukee Iowa. Louise Noun, Speech at Temple B'nai Jeshrun.

[4] Louise Noun. *Journey to Autonomy: A Memoir*. (Ames, IA: Iowa State University Press, 1990).

[5] Noun, *Journey to Autonomy, 14*.

[6] Noun, *Journey to Autonomy*.

The Des Moines Register. Rose Rosenfield Obituary, September 16, 1960.

[7] Louise Noun, *Journey to Autonomy*, 3-4.

[8] Little, Fred. Interview by author, San Francisco, California, 17/18 March, 2016.

[9] Noun, *Journey to Autonomy*, 4.

[10] Noun, *Journey to Autonomy*, 4.

[11] Noun, *Journey to Autonomy*, 17

[12] Noun, *Journey to Autonomy*, 12.

[13] Noun, *Journey to Autonomy*. 4.

[14] Noun, *Journey to Autonomy*. 4.

[15] Noun, *Journey to Autonomy*. 4.

[16] Noun, *Journey to Autonomy*. 5.

[17] Noun, *Journey to Autonomy*. 5.

[18] Noun, *Journey to Autonomy*. 6.

[19] Iowa Jewish Historical Archives, Waukee, Iowa. Reminiscence of Isaiah Frankel, The Rosenfield and Frankel Papers.

[20] Noun, *Journey to Autonomy*, 6.

[21] Iowa Jewish Historical Archives, Waukee, Iowa. Obituary of Isaiah Frankel, 1897, The Rosenfield and Frankel Papers.

[22] Iowa Jewish Historical Archives, Waukeed Iowa. Babette's Story, The Rosenfield and Frankel Papers.

[23] Noun, *Journey to Autonomy*, 8.

[24] Noun, *Journey to Autonomy*. 8.

[25] *Grinnell Herald*. On the Occsasio of Babette Frankel's 80th Birthday.

[26] Noun, *Journey to Autonomy,* 9.

[27] Noun, *Journey to Autonomy.* 9.

[28] Iowa Jewish Historical Archives, Waukee, Iowa. Des Moines History Project Interview with Joseph Rosenfield, 1998, The Rosesnfield and Frankel Papers.

[29] Noun, *Journey to Autonomy,* 9-10.

[30] Noun, *Journey to Autonomy.* 11.

[31] Noun, *Journey to Autonomy.* 83-84.
Interview with Mary Beth Tinker. Interview by the author. Grinnell, Iowa, October 4, 2017.

[32] Noun, *Journey to Autonomy.* 91.

[33] *Des Moines Register.* Interview with Joseph Rosenfield, May 10, 1951.

[34] Jill June. Interview by author, Ankeny, Iowa, 17 December, 2014.

[35] Kay Bucksbaum. Interview by author, Chicago, Illinois, 3 December, 2014.

[36] Noun, *Journey to Autonomy,* 21.

[37] Noun, *Journey to Autonomy,* 27.

[38] Fred Little. Interview by author, San Francisco, California, 17-18 March, 2016.

[39] Noun, *Journey to Autonomy,* 22.

[40] State Historical Society of Iowa, Younkers Inc. Archives, Box 31B. *Younker Reporter,* August, 1957.

[41] Noun, *Journey to Autonomy,* 20.

[42] Iowa Jewish Historical Society, Waukee, Iowa. The Rosenfield and Frankel Papers, Louise Noun talk at Temple B'nai Jeshrun.

[43] Iowa Jewish Historical Archives, Waukee, Iowa. The Rosnefield and Frankel Papers.

[44] Michael Gartner. Interview by author. Des Moines, Iowa, 11 November, 2014.

[45] The information about Dannie comes from her Obituary in the *Des Moines Register,* December 12, 1977; and from the Interview with Kay Bucksbaum in Chicago, Illinois, December 3, 2014; and from a conversation with Charles Duke relaying what he had learned during a dinner with Dannie Rosenfield.

[46] Jill June Interview.

[47] *Des Moines Register,* Obituary, December 12, 1962.

KAY BUCKSBAUM INTERVIEW.
[48] Grinnell College Archives, Burling Library. *Class Letters for 1925*.
[49] William Knapp. Interview by the author, February 4, 2014.

YOUNKERS
[50] State Historical Society of Iowa, Des Moines. Younker Inc. Archives, Box 36.
[51] Vickie Ingram, *Younkers: The Friendly Store* (Charlston, S.C.: The History Press, 2016), 11-13.
[52] Younker Inc. Archives, Box 36.
[53] Ingram, *Younkers,* 16.
[54] Joseph Rosenfield, "A Short History of Younkers." *The Iowa Magazine,* Vol. 16, No.4.
[55] Joseph Rosenfield, "A Short History of Younkers" is the source for the Frankel family business.
[56] Younkers Inc. Archives, Box 36.
[57] Joseph Rosenfield, "A Short History of Younkers."
[58] William Friedman. Interview by author, Des Moines, Iowa, May 23, 2014.
[59] Joseph Rosenfield, "A Short History of Younkers."
[60] Younkers Inc. Archives, Box 44.
[61] Iowa Jewish Historical Archives, Waukee, Iowa. The Rosenfield and Frankel Papers containing a 1998 Des Moines History Project with Joseph Rosenfield.
[62] Younkers Inc. Archives, Box 36.
Ingram, *Younkers, 28.*
[63] Joseph Rosenfield. 1998 Des Moines History Project Interview.
[64] Joseph Rosenfield. 1998 Des Moines History Project Interview.
[65] Younkers Inc. Archives, Box 32.
[66] William Friedman Interview.
[67] Joseph Rosenfield, "A Short History of Younkers."
[68] Youkers Inc. Archives, Box 31A.
[69] Younkers Inc. Archives, *The Reporter,* June, 1969, Box 32.
[70] Younkers Inc. Archives, Box OS/10.
[71] Joseph Rosenfield. 1998 Des Moines History Project Interview.
[72] Younkers Inc. Archives, Box 36.
[73] Joseph Rosenfield. 1998 Des Moines History Project Interview.

[74] Younkers Inc. Archives, Box 8.
[75] Ingram, *Younkers,* 48.
[76] *Des Moines Register,* May 10, 1981. Wendell Cochran, "Joseph Rosenfield: Patron of Business."
[77] Joseph Rosenfield, "A Short History of Younkers."
[78] Joseph Rosenfield. 1998 Des Moines History Project Interview.
[79] William Friedman Interview
[80] Younkers Inc. Archives, Box 36; and the author's memory.
[81] Younkers Inc. Archives, Box 32.
[82] Younkers Inc. Archives, Box 32.
[83] Younkers Inc. Archives Box 7.
[84] Younkers Inc. Archives, Box 36.
[85] Younkers Inc. Archives, Box 36.
[86] Younkers Inc. Archives, Box 32.
[87] Younkers Inc. Archives, Box 32.
[88] Joseph Rosenfield, "A Short History of Younkers."
[89] Examples in Younkers Inc. Archives, Box 28.
[90] Younkers Inc. Archives, Box 28.
[91] Younkers Inc. Archives, Box 28.
[92] Younkers Inc. Archives, Box 29.
[93] Younkers Inc. Archives, Box 29.
[94] Younkers Inc. Archives, Box 32.
[95] Younkers Inc. Archives, Boxes 28, 29, 31A, 32.
[96] Joseph Rosenfield, "A Short History of Younkers." Younkers Inc Archives, Box 36.
[97] *Good Morning,* March 10, 1947. Younkers Inc. Archives, Box 28.
[98] *Good Morning,* June 11, 1952. Younkers Inc. Archives, Box 28.
[99] *Good Morning,* July 14, 1952. Younkers Inc. Archives, Box 29.
[100] Younkers Inc. Archives, Box 28.
[101] Younkers Inc. Archives, Box 29.
[102] Younkers Inc. Archives, Box 28.
[103] *Good Morning,* January 18, 1960. Younkers Inc. Archives, Boxn29.
[104] Christopher Green. Interview by author, Des Moines, Iowa, November 19, 2014.
[105] *The Des Moines Register,* October 4, 2014.
[106] Younkers Inc. Archives, Box 29.
[107] Younkers Inc. Archives, Box 29.

[108] Younkers Inc. Archives, Box 29.
[109] *Good Morning,* May 26, 1952. Younkers Inc. Archives, Box 29.
[110] Younkers Inc. Archives, Box 27.
[111] Younkers Inc. Archives, Box 29.
[112] William Friedman Interview.
[113] William Friedman Interview.
[114] Younkers Inc. Archives, Box OS/8.
Ingram, *Younkers,* 124.
[115] Joseph Rosenfield. 1998 Des Moines History Project Interview.
[116] *Younker Reporter,* December, 1967. Younker Inc. Archives, Box 32.
[117] Frederich Hubbell. Interview by author, Des Moines, Iowa, October 8, 2014.
[118] James Cownie. Interview by author, Des Moines, Iowa, October 8, 2014.
[119] Frederich Hubbell Interview.
[120] *The Des Moines Register,* May 10, 1981, "Joe Rosenfield. Patron of Iowa Business,
Wendel Cochran.
[121] Michael Gartner. Interview by author, Des Moines, Iowa, November 11, 2014.
[122] *The Des Moines Tribune,* August 4, 1978.
[123] Younkers Inc. Archives, Box 33.
[124] Younkers Inc. Archives, Box 33.
Frererich Hubbell Interview.
Postscript
[125] Joseph Rosenfield. 1998 Des Moines History Project Interview.
[126]*The Des Moines Register,* April 19, 2018.
[127] *The Des Moines Register,* April 29, 2018.
[128] All quotes from *The Des Moines Register, April 29, 2018.*

PART 3:
JOE ROSENFIELD, COMMUNITY CATALYST
DES MOINES' CATALYST

[1] William Knapp. Interview by author, West Des Moines, Iowa, Feb 4, 2014.
[2] Michael Gartner. Interview by author, Des Moines Iowa, November 11, 2014.

[3] James Cownie. Interview by author, Des Moines, Iowa, October 8, 2015.
Michael Gartner Interview.
[4] Richard Leavitt. Interview by author, West Des Moines, Iowa, May 23, 2014.
[5] Jon Batesol. Interview by author, Des Moines, Iowa, May 23, 2014.
Stanley Richards. Interview by author, Des Moines, Iowa, June 10, 2014.
[6] Robert Burnett. Interview by author, West Des Moines, Iowa, October 8, 2014.
[7] James Cownie Interview.
[8] William Friedman Interview. Des Moines, Iowa, May 23, 2014.
[9] Thomas Miller Interview. Des Moines, Iowa, May 2, 2016.
[10] John Bucksbaum Interview. Chicago, Illinois, December 3, 2014.

THE UNIVERSITY OF IOWA LAW SCHOOL
[11] Iowa Jewish Historical Archives. The Rosenfield and Frankel papers, *Iowa Law School Campaign Brochure*.
[12] *Iowa Law School Campaign Brochure*.
[13] *Iowa Law School Campaign Brochure*.
[14] Richard Leavitt Interview.
[15] Kay Bucksbaum. Interview by author, Chicago, Illinois, December 3, 2014.
[16] Joseph Rosenfield. Taped interview by the author and Joseph Wall, 1990.
[17] Iowa Jewish Historical Archives, Waukee, Iowa. Rosenfield and Frankel Papers, Des Moines Historical Project Interview with Joseph Rosenfield, 1998.

THE GAMBLE LAW FIRM
[18] Chris Green. Interview by author, Des Moines, Iowa, November 19, 2014.
[19] Most of this information is from: William B. Friedricks, *In For the Long Haul: The Life of John Ruan* (Iowa City, Iowa: The University of Iowa Press, 2003).
Chris Green Interview.
[20] Joseph Rosenfield. Des Moines Historical Project Inteview.
Chris Green Interview.

[21] Stanley Richards. Interview by the author, Des Moines, Iowa, June 10, 2014.
[22] Fred Little. Interview by author, San Francisco, California, March 16-17, 2016.
[23] *The Des Moines Register.* Profile of Joe Rosenfield by Wendell Cochran, May 10, 1981.

DES MOINES' CATALYST
[24] Michael Gartner. All of this section from the Interview by the author.
[25] Connie Wimer. Interview by author, Des Moines, Iowa, June 10, 2014.
[26] James Cownie Interview.
[27] Bob Burnett. Interview by author, West Des Moines, Iowa, October 8, 2014.
[28] Stanley Richards Interview.
[29] Jon Batesole. Interview by author, Des Moines, Iowa, May 23, 2014.
[30] Connie Wimer Interview.
[31] John Bucksbaum. Interview by author, Chicago, Illinois, December 3, 2014.
[32] Richard Leavitt Interview.
[33] Frederick Hubbell. Interview by author, Des Moines, Iowa, October 8, 2014
James Cownie Interview.

JOE ROSENFIELD, BUSINESSMAN
[34] Grinnell College Archives, Burling Library. Joe Rosenfield Files, *Iowa Business Hall of Fame Brochure, 1979.*
[35] *Des Moines Register.* Joe Rosenfield Profile, 1981.
[36] William B. Friedericks, *The Real Deal: The Life of Bill Knapp* (Des Moines: Business Publications Corp Corporation Inc.), 83,
[37] Friedricks, *The Real Deal,* 105-6.
[38] William Knapp. Interview by author, West Des Moines, Iowa, February 4, 2014.
[39] William Knapp Interview.
[40] Friedricks, *The Real Deal,* 34.
[41] Friedricks, *The Real Deal,* 106-7.

[42] *Wall Street Journal,* March 19, 1964
Friedricks, *The Real Deal,* 126-7.
[43] *Des Moines Register,* Joe Rosenfield Profile.
[44] James Cownie Interview.
[45] Friedricks, *The Real Deal.*
[46] Friedricks, *The Real Deal.*

JOE ROSENFIELD AND THE DES MOINES JEWISH COMMUNITY

[47] Elaine Steinger, (Des Moines Jewish Federation Director, 1877-2009) Telephone conversation with the author, January 20 2017.
Stanley Richards Interview.
[48] Stanley Richards Interview.
[49] Kay Bucksbaum Interview.
[50] Elaine Steinger Telephone Conversation.
[51] Fred Little Interview.
[52] William Knapp Interview.
[53] Richard Leavitt Interview.
[54] Stanley Richards Interview.
[55] Kay Bucksbaum Interview.
[56] Stanley Richards Interview.
[57] William Friedman Interview.

JOE ROSENFIELD , PHILANTHROPIST

[58] *Des Moines Register,* Joe Rosenfield Profile.
[59] James Cownie Interview.
[60] *Des Moines Register,* October 9, 1976/ Iowa Historical Archives, Waukee, Iowa. The Rosenfield and Frankel Papers, 1998 Des Moines History Project with Joe Rosenfield.
[61] Richard Leavitt Interview.
[62] Joe Rosenfield, Videotaped Interview by the author and Professor Joseph Wall, Grinnell, Iowa November 26, 1990.
[63] *Des Moines Register,* Joe Rosenfield Profile.
[64] Jill June, Interview by the author, Ankeny, Iowa, December 17, 2014.
[65] Jill June Interview
[66] Joseph Rosenfield Will
Research by the Grinnell College Development Office.

[67] Pat Gessman. Interview by author, Chicago, Illinois, December 3, 2014.
[68] William Knapp Interview.
[69] Jill June Interview.
[70] Grinnell College Archives, Burling Library. Letter in the Iowa Philanthropy Award File.

JOE ROSENFIELD, MENTOR
[71] Fred Little Interview.
[72] Fred Little Interview.
[73] Joseph Rosenfield. Des Moines Historical Project Interview.
[74] Recollection by the author.
[75] Stanley Richards Interview.
[76] Connie Wimer Interview.
[77] Jill June Interview.
[78] David Clay. Interview by author, Grinnell, Iowa, November 20, 2014.

HERITAGE COMMUNICATIONS
[79] James Cownie Interview.
[80] James Cownie. Telephone Conversation with the author, March 14. 2018.
[81] James Hoak. Interview with the author, Dallas, Texas, March 17, 2016. Much of the Heritage story comes from this interview as well as the authors October 8, 2014 with Hoak's partner, James Cownie.
[82] Connie Wimer Interview.
[83] James Hoak and James Cownie. The Heritage story is based on Interviews with them.

JOE ROSENFIELD & GENERAL GROWTH
[84] Grinnell College Archives, Burling Library. Joe Rosenfield Files.
[85] John Bucksbaum Interview.
[86] John Bucksbaum Interview.
[87] Jon Batesol. Interview by author, Des Moines, Iowa, Mayi 23, 2014.
Stanley Richards Interview.
[88] Kay Bucksbaum Interview.
William Friedman Interview.
[89] Joeseph Rosenfield. Des Moines Historical Project Interview.
[90] Fred Hubbell. Interview by author, Des Moines, Iowa, October 8, 2014.
[91] John Bucksbaum Interview.

[92] John Bucksbaum Interview.
[93] Kay Bucksbaum Interview.
[94] Pat Guessman Interview.
[95] *Des Moines Register.* Joe Rosenfield Profile, 1981.
[96] *Des Moines Register.* Joe Rosenfileld Profile, 1981.
[97] Jill June Interview.
[98] Joe Rosenfield. Des Moines Historical Project Interview.
[99] Joe Rosenfield. 1990 Videotaped Interview.
[100] Connie Wimer Interview.
[101] Fred Hubbell Interview.
[102] Connie Wimer Interview.
[103] Jill June Interview.
[104] Pat Gessman Interview.
[105] Jill June Interview.
[106] Jill June Interview.
[107] Fred Hubbell Interview.
[108] Joe Rosenfield. 90th Birthday Program.
[109] The information for this section comes from the Interviews with Jill June and Connie Wimer.
[110] *Des Moines Register.* June, 1990.

DEMOCRATIC POLITICS
[111] *Des Moines Register.* Joe Rosenfield Profile, 1991.
[112] Stanley Richards Interview.
[113] Michael Gartner Interview.
[114] Fred Little Interview.
[115] Tom Miller. Interview by author, Des Moines, Iowa, May 2, 2016.
[116] Joe Rosenfield. Des Moines Historical Project Interview.
[117] *Des Moines Register.* Joe Rosenfield Profile, 1981.
[118] Jill June Interview.
[119] Joe Rosenfield. 1990 Videotaped Interview.
[120] Jon Batesole Interview.
[121] *Des Moines Register.* Joe Rosenfield Profile, 1981.
[122] Joe Rosenfield. Des Moines Historical Project Interview.
[123] Jim Cownie Interview.
[124] Friedricks, *The Real Deal*.
[125] Most of this section is drawn from a Telephone Conversation by

the author with Tom Harkin, October 9, 2017. Also and the Interview with Jill June by the author on December 17, 2014.

[126] John Culver. Telephone conversation with author, June 7, 2017.

[127] Thomas Miller. Interview by author, Des Moines, Iowa, May 2, 2016. *Des Moines Register,* Joe Rosenfield Profile, 1981.

[128] Bill Knapp Interview.

[129] *Des Moines Register,* Joe Rosenfield Profile, 1981.

[130] Tom Harkin Interview.

[131] Thomas Miller Interview.

[132] Joe Rosenfield. Des Moines Historical Project Interview.

JOE ROSENFIELD & THE CHICAGO CUBS

[133] *Des Moines Register,* Joe Rosenfield Profile, 1981.

[134] *Des Moines Register,* June 8, 2000.

[135] Jill June Interview.

[136] *Younker Reporter,* August, 1951.

[137] Joe Rosenfield. Videotaped Interview, 1990.

[138] Joe Rosenfield. Videotaped Interview, 1990. Also, Interviews with Kay Bucksbaum and William Friedman.

[139] Richard Leavitt Interview.

[140] *Des Moines Register.* Joe Rosenfield Profile, 1981.

[141] George Will. Column, March 13, 1997.

[142] *Des Moines Register.* Joe Rosenfield Profile, 1981.

[143] Pat Gessman Interview.

[144] John Bucksbaum Interview.

[145] *Des Moines Register.* Joe Rosenfield Profile, 1981.

[146] The author.

PART 4:
JOE ROSENFIELD, TRUSTEE
THE COLLEGIATE SCENE
GRINNELL COLLEGE

[1] Joseph Frazier Wall, *Grinnell College in the Nineteenth Century: From Salvation to Service* (Ames: Iowa State University Press, 1997). Much of this section is based on Professor Wall's excellent book.

JOE ROSENFIELD, TRUSTEE & SAM STEVENS, PRESIDENT

[2] Grinnell College Archives, Burling Library. *Board of Trustees Minutes,* November 29, 1941.

[3] Iowa Jewish Historical Archives, Waukee, Iowa. The Rosenfield and Frankel Papers, December 1998 Des Moines Historical Project Interview with Joseph Rosenfield.

[4] I am indebted to Grinnell College Emeritus History Professor, Daniel Kaiser, who found this letter in the Smithsonian Institution Archives, Washington, D.C.

[5] Described in the *Board of Trustee Minutes,* June 2, 1949.

[6] *Board of Trustee Minutes,* May 26, 1945.

[7] *Board of Trustees Minutes,* May 29, 1942.

[8] *Board of Trustee Minutes,* January 8, 1944.

[9] *Board of Trustee Minutes,* December 12, 1942.

[10] *Board of Trustee Minutes,* December 12, 1942.

[11] *Board of Trustees Minutes,* June 4, 1951.

[2] Joseph Rosenfield. 1990 Videotaped Interview by the author and Professor Joseph Wall.

[3] *Board of Trustees Minutes.* May 21, 1943.

[4] James MacGregor Burns. *Roosevelt: Soldier of Freedom 1940-1944 (New York: Open Road), Kindle, 464.*

[5] *Board of Trustees Minutes,* January 8, 1944.

[6] Grinnell College Archives, Burling Library. *Board of Trustees Executive Committee Minutes,* February 10, 1944.

[7] *Executive Committee Minutes,* April 1, 1944.

[8] *Executive Committee Minutes,* June 16, 1945.

[9] *Board of Trustees Minutes,* December 12, 1947. Dean Strong's report that indicated 35 new faculty hires in that academic year.

[20] *Executive Council Minutes,* April 24, 1947. President Stevens recommended purchase of 15 standard sized prefabricated houses at a cost of $120,000. The College had most of the needed lots on which to locate the houses. In fact, only 10 houses were purchased.

[21] This information is drawn from the manuscript of a continuation of Joseph Wall's history of *Grinnell College in the Nineteenth Century* by his widow, Bea. Bea's manuscript is being edited by Terry Bissen. The particular reference is on page 107 of the manuscript.

[22] *Board of Trustees Minutes,* October 29, 1949.

[23] *Board of Trustees Minutes,* June 4, 1948/June 9, 1952.
[24] *Board of Trustees Minutes,* June 5, 1950.
[25] *Board of Trustees Minutes,* October 29, 1949/June 5, 1950.
[26] *Board of Trustees Minutes,* December 12, 1947.
[27] *Board of Trustees Minutes,* June 4, 1948.
[28] *Board of Trustees Minutes,* June 5, 1950.
[29] I am indebted to former Grinnell College Chemistry Professor, Gene Wubbels for providing me with a 1950's NSF study, "Research and Teaching in the Liberal Arts Colleges." This study details the postwar construction of science facilities in leading liberal arts colleges, including costs per square foot.
[30] *Board of Trustees Minutes,* October 29, 1949.
[31] *Board of Trustees Minutes,* October 28, 1950/ June 4, 1951.
[32] *Executive Committee Minutes,* April 22, 1952.
[33] *Board of Trustees Minutes,* June 9, 1952.
[34] *Executive Committee Minutes,* May 27, 1952. "Mr. Rosenfield explained that the bankers were insisting that some assets be liquidated for the purposes of establishing working capital. At the beginning of the year the College possessed little or no working capital and the deficit situation of the budget has resulted in a situation whereby the working funds of the college could not be fully satisfied with bank loans. It was felt that some assets would have to be sold so that the budget operations could be balanced. In addition, there should be made available some working fund capital so that the bank borrowing could be reduced."
[35] *Executive Committee Minutes,* May 27, 1952.
[36] *Board of Trustees Minutes,* November 3, 1951. President Stevens, who had a seminary degree habitually began each board meeting with what many must have regarded as a "sermon" to the Board.
[37] *Board of Trustee Minutes,* November 11, 1952. The Board also had met in September in this crisis year.
[38] *Executive Committee Minutes,* October 15, 1952.
[39] *Board of Trustees Minutes,* November 11, 1952.
[40] Bea Wall Manuscript.
[41] *Board of Trustees Minutes,* May 21, 1953.
[42] *Board of Trustees Minutes.* May 21 1953.
[43] *Board of Trustees Minutes,* June 8, 1953.

[44] Bea Wall Manuscript, 115. Based on a Memoir by Grant Gale.
[45] *Executive Committee Minutes*. August 5, 1953.
[46] *Board of Trustees Minutes,* January 29, 1954.
[47] *Board of Trustees Minutes,* June 7, 1954.
[48] "Grant Gale's Memoire." Quoted in Bea Wall's Manuscript, 114-116. The author also has read the Gale Memoire several years ago at Grant Gale's invitation, though he was not able to find it in the Gale Manuscripts in Burling Library when he was researching for this book.

THE PARTNERSHIP OF JOE ROSENFIELD & HOWARD BOWEN

[49] Grinnell College Archives, Burling Library. "1925 Class Letter," April, 1954.
[50] *Board of Trustees Minutes,* Special Meeting of April 8, 1955 (Introduction of Howard Bowen to the Board).
[51] *Board of Trustees Minutes,* December 4, 1954.
[52] *Board of Trustees Minutes,* June 6, 1955.
[53] *Board of Trustees Minutes,* December 4, 1954. The discussion at this meeting makes it clear that the Darby Estate was critical to the survival of the College.
[54] *Board of Trustees Minutes,* December 4, 1954.
[55] *Board of Trustees Minutes,* June 6, 1955.
[56] *Board of Trustees Minutes,* December 4, 1954.
[57] *Board of Trustees Minutes,* June 6, 1955.
[58] *Board of Trustees Minutes,* November 14, 1955.
[59] I am indebted to Paige Carlson of the Grinnell College Treasurer's Office for the Endowment Figures in this chapter.
[60] *Board of Trustees Minutes,* November 14, 1955.
[61] Grinnell College President, Raynard Kington. Conversation with the author, Grinnell, Iowa, March 4, 2016.
[62] *Board of Trustees Minutes,* October 28, 1957.
[63] *Board of Trustees Minutes,* February 4, 1956.
[64] *Board of Trustees Minutes,* October 28, 1957.
[65] *Board of Trustees Minutes,* June 8, 1959.
[66] *Board of Trustees Minutes,* June 10, 1957.
[67] *Board of Trustees Minutes,* October 27, 1958.

[68] *Board of Trustees Minutes,* June 8, 1959.
[69] *Board of Trustees Minutes,* June 4, 1956.
[70] *Board of Trustees Minutes,* February 4, 1961.
[71] *Board of Trustees Minutes,* June 5, 1961.
[72] *Board of Trustees Minutes,* October 30, 1961.
[73] *Board of Trustees Minutes,* February 3, 1963.
[74] *Board of Trustees Minutes,* October 15, 1962.
[75] *Board of Trustees Minutes,* June 10,1963/ *Executive Committee Minutes,* June 26, 1964.
[76] *Board of Trustees Minutes,* February 6, 1960/ June 5, 1961.
[77] The author's memory.
[78] *The Cedar Rapids Gazette,* March 14, 1988. An article on Joe's 1988 Outstanding Trusteeship Award of the Association of Governing Boards which quotes Howard Bowen.
[79] *Board of Trustees Minutes,* June 8, 1959.
The authors Memory as he taught in the Historical Studies course as a sabbatical replacement faculty member in the 1960-61 academic year.
[80] *Board of Trustees Minutes,* June 10, 1957.
[81] *Board of Trustees Minutes,* June 5, 1961.
[82] *Board of Trustee Minutes,* June 5, 1961.
[83] *Board of Trustees Minutes,* February 3, 1963.
[84] *Board of Trustee Minutes,* June 10, 1963.
[85] *Board of Trustees Minutes,* February 4, 1961.
[86] This summary of Grinnell College Endowment growth in five year increments was provided by Paige Carlson of the college's Development Office.

ENDOWMENT GROWTH & STUDENT UNREST
[87] *Board of Trustees Minutes,* February 6, 1960.
[88] *Board of Trustees Minutes,* February 3, 1963.
[89] *Board of Trustees Minutes,* June 10, 1963.
[90] The author's memory.
[91] *Board of Trustees Minutes,* February 3 1963.
[92] *Board of Trustees Minutes,* October 28, 1963.
[93] *Board of Trustees Minutes,* March 9, 1964.
[94] *Board of Trustees Minutes,* November 1, 1964.
[95] *Board of Trustees Minutes,* October 30-31, 1967.

NOTES

[96] *Board of Trustees Minutes,* January 28-29, 1968/May 26, 1968.

[97] *Executive Committee Minutes,* March 16, 1964.

[98] The author's memory.

[99] Bea Wall. Manuscript of her continuation of her husband, Joe's history of Grinnell College, 128.

[100] Warren Buffett. Interview by author, Omaha, Nebraska, June 5, 2014.

[101] Jason Zweig, "The Best Investor You've Never Heard Of." *Money,* June, 2000, 142.

[102] Kay Bucksbaum, Interview by author, Chicago, Illinois, December 3, 2014.

[103] Zweig, "Investor," 142

[104] Warren Buffett Interview.

[105] Warren Buffett Interview.

[106] Fred Little. Interview by author, San Francisco, California, March 17-18, 2016.

[107] Warren Buffett Interview.

[108] Warren Buffett. Conversation with the author, mid-1980's.

[109] *Board of Trustees Minutes,* January 18, 1970.

[110] *Board of Trustees Minutes,* June 3-4, 1973.

[111] Warren Buffett Interview.

[112] Warren Buffett Interview.

[113] Bea Wall. Manuscript continuation of her husband, Joe's history of Grinnell College, edited by Terry Bissen, 168.

[114] *Board of Trustees Minutes,* November 1-2. 1969.

[115] *Board of Trustees Minutes,* November 4-5, 1972.

[116] Zweig, "Investor," 143.

[117] *Board of Trustees Minutes,* June 1-2, 1975. Also the author's memory, as I was a Board member at that time and remember well the persuasive case for purchase made by Warren and backed by Joe. In fact discussion of how to manage the station was much more extensive than discussion before voting on Warren's proposal.

[118] Zweig, "Investor," 143.

[119] *Board of Trustees Minutes,* February 25-26, 1978.
Interview with Warren Buffett
The author's memory.

[120] Zweig, "Investor," 143.

[121] The Endowment figures were compiled by Paige Carlson of the

Grinnell College Treasurer's Office.

[122] Jason Zweig, "The Best Investor You've Never Heard Of," *CNNMoney,* June I, 2000,http:/money.cnn.com/magazines/moneymag__archiv.

[123] Zweig, "Investor," *CNNMoney*.

[124] Warren Buffett Interview.

[125] Zweig, "Investor," 144. After his interview with Joe, Jason Zweig wrote that he did not have the heart to tell Joe, who was in the last year of his life, that instead of the $50,000,000 that Joe had suggested the College had forsaken by premature sale of its Intel stock, "that the shares he sold would today be worth several billion dollars."

[126] Warren Buffett Interview.

[127] Warren Buffett Interview.

[128] Warren Buffett Interview.

[129] Warren Buffett Interview.

[130] Warren Buffett Interview.

[131] Warren Buffett Interview.

[132] Warren Buffett Interview.

[133] Joesph Rosenfield. Iowa Jewish Historical Archives, Waukee, Iowa. The Rosenfield and Frankel Papers, 1998 Interview for the Des Moines History Project.

[134] *Board of Trustees Minutes,* November 4-5, 1972.

[135] Grinnell College Archives, Burling Library. Letter of Joseph Rosenfield to E.A. Norelius, June 11, 1970. Norelius was captain of the football team when he and Joe were students at Grinnell. The team played "big-time football," competing against teams such as Missouri, Kansas and Iowa State.

[136] Author's Conversation with the 1967 Reunion Planning Committee, May 5, 2016.
Author's Conversation with Henry Wilhelm, December 8, 2017.
Grinnell College Newspaper, *The Scarlet and Black,* February 17, 1967.

[137] *Board of Trustees Minutes,* November 2-3, 1968.

[138] *Board of Trustees Minutes,* May 26, 1968.
Board of Trustees Minutes, March 15-16, 1969.

[139] *Board of Trustees Minutes,* June 1, 1969.

[140] *Board of Trustees Minutes,* November 1-2, 1969.

[141] *Board of Trustees Minutes,* May 31-June 1, 1970.

[142] *Board of Trustees Minutes,* November 14-15, 1970.
[143] *Board of Trustees Minutes,* November 4-5, 1972.
[144] Beryl Clotfelter, "Adoption of the No-Requirements Curriculum," January 2003. This paper was generously given to me by Professor Clotfelter.
[145] *Board of Trustees Minutes,* April 6-7, 1974.
[146] *Board of Trustees Minutes* February 5-6, 1977.
[147] *Board of Trustees Minutes,* November 2-3, 1968.
[148] *Board of Trustees Minutes,* March 15-16, 1969.
[149] *Board of Trustees Minutes,* May 10-11, 1969.
[150] *Board of Trustees Minutes,* June 1, 1969.
[151] *Board of Trustees Minutes,* March 7-8, 1970.
[152] All of this section from the author's memory.
[153] *Board of Trustees Minutes,* April 14-15, 1973.
[154] *Board of Trustees Minutes,* November 5-6, 1977.
[155] The author's memory.
[156] *Board of Trustees Minutes,* November 5-6, 1966.
[157] *Executive Committee Minutes,* January 9, 1967.
[158] *Executive Committee Minutes,* March 12, 1968.
[159] *Board of Trustees Minutes,* October 30-31, 1971.
[160] Interview with Henry Wilhelm, December 8, 2017.
[161] The author's memory of board discussions.
[162] *Executive Committee Minutes,* April 13, 1967.
[163] *Board of Trustees Minutes,* February 5-6, 1977. Mears Cottage was one of two buildings of the early post tornado construction after 1882 that remained on campus.
[164] *Board of Trustees Minutes,* June 5-6, 1977.
[165] *Board of Trustees Minutes,* June 22-23, 1979.
[166] *Board of Trustees Minutes,* June 4-5, 1978.
[167] Waldo Walker. Interview by the author, Grinnell, Iowa, June 5, 2014. Wally was responsible for the budget in these years and was in frequent contact with Joe abour budgetary matters.
[168] Waldo Walker Interview.
[169] *Board of Trustees Minutes,* March 7-8, 1970.
[170] *Board of Trustees Minutes,* October 30-31, 1971.
[171] *Board of Trustees Minutes,* April 15-16, 1972.
[172] *Board of Trustees Minutes,* June 1-2, 1975.

[173] *Board of Trustees Minutes,* February 28-29, 1976.
[174] *Board of Trustees Minutes,* June 5-6, 1977.
[175] *Board of Trustees Minutes,* November 5-6, 1977.
[176] *Board of Trustees Minutes,* February 25-26, 1978.
[177] *Board of Trustees Minutes,* January 25-26, 1975.
[178] *Board of Trustees Minutes,* October 16-17, 1976.
[179] *Board of Trustees Minutes,* June 5-6, 1977.
[180] *Board of Trustees Minutes,* June 5-6, 1976.
The author's memory.
[181] *Board of Trustees Minutes,* June 1-2, 1975.
[182] *Board of Trustees Minutes,* February 5-6, 1977.

THE ELDER STATESMAN
[183] Endowment Figures in five-year increments by Paige Carlson of the Grinnell College Treasurer's Office.
[184] Jason Zweig, "The Best Investor You've Never Heard Of," *Money,* May 2000.
[185] Zweig, "Investor."
[186] Zweig, "Investor."
[187] Zweig, "Investor."
[188] Warren Buffett. Interview by author, Omaha, Nebraska, June 5, 2014.
[189] Zweig, "Investor."
[190] James Hoak. Interview by author, Dallas, Texas, March 17, 2016.
[191] The author's memory.
[192] *Board of Trustees Minutes,* February 5-6, 1982.
[193] *Board of Trustees Minutes,* May 8-9, 1997.
[194] *Board of Trustees Minutes,* February 24-25, 1989.
[195] Various articles in *The Des Moines Register.*
[196] *Board of Trustees Minutes,* 1980's.
[197] *Board of Trustees Minutes,* 1990's
US News and World Report.
[198] *Board of Trustees Minutes,* 1980's
The author's memory.
[199] *Board of Trustees Minutes,* November 2-3, 1984.
[200] This section on building relies on the author's memory of his time as president.
[201] The author's memory.

[202] *Board of Trustees Minutes,* May 13-14, 1992.
[203] *Board of Trustees Minutes,* May 10-11, 2002.
[204] *Board of Trustees Minutes,* February 10-11, 1984.
[205] *Board of Trustees Minutes,* November 4-5, 1983.
[206] *Board of Trustees Minutes,* February 1-2, 1985.
[207] *Board of Trustees Minutes,* February 22-23, 1990.
[208] *Board of Trustees Minutes,* May 1-2, 1985.
[209] The author's memory.
[210] *Board of Trustees Minutes,* May 2-3, 1980.
[211] The author's memory.
[212] *Board of Trustees Minutes,* October 29-31, 1981.
[213] *Board of Trustees Minutes,* May 2-3, 1980.
[214] The author's memory.
[215] *Board of Trustees Minutes,* May 4-5, 1984. President Drake reported to the Board that the "Parslow Proposal" had been defeated by a proportional 2-1 vote.
[216] *Board of Trustees Minutes,* May 6-8, 1988.
The author's memory.
[217] The author's memory and judgment.
[218] *Board of Trustees Minutes,* October 24-25. The College Experience Study is included in an Appendix.
[219] The author's memory.
[220] *Board of Trustees Minutes,* February 11-12, 1983. The Venture Fund was a classic iteration of Warren's and Joe's capacity to think creatively.
[221] *Board of Trustees Minutes,* October 8-9, 1998.
[222] The author's memory and judgment.
[223] *Board of Trustees Minutes,* November 14-15, 1986/February 12-13, 1988.
[224] The author's memory.
[225] Grinnell College. *Academic Catalogs for the 1990's.*
[226] *Board of Trustees Minutes,* May 6-7, 1999.
[227] The author's memory and knowledge based on his 1991-1993 Peace Corps experience in Lesotho which is totally surrounded by South Africa. After his return to teach at Grinnell in 1994, he introduced a history course on Southern Africa that concentrated on South Africa.
[228] The author's memory.

[229] *Board of Trustees Minutes,* September 28-29, 1979.
[230] *Board of Trustees Minutes,* October 29-31, 1981.
[231] *Board of Trustees Minutes,* May 7-8, 1982.
[232] *Board of Trustees Minutes,* November 5-6, 1982.
[233] The author' memory.
[234] *Board of Trustees Minutes,* February 4-5, 1984/ November 2-3. 1984.
[235] *Board of Trustees Minutes,* May 1-2, 1985.
[236] The author's memory.
[237] *Board of Trustees Minutes,* May 1-3, 1986.
[238] *Board of Trustees Minutes,* November 14-15, 1986.
[239] *Board of Trustees Minutes,* May 8-9, 1987,
[240] *Board of Trustees Minutes,* May 6-7, 1988.
[241] *Board of Trustees Minutes,* October 28-29, 1988.
[242] *Board of Trustees Minutes,* September 17-18, 1993.
[243] The author's memory.
[244] The author's memory and judgment.
[245] *Board of Trustees Minutes,* October 13, 1989.
[246] *Board of Trustees Minutes,* February 22-23, 1990.
[247] Grinnell College. "Report of the Admission Office." 2016.
[248] All from the author's memory.
[249] Fred Little. Interview by the author, San Francisco, California, March 17-18, 2016.
[250] *Board of Trustees Minutes,* February May 6-7, 1988.
[251] The author's memory.
[252] *Board of Trustees Minutes,* May 10, 2002.

EPILOGUE & OBITUARY

[1] Grinnell College, Office of the President. "Report Prepared for Warren Buffett," May 18, 2016. All of the information in this section comes from this report that was presented on slides in Warren Buffett's office, Omaha, Nebraska.
[2] Pat Gessman. Interview by author, Chicago, Illinois, December 3, 2014.
[3] Jill June, Interview by author, Ankeny, Iowa, December 17, 2014.
[4] Robert Burnett. Interview by author, West Des Moines, Iowa, October 8, 2014.
[5] Warren Buffett. Interview by author, Omaha, Nebraska, June 5, 2014. Interview in a videotaped tribute to Joe entitle, "Joe Rosenfield '25,"

produced by David Buck, 2000.
[6] William Knapp. Interview by author, West Des Moines, Iowa, February 4, 2014.
[7] Jill June Interview.
[8] Connie Wimer. Interview by author, Des Moines, Iowa, June 10, 2014.
[9] Richard Leavitt. Interview by author, West Des Moines, Iowa, May 23. 2014.
[10] Stanley Richards. Interview by author, Des Moines, Iowa, June 10, 2014.
[11] James Cownie. Interview by author, Des Moines, Iowa, October 8, 2014.
[12] Fred Little. Interview by author, San Francisco, California, March 17-18, 2016.
[13] Thomas Marshall. Interview by author, Grinnell, Iowa, January 8, 2015.
[14] Michael Gartner. Interview by author, Des Moines, Iowa November 11, 2014.
[15] Fred Hubbell. Interview by author, Des Moines, Iowa, October 8, 2014.
[16] William Friedman. Interview by author, May 23, 2014.
[17] John Culver. Telephone conversation with author, June 7, 2017.
[18] James Cownie Interview.
[19] George Drake. "Joe Rosenfield '25," A video tribute produced by David Buck. Drake was one of those interviewed for this taped tribute, 2000.

INDEX

A

AAUP (American Association of University Professors), 183
abortion, 142
ACM (Associated Colleges of the Midwest), 183, 218
Addams, Jane, 44
administration: cuts, 212; faculty ratio, 9. *See also* Board of Trustees; Board of Trustees and JR; presidents, Grinnell College
admissions: need-blind, 244; office, 10, 219, 221–222; policy, 204
advertising: Heritage Communications, 136; in *Malteaser,* 26
Affirmative Action Officer, 212
African American students, 191, 204–206
African American Studies Program, 205
AIM Campaign, 210
air conditioning, 74
Air Force ROTC, 166, 201, 202

alcohol: campus pub, 194, 199, 234–235; rules for, 186, 187, 234–235
Alumni Association, divestment in South Africa, 233
alumni giving, 222
Alumni Recitation Hall, 220
American Association of University Professors (AAUP), 183
Amherst College, 184, 244
Anglican Church and origins of colleges, 155–156
anti-German sentiment, 14
anti-Semitism, 7–8, 27–28, 124
applications, 187, 217, 226
Armstrong, Louis, 192
Associated Colleges of the Midwest (ACM), 183, 218
Association of Governing Boards, 238
athletics: Bowen years, 185; facilities, 162, 207, 222; during JR's college days, 9, 15–16; JR's love for, 16; Olympic athletes, 15, 16, 38; participation rates,

227; recruitment, 185; secret fraternities and societies, 32–33, 35; tennis, 56–57; University of Iowa, 112–113; Younkers, 72, 75. *See also* baseball
AT&T, xii, 196
Austin, Kenneth, 77
awards, 112, 127, 238

B

Bach, Emanuelle, 50
Banker's Trust, 121
banking: bank failures, 20, 61, 63; Becker and Cownie, 133; Community Bank, 197; by Isaiah Frankel, 50; by Joseph Rosenfield, 49; Ruan and, 121
Banks, Ernie, 135
Baptist Church and origins of colleges, 156
baseball: Chicago Cubs, xiii, 16, 111, 148–151; Des Moines Bruins, 72, 149; Younkers, 72, 75
basketball, 15, 16, 185
Batesole, Jon, xvi, 110, 118
bathrooms, coed, 208
Bear, Charles, 222, 237
Becker and Cownie, 133
Beloit College, 183, 218
Bergson, Rollo, 126
Berkshire Hathaway, 214. *See also* Buffett, Warren
Bernie Lorens Recovery House, 127

Blair Hall, 164, 165
"Blairsburg Sketches," 18–19
Blank, Myron, 143
Bluebook. See *The Cyclone*
Board of Trustees: Bowen, 237; Buffett, xii, 192–197, 199–200, 209–210, 213–217, 236, 243–246; Chrystal, 237; Drake, xiii, 237; Little, 129, 210, 237. *See also* Board of Trustees and JR; Executive Committee (Grinnell College); Finance Committee
Board of Trustees and JR: appointment to, 129, 161; awards, 238; baseball meetings, 151; Board after departure, 238; as Board President, 164; Bowen years (1955-1964), 173–190; building Board strength, 204, 236; as decision-maker, 181–182; divestment in South Africa, 206–207, 230–231, 233, 234; Drake years (1979-1991), 213–217, 218, 220, 223, 227–229, 230–231, 233, 234–235; endowment growth, xii, 170, 177–178, 185, 193–197, 199, 213–217, 243; Leggett years (1965-1975), 181–182, 190–191, 193–197, 199–201; metrics, 228; multiculturalism, 204–206;

Osgood years, 221; rejoining, 175; resignation, 171, 173; Stevens years (1941-1954), 161–173; student activism, xix, 31–32, 188, 200–201, 230–235; Turner years (1975-1979), 181–182, 206–207, 210, 211–212; Venture Fund, 227. *See also* Executive Committee (Grinnell College); Finance Committee
boards, other JR service: General Growth Properties, 69, 137; Hospital Services of Iowa, 72; law school, 112; list of, 251; in obituary, 246
Boesen, Connie, 79
Bohnenkamp, Ashley, xvi
bond ratings, 132, 217
Bon-Ton Stores, 78
Booth, Dick, 237
Boston Herald Traveller, 121
Botanical Center, 116
Bowdoin College, 225, 244
Bowen, Howard: appointment, 172, 173, 175; background and career, 173–174, 177, 180, 189, 190; on compound interest, 216–217; as fundraiser, 178, 180, 182; improvements under, 173–186; on JR as trustee, 182; on minority students, 205; resignation, 173, 180, 189–190; science building

name, 221; student activism under, 186–190; on tuition, 9
Bowen, Lois, 181, 189, 221
Boy Scouts, 57, 65, *81,* 109
Bradford, Curtis, 170
Bradley, Bill, 135
Brandeis (store), 77
The Breakfast Club, 118
Brenton, William, 116
Bridenstine, Ellen, xv
Brogan, Dennis, 183
Brooks, Archie, 117
Brown University, 156, 224
Bryn Mawr College, 184
Buck, David, xvii
Buck, Jane, 79
Bucksbaum, John, xvi, 110–111, 118–119, 128, 137–138, 151
Bucksbaum, Kay: on being Jewish student, 6, 124; Fine Arts building, 221; friendship with JR, 69; on JR and football, 112; JR's influence on philanthropy, 128; on JR's mentoring, 139; on JR's relationship with Louise, 56; as resource, xvi; on Rose Rosenfield, 43
Bucksbaum, Martin, *90*; JR's influence on philanthropy, 130; JR's mentoring of, 111, 132, 138–139; Planned Parenthood, 143. *See also* General Growth Properties
Bucksbaum, Matthew, *90*; Fine Arts building, 221; JR's

influence on philanthropy, 128, 130; JR's mentoring of, 111, 132, 138–139; Planned Parenthood, 143. *See also* General Growth Properties
Bucksbaum Center for the Fine Arts, 221, 229
Buffett, Susie, 141, 142
Buffett, Warren: and Chicago Cubs, 150; foreword by, xi–xii, xvi; friendship with JR, xi–xii, 191–192, 198–199, 247; General Growth Properties, 139; Grinnell endowment, xii, 192–197, 199, 213–217, 227, 243–246; Grinnell's television station purchase, xii, 182, 194–195, 215, 216; as Grinnell trustee, xii, 192–197, 199–200, 209–210, 213–217, 236, 243–246; on JR's investment acumen, 196–197; on JR's love of Grinnell, xii, 39; Planned Parenthood, 127, 141, 143, 197; as resource, xvi
buildings, Grinnell College: under Bowen, 177, 180–181, 188; Cubs Room, 148–149; funding with endowment income, 218, 222; government loans for, 207; grants for, 179; under Leggett, 207–209; Main's vision for, 13, 160, 207; new buildings in 1980's and 1990's, 220–222; new buildings in 2000's, 221–222; new buildings post-WWII, 163, 164–166; president's house, 181, 219; renovations in 1970's, 207–209; renovations in 1980's and 1990's, 219–220, 229; science building, 164–166, 180, 220, 221, 229; Skidmore, Owens, and Merrill, 179, 181, 188, 207; WWII expenditures, 162. *See also* dormitories
Buildings and Grounds Committee, 189
Bulletin, 3
Burke, Dannie. *See* Rosenfield, Dannie
Burling, Edward, 179, 219
Burling Library, 179, 181, 210, 211, 219
Burnett, Bob, xvi–xvii, 110, 118, 237, 247

C

Calvinism, 159
Cambridge University debate visits, 12, 38
Campbell, Bonnie, 143
The Capitol City Woolen Mills, 52
Cardinal, José, 150
Carleton College: associations, 183, 218; comparison groups, 184,

244; founding, 156; student unrest, 187; teaching load, 225
Carlson, Sarah, xv
Carnegie Foundation, 38
Carroll, Shelby, xvi
cars, rules for, 37, 186, 187
Catholic Church and and origins of colleges, 157, 158
CBS (Concerned Black Students), 204–205
Cech, Tom, 200, 226
Chapel talks, 12, 14
Chicago Cubs, xiii, 16, 111, 148–151
Chicago Tribune, 148–149
China programs, 12, 185, 219, 228
Chrestomathia, 7–8
Christian Reform Church and origins of colleges, 157
Chrysalis Foundation, 58, 127
Chrystal, John, 121, 126, 146, 151, 222, 237
cigars, 150
Civic Center (Des Moines), 116, 119, 125
Civil War, 159, 162
Clarke University, 158
Clark Hall, 209
Class Letters, 174–175
Clay, David, xvi, 131–132
Clotfelter, Beryl, 203
Coble, Genevieve B., 18
Cochran, Wendell: profile of JR, 57, 119–120, 122–123, 126, 143, 145; testimonial, 248
Coe College, 183, 218

Colorado College, 156, 244
color-blindness, 66, 122
Columbia University, 156, 160
Committee on Trustees, 175
Commonwealth Fund study, 9
Community Bank, 197
community service: Younkers, 70, 74, 75. *See also* philanthropy
comparison groups, college, 184, 244
comprehensive fees, 168
Conard, Henry, 161
Concerned Black Students (CBS), 204–205
Congregational Church, 10, 156, 157–158, 159–160, 184
Convocation of 1957, 185
Cook, Wayne, 112
Cooney, Jim, 134
Cooper, Frank. *See* Cooper, Gary
Cooper, Gary, 6, 16–17
Cornell College, 183, 218
cottages, 6
Covington and Burling, 179
Cowles Foundation, 163, 219, 228
Cowles Hall, 162
Cowles-Kruidenier Chinese Studies Program, 219, 228
Cownie, Jim: background and career, 133; Heritage Communications, xiv, 133–137; JR's mentoring of, xiv, 110, 111, 132, 136; on JR's philanthropy, 117, 118, 125–126; Marriott

Hotel, 119; as source, xvi; as sponsor of biography, xiii, xiv, xv, 110; testimonials, 110, 248
Crady, Tom, 235
Crone, Neil, 17
Cubs Room, 148–149
Culver, John, xvii, 144, 146, 249
curriculum: changes under Bowen, 182–183; current, 183, 202–203, 224–225; expansion in 1980's, 228–229; individually advised, 202–203, 224–225; interdisciplinary offerings, 229; in JR's college days, 6–7; non-Western canon in, 184; requirements, 6–7, 182–183, 191
The Cyclone, 3, 5–6, 16, 28–29, 30, 34

D

Danforth Foundation, 183
Darby, Fred, 165, 167
Darby Fund, 165, 167, 170, 175, 177, 178, 185
Darby Gymnasium, 162
Darling, Ding, 45
dating and sexual relations, rules for, 36, 37, 186
Davenport, Iowa: founding of Iowa College, 10, 158; move from, 7, 10, 158–159, 162
Davidson College, 244
Davidson's, 67
Davis, Chester, 160
Davis, Gladys Foster, 57, 69
debate visits, 12, 38
debt, student, 217–218, 234, 235, 244, 245
deferred giving progams, 194
Delta Phi Rho, 33
Demerosch, Walter, 12
demonstrations and protests: by CBS, 205; closure of College, 200–201, 202; gay rights, 236; Vietnam War, 55, 190. *See also* student activism and politics
Dentel, Georgia, 185
Des Moines: Isaiah Frankel activities, 51; Jewish community, 45, 51, 123–124, 127, 130; JR as community leader, 109–111, 115, 116–117; JR's philanthropy to, 111, 116–119, 123–128; Rose Rosenfield activities, 44–45; Younkers philanthropy, 75; Younkers shift to, 61
Des Moines Art Center, 45, *94,* 125
Des Moines Bruins, 72, 149
Des Moines Cable Network, 133–134, 135. *See also* Heritage Communications
Des Moines Civic Center, 116, 119, 125
Des Moines Community Playhouse, 58
Des Moines Enterprises, 149
Des Moines Garden Club, 45

Des Moines Metro Opera, 127
The Des Moines Symphony, 127
Distinguished Alumni Achievement Award, 112
Distinguished Service Award in Trusteeship, 238
Dober, Dick, 208
"DORIC" column, 5–6, 18, 19, 20–25, 66, *104*
dormitories: African American students, 205; architecture, 13, 160, 181, 207; coed, xix, 189, 208; coed bathrooms, 208; crowding, 163, 188; during JR's college years, 6; new in 1940's and 1950's, 162, 163, 164; new in 2000's, 221; as part of endowment, 162–163, 194; proposal for "dorm that never was," 187, 188–189; renovations, 207–209, 210, 211, 219; rules for, 186, 187, 201. *See also* housing
Dowling High School, 125–126, 127
draft: Korean War, 166; Vietnam War, 190
Drake, George: background and career, 212–213; on Buffett's endowment comments, 243–246; capital campaign, 211; on Chicago Cubs sale, 148; on comparisons to Main, 13; faculty interaction program with University of Iowa, 219; new buildings in 1980's and 1990's, 220–222; as president, xiii, 212, 213, 223–226; on strength of Board, 236–237; on student activism, 230, 232; tenure policy, 223–224; testimonial, 249; as trustee, xiii, 237
Drake, Sue, xvii
Drake Law School, 55
Drake University, 55, 75
Draper Prize in Engineering, 226
drinking. *See* alcohol
Duchen, Charles (Chuck), 73, 77, *96*, 128
Duck Creek Shopping Center, 68
Dudley, De, xv
Duke, Charlie, 213
Duncan, Randy, 118
Dunlap, Flora, 44
Dutton, Gardiner, 195, 237

E

Eckhardt, Christopher, 55
Economics, 183
Education Department and offerings, 184, 220, 228–229
education of JR. *See* student, JR as
Eisley, Loren, 192
Elementary Education, 184
endowment: "DORIC" column on, 23; effect on alumni giving, 222; endowed chairs, 183, 222–223; farms and dorms

in, 162–163, 167, 175, 177, 194; Ford Foundation grant, 180; funding capital projects with, 218, 222; growth under JR and Buffett, xii, 170, 177–178, 185, 193–197, 199, 213–217, 243; investment philosophy, 132, 193–197, 213–217; mentoring of Clay, 131–132; oil royalties, 165, 167, 170, 175, 177, 178, 185; Stevens on need to increase, 168; and study abroad, 185; use for programs, 185, 227–228, 243–246; Venture Fund, 227

Enright, Jim, 115, 143, 151

enrollments: declines in 1950's and 1960's, 166, 168; declines in 1960's and 1970's, 187, 191; increase in 1950's, 179; increase in 1980's and 1990's, 217; increase in 2000's, 244; Jewish students, 10; during JR's college days, 8–9; post-WWII, 163–164, 176; World War I, 14

Equitable of Iowa Insurance Company, 60, 76–77, 119, 129, 139

Erickson, Karla, xvi

Evangelism, 159

E.W. Variety Stores, 55

Executive Committee (Grinnell College): ability to sell real property, 167; appointment to, 162; dorm renovations, 208; faculty housing, 164; faculty salaries, 170–171; need for fundraising, 164, 167; Physical Education Complex, 207

Executive Committee (Younkers), 65, 134

F

faculty: administration ratio, 9; cuts, 169, 210; endowed chairs, 183, 222–223; evaluations, 203, 228; Harvard University exchange, 9; hiring post-WWII, 163–164, 176; housing, 164; during JR's college days, 9–10, 13–15; leave program, 223; publications, 226; quality of, 7, 9, 182, 183, 225–226; recruitment, 13, 177; retirement policy, 224; salaries, 170–171, 179, 183, 218, 223, 228; student involvement in hiring, 203; teaching load, 225–226; tensions with Board, 227–228; tensions with Stevens, 170, 177; tensions with Turner, 211–212; tenure policy, 183, 211–212, 223–224; University of Iowa interaction program, 219; Venture Fund grants, 227

Faculty Committee on Student Affairs, 187
farms, as part of endowment, 162–163, 175, 177
Farnam, Henry, 158
FBI, 201–202
Fell, Bob: as Class Agent, 59, 174; "DORIC" column, 5–6, 18, 19, 20–25, 66, *104*. See also *Malteaser*
feminism: Dannie Rosenfield, 58; JR, 142; Louise Noun, 58, 142; Rose Rosenfield, 43, 45
Ferguson, Pamela, 212, 213, 229
field house, 222
Finance Committee: ability to buy and sell, 163; Buffett as chair, xii, 192–193, 209; divestment in South Africa, 206–207, 230–234; JR as chair, 175, 181, 192; proposed new dorm, 188; Second Century Fund, 169–170
finances, Grinnell College: balancing of budget with gifts, 209; debt, 160, 161, 162, 163, 166, 167–169, 175, 177; divestment in South Africa, 206–207, 230–234; financial ratings, 132, 217; investment in Intel, xii, 122, 130, 196, 214–215; plant funds deficit, 207, 209, 210; summer borrowing, 167, 177, 178, 209, 217; television station purchase, xii, 182, 194–195, 215, 216. *See also* endowment; Finance Committee; fundraising, Grinnell campaigns; grants
financial aid: African American students, 204, 205; building, 221–222; forgivable loans for teachers, 229; grants to students, 217–218, 244–245; *Malteaser* Class Fund, 27; in 1980's and 1990's, 217–218; scholarships funded by JR, 112, 127; South African student program, 231–232, 233; in 2000's, 244–245
Fine Arts buildings, 179, 181, 221, 229
fire safety, 201
First Year Tutorial, 202–203
Flanagan, Hallie, 12, 36, 160
Fleming, Bob, 114, 118
Flunk (Skip) Day, 24
football, 15, 16, 112–113, 185
Ford Foundation, 177, 179–180, 183, 185, 219
Fortas, Abe, 55
Forum, 181
Foster, Charlie, 170
Founder's Garden Club, 45
Frankel, Allie, 43
Frankel, Anselm, 44, 50
Frankel, Babette Sheuerman, 43, 49, 51–54

Frankel, Henrietta, 50
Frankel, Henry: birth, 50; home, 43–44; travels, 53; Younkers, 64, 65, 66, 70, 74
Frankel, Isaiah, 49–51, 52, 62, 123
Frankel, Manassa, 50, 62, 63
Frankel, Mrs. Henry, *94*
Frankel, Nathan (Nate), 43, 50, 62
Frankel, Rose. *See* Rosenfield, Rose Frankel
Frankel Clothing Company of Oskaloosa, 62
Frankel Memorial Terrace, *94*
Frankel Men's Clothing Store, 65–66
Frankel's (store), 26, 50, 62, 67
fraternities and sororities, 4, 6, 32–34
Freddie Mac, 215
Freshman Tutorial, 202–203
Fridricks, William B., xvii
Friedman, Stanley B., *96*
Friedman, William, Jr., 77, *96*
Friedman, William (Bill), *96*; on influence of JR, 110; investment in cable television, 134, 135; on JR's appearance, 122; on JR's investmant ability, 75; on JR's Jewishness, 124; as resource, xvi; testimonial, 249
Friendly, Fred, 192
Fry, Hayden, 112
Fund for Excellence, 227
fundraising, Grinnell campaigns: under Bowen, 178, 179–180, 182, 185; deferred giving progams, 194; dorm renovations, 209; under Drake, 211; Gale Observatory, 219–220; gift annuity program, 194; under Leggett, 210–211; new buildings in 1980's and 1990's, 220–222; new buildings in 2000's, 222; sesquicentennial, 229; under Stevens, 164, 165, 167, 168–171; Symposium in 1967, 192, 210; under Turner, 210
fundraising by JR: for endowment in 1960's, 178, 180; JR as leader, 125, 126, 128; JR's advice on fundraising, 128; Living History Farms, 126; to match Ford grants, 179–180; Planned Parenthood, 142–143, 197; political, 145–146, 147; for University of Iowa, 112. *See also* philanthropy by JR

G

Gale, Grant, 170, 171, 172, 220
Gale Observatory, 219–220
Gamble, Graham, 64, 113
Gamble, Read, Howland, 63, 64, 113–115
gambling, 114–115, 143
Ganaway, John, 7
Garang, John, 205

Gartner, Michael, xvi, 109, 115–117, 122, 143, 248
Gaskell, Jon, 136
Gates, George, 160
Gates Lectures, 10, 12
gay rights, 234, 235–236
General Growth Development Corporation, 138
General Growth Management, 139
General Growth Properties, 68–69, 111, 120, 132, 137–139
Geo. Innes Co., *99*
Gessman, Pat, xvii, 127, 128, 139, 150–151, 247
GI Bill, 163–164, 166
gift annuity program, 194
Ginther, Joseph M., *96*
"The Girl in my English Class," 21–22
Glynn, Frederick A., *96*
Good Morning, 70, 72, 73, 74, 77
Goodnow Hall, 209, 210, 220
Gordon family, 143
government, student, 37–38. *See also* political activity
graduation rates, 30, 218, 245
Grand Department Store, 61
grants: Carnegie Foundation, 38; Cowles Foundation, 163, 219, 228; faculty interaction grant, 219; faculty salaries, 183; Ford Foundation, 177, 179–180, 183, 185, 219; Hewlett Foundation, 219; Howard Hughes Foundation, 219; Joyce Foundation, 219; Kresge Foundation, 219; land grants, 156; Mellon Foundation, 219; National Science Foundation, 179, 180, 219; Pell Grant, 244, 245; PEW Foundation, 219; Rockefeller Foundation, 180, 204; Sloan Foundation, 179, 183, 219; to students, 217–218, 244–245; Venture Fund, 227
Great Depression, 14–15, 160, 161
Green, Chris, xvii, 114, 118
Griner, John A., III, *96*
Grinnell, Iowa: move to, 7, 10, 158–159, 162; tornado, 159, 279n163
Grinnell, Josiah Bushnell, 158–159
Grinnell College: admissions, 10, 204, 244; applications, 187, 217, 226; associations, 183, 218; closure, 200–201, 202; cultural programming, 184–185; founding, 10, 156, 157–158; graduation rates, 30, 218, 245; history, 156, 157–160; during JR's college days, 3, 4, 6, 7–8, 10–21, 30–38; JR's decision to attend, 3–5; JR's love for, xii, 3–4, 8, 39; legal work by JR,

114; move to Grinnell, 7, 10, 158–159, 162; philanthropy by JR, 126, 127, 179, 209, 221, 222–223, 238–239; reputation and teaching quality, 4, 7, 9, 38, 182, 183, 186, 225–226; Rose Rosenfield lecture endowment, 45; sesquicentennial, 220, 229; tuition, 9, 168, 244; water supply, 20. *See also* athletics; Board of Trustees; Board of Trustees and JR; buildings, Grinnell College; curriculum; dormitories; endowment; enrollments; faculty; finances, Grinnell College; fundraising, Grinnell campaigns; presidents, Grinnell College; student activism and politics; students; women students
Grinnell Corps, 227
Grinnell House, 219
Grinnell Investment Committee, 215
The Grinnell Magazine, 104–105
The Grinnell Register, 32
Grinnell Savings Bank, 20
Grinnell Travel Fellowships, 185
Grove, Andy, 214
gyms, 162, 207, 222

H

Haack, Allison, xv
Hackes, Peter, 192
Hall, James Norman, 11
Halloran, Beth, xiii, xv
Harkin, Ruth, 146
Harkin, Tom, xvii, 144, 145–146, 147
Harris, Hardy, 62
Harris, Henry C., 62
Harris, Jack, 220, 223
Harris, Lucile, 220, 223
Harris Center, 220
Harris Dry Goods Store, 62
Harris-Emery: acquisition by Frankel's, 50, 62; history, 62–63; JR's working at, 65–66; merger with Younkers, 48, 50, 61, 63–64, 113; Meyer's role, 47–48, 62; *Tips*, 66
Harris Fellowship, 223
Hartung, John, 185
Harvard University: faculty exchange, 9; founding, 155; New Deal, 160; Noun at, 47; South African student program, 231–232
Haverford College, 156, 184
Hawk, Rupert, 167, 171, 175–176
Hawkeye Television Network, 134. *See also* Heritage Communications
Hayakawa, S. I., 192
"Haystack Prayer Meeting," 158
hazing, 186

health insurance, 72
Heath Visiting Professor Program, 183
Heller, Walter, 139
Henderson, Stacey, xvii
Henry Luce Foundation, 223
Heritage Communications: history, 66, 133–137; mentoring by JR, xiv, 111, 132, 133, 135, 136, 216; Ruan investment in, 121, 135
Herr, Kathrin, xv
Herrick Chapel, 10
Herron, George, 13, 160
Hess, Mike, 125–126
Hewlett Foundation, 219
Hiller, Betty, 191
Hiller, Dick, 191, 192
Historical Studies, 183
history, as JR's minor, 6, 7
Hoak, Jim: background and career, 133; Heritage Communications, xiv, 133–137, 216; mentoring by JR, 111, 132, 136, 216; as source, xvi
Homerin, Dennis, 185, 237
Homes at Oakridge, 127
Hopcus, Jeanie, 79
Hopkins, Harry, 160
Hornets. See *The Cyclone*
Hospital Services of Iowa, 72
housing: cottages, 6; faculty, 164; married students, 235–236; off-campus, 187, 188, 235–236; women students, 6, 188, 201. *See also* dormitories
Howard Hughes Foundation, 219
Hoyt, Chuck, 16
Hubbell, Fred, Jr.: on General Growth Properties, 138–139; on Joe's interest in women's rights, 142; Marriott Hotel project, 119; Planned Parenthood, 140, 143; as resource, xvii; on sale of Younkers, 77; testimonial, 248
Hubbell, Fred, Sr., 118
Hubbell, Frederich M., 119
Hubbell, James W., Jr., 77, 116
Hubbell family, legal work for, 114
Huff, Doc, 15
Hughes, Harold, 76, 120, 122, 126, 144–145, 147
Humanities course, 183
Hunter, Judy, xv
Hutchison, Tom, 122, 151

I

ICLU (Iowa Civil Liberties Union), 54–55
I Have a Dream Foundation, 127
The Imp. See *The Cyclone*
Ingham, Vicki, xvii
Innes, Walter P., Jr., 99
Innes, Walter P., Sr., 99
Innes Department Store, 67, 99
insurance, health, 72
Intel: mentoring by JR, xiv,

129–130; Ruan investment in, 110, 117, 121–122; startup investment, xii, 122, 130, 196, 214–215; World Food Prize, 110, 117, 122
interdisciplinary programs, 229
International Relations, 45, 222
International students, 235
Investor Responsibility Committee, 231, 233
Investor Responsibility Research Center, 233–234
"Iowa Band," 158
Iowa Business Hall of Fame, 119
Iowa Civil Liberties Union (ICLU), 54–55
Iowa College: founding, 10, 158–159; move to Grinnell, 7, 10, 158–159, 162. *See also* Grinnell College
Iowa Cubs, 151
Iowa Democratic Party, 111, 143–148
Iowa Natural Heritage Foundation, 127
Iowa Peace Institute, 127
Israel, 125, 145

J

James Hall, 209
Janisch, Julia, 226
Jansen, H. W., 211
Jenkins, Dick, 194
Jester, Ralph, 68
Jesuit Monastery site, 68
Jewish Community Center, 45
Jewish Federation of Greater Des Moines, 123–124, 127, 130
Jewishness: assimilation by Rosenfield family, 57; on campus, 6, 7–8, 10, 124; influence on JR's philanthropy, 117; Jewish community in Des Moines, 45, 51, 123–124, 127, 130; JR as Jewish community leader, 123–124; JR's lack of religiosity, 123, 124; in Keokuk, 61; philanthropy by JR to Jewish community, 123–124, 127. *See also* anti-Semitism; religion
Jewish Settlement House, 45
J. Mandelbaum & Sons, 64
Jobs, Steve, 236
"Joe Rosenfield Fund" (Planned Parenthood), 141
John Blair and Company, 121
Johnson, Alf, 237
Johnson, Bettie, 39
Johnson, Dan, 55
Johnson, Wilbur, 201
Jones, Allan, 203
Jones, Chris, xv
Joseph and Dannie Rosenfield Program in Human Rights and International Relations, 222
Journey to Autonomy (Noun), xvii, 44, 46–47, 48, 54
Joyce Foundation, 219
June, Jill: on Dannie Rosenfield, 58; on JR's advice for fundraising,

128; on JR's declining health, 247; on JR's gifts to Planned Parenthood, 127, 140, 141–143; on JR's love of Chicago Cubs, 149; on JR's political activity, 144, 146; on JR's relationship with Louise, 55–56; mentoring by JR, 131, 132; as resource, xvi; testimonial, 248

Junior Liberal Arts Examination, 183

Junto, 12, 18–19

K

Kaiser, Daniel, 222
Kakert, Arnold, *90*
Kenyon College, 244
Keokuk, Iowa, 60–61
Kerr, Florence, 160
King, Martin Luther, Jr., 191, 210
King's College. *See* Columbia University
Kington, Raynard, 243–246
Kinsey, Bob, 177, 178
Kintner, Phillip, 202
KIOA, 121
Kirk, J. Stuart, *96*
Kirkpatrick, Stewart, 172
Kissane, James, 18
Knapp, Bill: cable television, 133–134; on death of James Rosenfield, 59; friendship with JR, 120; on JR's influence and reputation, 109, 120, 247; on JR's Jewishness, 124; and JR's philanthropic leadership, 116, 117, 118, 128, 130; on JR's political activity, 145, 147; Merle Hay purchase attempt, 120; Planned Parenthood, 141, 143; political activity, 145; as resource, xvi, xvii
Knox College, 183, 218
Korean War, 166
Kosak, Jake, 226
Kresge Foundation, 219
Kruidenier, David, 116, 118, 125
Kruidenier, Elizabeth, 237
Krum, Stanley H., *96*

L

Lake Forest College, 187, 218
land grants, 156
Langan Hall, 6
language departments, 183, 228
Laug, Adam, xvi
Lauterbach, Karen, 201
law practice, JR: Gamble, Read, Howland firm, 63, 64, 113–115; law school, 5, 64, 111–113, 127; work for Grinnell, 114; work for Ruan, 114–115; for Younkers, 44, 60, 64, 65, 113–114
Lawrence College, 183, 218
law school: JR, 5, 64, 111–113; Louise Noun, 55; philanthropy to, 112, 127
Law School Foundation

Board, 112
Lazier, Bill, 237, 238
League Board, 37–38
Leavitt, Dick, 110, 112, 124, 126, 149, 248
Leavitt, Ellis, 119
Leggett, Glenn: career, 190–191; as president, 190–191; on proposed dorm, 189; resignation, 210; student activity and unrest, 190, 200–201
liberal arts colleges: compared to universities, 155; history and background, 155–157; JR on, 4–5
libraries: Burling Library, 179, 181, 210, 211, 219; pilfering from, 24
Lilac Arboretum, 45
Lilly Foundation, 183
Lipschutz, Sarah, 51, 52
literary magazines, 12, 18–19
literary societies, 7–8, 35–37
Little, Fred: as campaign chair, 210; interview with JR, 4, 8; on JR as a lawyer, 114; on JR as mentor, 128–129; on JR's goal to strengthen Board, 192, 204, 236; on JR's Jewishness, 124; on JR's love of Grinnell, 39; on JR's political activity, 143; on JR's privacy, 46, 56; as resource, xvi; testimonial, 248; as Trustee, 129, 210, 237

Living History Farms, 111, 126, 127
Loeb, Schlosser, and Bennett, 181
Loewi, Andrew, 203
Loose Hall, 163, 164
Loras, 158
Lovejoy, Ted, 237
Lovell, Cecil, 7, 170
Lowden, Eleanor, 7
Lowry, Jim, 185, 204, 237
Lubetkin, Robert, *96,* 191
Lutheran Hospital, 75
Lyons, Howard, 70
Lyons, Selma Sheurerman, 47

M

Macalester, 156, 244
MacDonald, Malcom, 12
MacNider, Hanford, 119
Macy, Jesse, 160
Magoun, George, 159
Main, John Hanson Thomas: Carnegie Foundation Board appointment, 9; as president, 13, 34, 160; resident halls vision, 13, 34, 160, 207; secret fraternities and sororities, 34
Malteaser, 84; anti-Semitism in, 27–28; in campus culture, 3; Class Fund, 27; influences on, 66; JR's role, 5–6, 25–26, 27; "Malteaser Follies," 26–27; origins, 26; topics, 30–31, 36
"Malteaser Follies," 26–27
Mandela, Nelson, 234

Mandelbaum, Julius, 64
Mandelbaum, Robert, *96*
Mandelbaum, Sidney, 63, 64
Mandelbaum family, 60, 64
MAP (Mentored Advanced Project Program), 229
Marriott Hotel, 119
Marshall, Tom, xvi, 248
Marshall Field Foundation, 165, 172
Marshall Scholarship, 226
Marshalltown Community College, 233
Martin Luther King Scholarship Fund, 204
Martz and Lundy, 180, 210
Mauch, Hilda, 10–11, 18, 24, 35–37
May, Henrietta. *See* Rosenfield, Henrietta May
Maytag, Fred, 171, 172, 237
McAlman, [Coach], 33
McCann, Mary, 73
McCarthy, Eugene, 144
McCarthy, Kenneth, *96*
McGinn, John, 121
McLuhan, Marshall, 192
Mears Cottage, 208–209, 219
media, general: on Buffett's endowment comments, 243; college ratings, 218, 245; on Grinnell student activists, 201; on JR, *86, 87*; on secret fraternities and sororities, 32; on Younkers, *89–92*. *See also* publications, campus; publications, store; radio; television
Mellon Foundation, 219
Men's Court, 38
Men's Glee Club, 12
Men's Senate, 37, 38
Mentored Advanced Project Program (MAP), 229
mentoring by JR: Bucksbaum brothers, 111, 132, 138–139; Clay, 131–132; Cownie, xiv, 110, 111, 132, 133, 136; General Growth Properties, 111, 120, 132, 138–139; Heritage Communications, xiv, 111, 132, 133, 135, 136, 216; Hoak, 111, 132, 136, 216; Intel, xiv, 129–130; June, 131, 132; Little, 128–129; Noyce, xiv, 129–130; in philanthropy, 130; role, 128–132; Wimer, 130–131
Merchants National Bank, 20
Merle Hay shopping center, 68, *91,* 120
Merryman, Marguerite, 18–19
Methodist Hospital, 75
metrics, 228
Meyer, Sidney, 223
Miller, Tom, xvii, 110, 144, 146–147
misogyny in "DORIC" column, 21–23
missionaries, Hall on, 11
Modern Languages, 183
Mohrman, Katherine, 237
Monmouth College, 183, 218
Montague, Ashley, 192

Montgomery, Ruth, 203
Moore, Gordon, 214
Morgan, Randall, 185, 204
Morningside College, 75
Morrill Act, 156
Morris, Willie, 192
Moyer, Wayne, 229
Murray, Bill, 126, 127
Murrow, Edward R., 185
Music, School of, 8
Musser, Bob, xvi, 8
Mutti, Jack, 223, 228
Mutual Aid Society, Younkers, 72

N

Nanjing University, 228
National By-Products, 114
National College Experience Study, 226
National Organization for Women (NOW), 58
National Science Foundation (NSF), 179, 180, 219
National Society of Fund-Raising Executives, 127
Nations and the Global Environment Chair, 223
need-blind admissions, 244
Netsch, Walter, 179
New Deal, 160
Nixon, Richard, 144, 148, 150
Nobel Laureates, 226
Nollen, John, 162
Norelius, E. A., 200
Norris, D. W., 27
Norris, John, 27, 119, 189, 237
Norris Hall, 181

Norton, Homer, 170, 176
Noun, Louise, *85, 88*; autobiography, xvii, 44, 46–47, 48, 54; birth, 44; Chrysalis Foundation, 127; death, 247; on family life, 46–47, 55–56; feminism, 58, 142; on grandparents, 49, 50, 51, 53, 54; influence on JR, 142; political activity, 54–55, 58, 148; relationship with JR, 54–56; religion, 123; as resource, xvii, 59; on Rose Rosenfield, 44, 46, 47
Noun, Maurice, 55
Noun Chair in Women's Studies, 223
Noyce, Bob: AIM Campaign, 210; Draper Prize in Engineering, 226; fame, 237; Gale Observatory, 219–220; mentoring, xiv, 129–130. *See also* Intel
Noyce Science Center, 164–166, 180, 220, 221, 229
NSF (National Science Foundation), 179, 180, 219

O

Oberlin: comparison groups, 184, 244; founding, 156; lack of fraternities, 33; student unrest, 187; teaching load, 225
obituary for JR, 246
occupations, student, 202

off-campus housing, 187, 188, 235–236
officer training programs: Air Force ROTC, 166, 201, 202; WW II, 162, 163, 176
oil royalties, 165, 167, 170, 175, 177, 178, 185
Olson, Dick, 134
Olympic athletes, 15, 16, 38
Oracle (secret society), 35, 36
Osgood, Russell, 212, 213, 221, 239
Outstanding Philanthropist Award, 127
Oxford University debate visits, 12, 38

P

Papper, Patricia, 223
Paramount-Gulf, 133–134
pareital rules, 186
Parslow, Morris, 225
Patton, O.K., 112
Pauling, Linus, 192
Paulu, Leonard, 15–16
Payne, Charles, 7, 10
PEC (Physical Education Complex), 207
Peck, Paul, 7
Pell Grant, 244, 245
Penn State, glee club competition, 12
PEW Foundation, 219
Pfitsch, John, 207
Phelps, Louis V., 9, 14–15, 23, 24, 27, 162
philanthropy: by Babette Frankel, 53–54; by Marshall Field Foundation, 165, 172; by Stanley Richards, 123–124, 130; by Younkers, 75
philanthropy by JR: awards, 127; as compulsion, 126; to Des Moines, 111, 116–119, 123–128; to Dowling High School, 125–126, 127; endowed chairs, 222–223; to Grinnell, 126, 127, 179, 209, 221, 222–223, 238–239; to Jewish community, 123–124, 127; leadership and influence on others, 116, 117–118, 125, 128, 130; to Living History Farms, 111, 126, 127; to Planned Parenthood, 127, 128, 131, 140–143, 197; to University of Iowa, 112, 127; and Younkers, 75. *See also* fundraising by JR
Philosophy and Religious Studies, 220
Physical Education Complex (PEC), 207
Physics Department, 223
Pickle, Steven, 226
Pike, James, 185
Pinney Woods Cotton Blossom Singers, 54
Pinney Woods School, 54
Pioneer Hybrid, 141
Planned Parenthood: birthday celebration, 142–143; Buffett, 127, 141, 143, 197;

Dannie Rosenfield, 58;
JR's role, 111, 128, 131,
140–143, 197; philanthropy
to, 127, 128, 131, 140–143,
197. *See also* June, Jill
plant funds deficit, 207, 209, 210
"Playboy Incident," 201
policing, 201
political activity: Dannie
Rosenfield, 58, 144; Iowa
Democratic Party, 111, 143–
148; Isaiah Frankel, 51;
JR, 54–55, 111, 143–148;
during JR's student years,
11; Louise Noun, 54–55, 58,
148; student government,
37–38; voting reminders
in Younkers magazines,
74; Wimer encouragement,
130–131
political science, as JR's
major, 6, 7
Pollard, Will, 185
Pomona College, 156, 244
Poppejohn, John, 143
Poppejohn, Mary, 143
Poweshiek Oil Company, 167
Presbyterian Church and
origins of colleges, 156, 157
Presidential Search
Committee, 175
presidents, Grinnell College:
Ferguson, 212, 213, 229;
Hawk, 175–176; house for,
181, 219; Kington, 243–
246; Main, 9, 13, 34, 160,
207; Osgood, 212, 213, 221,
239; role, 176; Turner, 210,
211–212. *See also* Bowen,
Howard; Drake, George;
Leggett, Glenn; Stevens,
Samuel
Price, John, 206, 237
Princeton, founding of, 156
privacy: and donations to
Planned Parenthood, 140,
141–143; of JR, 46, 56, 140,
141–143; Rosenfield name
on Campus Center, 221, 239
Proffits, 77
profit sharing at Younkers, 71, *104*
pub, 194, 199, 234–235
publications, campus: in
campus culture, 3; *The
Cyclone,* 3, 5–6, 16, 28–29,
30, 34; "DORIC" column,
5–6, 18, 19, 20–25, 66, *104*;
first female editor, 10–11,
18; *The Grinnell Magazine,
104–105*; *Junto,* 12, 18–19.
See also *Malteaser; Scarlet
and Black (S&B)*
publications, faculty, 226
publications, store: *Good
Morning* (Younkers), 70,
72, 73, 74, 77; *Reporter*
(Younkers), 39, 65, 70–71,
72, 74, 77, *95–101*; *Tips*
(Harris-Emery), 66
Puritan origins of colleges,
155–156

R

Radcliff College: Noun at, 47;

student unrest, 187
radio, 11, 121
Ragsdale, Bradford, 170
ratings: bond, 132, 217; college, 218, 245
Rauschenberg, Robert, 192
Rawlings, Hunter, 219
Ray, Robert, 127
recruitment, faculty, 13, 177
recruitment, student: athletes, 185; and Congregational Church, 10; international students, 235; JR's college years, 10; students of color, 204, 235
Reed College, 184, 244
religion: Grinnell's founding, 10, 157; JR's lack of religiosity, 123, 124; Louise Noun, 123; private colleges, 155–157; in Rosenfield family, 57, 123; student demographics, 10. *See also* Jewishness
Religious Studies, 223
Reporter: cuts to, 77; images and clips, *95–101*; on JR, 39, 65; Mutual Aid Society soliciations, 72; voting campaign, 74; Younkers culture, 70–71
retirement plans, Younkers, 71–72
retirement policy, Grinnell, 224
Reynolds, Arthur, 62
Rhodes Scholars, 17, 18, 38, 226
Richards, Stanley: on JR's leadership, 110, 118; on JR's political activity, 143; philanthropy by, 123–124, 130; as resource, xvi; testimonial, 248
Richey, Wayne, 58
Riesman, David, 185
Ripon College, 183, 218
River Hills Redevelopment Group, 138
Roadside Settlement House, 44
Rockefeller Foundation, 180, 204
Rock Island Railroad, 113
Roosevelt, Theodore, 57, *81*
Rosenfield, Dannie, 57–59, *87,* 140, 144
Rosenfield, Henrietta May, 49
Rosenfield, James, 57–59, *93*
Rosenfield, Joe: business career, 119–123; childhood, 43, 57, *80, 81, 82*; Class Letter, 174–175; college images, *81, 83*; community leadership, 109–111, 115, 116–117; death and memorial service, 246–247; family life, 46–47, 48, 55–56, 57; friendship with Buffett, xi–xii, 191–192, 198–199, 247; health, 236, 238, 247; images as an adult, *86, 87, 90, 91, 96, 99, 100, 102–105*; love for Grinnell, xii, 3–4, 8, 39; marriage and fatherhood, 57–59, *87*; obituary, 246; as private, 46, 56, 140,

141–143; relationship with Louise, 54–56; sense of humor, xix, 21, 28, 29, 39, 46, 48; will, 123, 127, 140, 221, 238–239; work with Ruan, 114–115, 120–123. *See also* Board of Trustees and JR; boards, other JR service; fundraising by JR; law practice, JR; mentoring by JR; philanthropy by JR; student, JR as; Younkers, JR at
Rosenfield, Joseph (grandfather), 49
Rosenfield, Louise. *See* Noun, Louise
Rosenfield, Meyer: birth, 49; career, 47–48, 62, 63; character, 48; death, 48; endowed lecture, 45; marriage, 44, 48, 62; privacy, 56; religion, 123; sense of humor, 48
Rosenfield, Rose Frankel: activities, 43, 44–45; birth and childhood, 45, 50, 53; character, 43, 44, 46, 47, 54; death, 45; education, 45–46; images, *85, 88, 94*; influence on JR, 43, 45; marriage, 44, 48, 62; religion, 123
Rosenfield, Ruth, 44, 48, 56, *85*
Rosenfield, Walter, 62
Rosenfield Campus Center, 221, 239

Rosenfield Chair in Social Studies, 222
Rosenfield Program, 45
Rosenthal, Sam, 122, 130, 196, 214
ROTC program, 166, 201, 202
Rovere, Richard, 192
Ruan, John: investment in *Boston Herald Traveller*, 121; investment in Intel, 110, 117, 121–122; investment in television, 121, 135; on JR's influence, 109–110; JR's influence on philanthropy, 117, 118, 128, 130; Marriott Hotel, 119; Merle Hay purchase attempt, 120; as resource, xvii; work with JR, 114–115, 120–123; World Food Prize, 110, 117, 122
Ruan, John, III, 117
Rutherford, Geddes, 7
Ryan, John, 7, 14

S

Sachs, 77
salaries: faculty, 170–171, 179, 183, 218, 223, 228; Younkers, 73
Sandler, Ron, 185
Sanford, Arthur, 120
Scarlet and Black (S&B): in campus culture, 3; "DORIC" column, 5–6, 18, 19, 20–25, 66, *104*; first female editor, 10–11, 18;

on graduates, 31; on library pilfering, 24; on literary societies, 35–37; on Oracle, 35, 36; on secret fraternities and sororities, 32–34; Steiner articles, 14
scholarships. *See* financial aid
School of Music, 8
Schwartz, Matilda, 52
science building, 164–166, 180, 220, 221, 229
SDS (Students for a Democratic Society), 201
Second Century Fund, 169–170
Sequoia Fund, 112, 214, 215
Settlement House (Des Moines), 44
sexual relations, rules for, 36, 37, 186
Sheuerman, Abraham, 52
Sheuerman, Babette. *See* Frankel, Babette Sheuerman
Sheuerman, Leopold, 52
Sheuerman, Rose, 52
Sheuerman, Sophie, 52, 53
Sheurerman, Manassa, 51, 52
shopping centers, Younkers' focus on, 67, 68
Sigma Delta Chi, 6, 26
Sioux City, IA, Younkers donations, 75
Skidmore, Owens, and Merrill, 179, 181, 188, 207
Skip Day, 24
Sloan Foundation, 179, 183, 219
Smith, Don, 183
Smith College, 244

"The Social Gospel," 159–160
Social Studies, endowed chair, 222
SOM. *See* Skidmore, Owens, and Merrill
sororities. *See* fraternities and sororities
Sostrin, Morey, *90, 96, 99*; on culture of Younkers, 70–71; focus on shopping centers, 67; on Henry Frankel, 70; hiring, 65, 66; on JR's love of negotiating, 120
South Africa: divestment in, 206–207, 230–234; students at Grinnell, 231–232, 233
Spencer, Kappie, 143
Stahl, Mary, xvi
Stauss, Jim, 170, 205
Steiner, Edward, 13–14, 24, 160
Steiner, Richard, 35
Steiner Hall, 220
Steinger, Ellain, xvii
Stevens, Samuel: deficit in 1950's, 167–169; dishonesty, 170–171, 172, 177; Great Depression, 161–162; leadership style, 176–177; officer training, 162, 163, 176; post-WWII building, 163–166; relationship with JR, 169, 170–171; resignation, 172, 173, 175; science building, 164–166
Stewart, Donald, 204, 237
St. Olaf College, 183, 218, 244

310 MENTOR

Stone, Herb, 220
Straus, Samuel, 30
Strauss, James, 188
student, JR as, *81, 83*; activities, 3–8, 21–31; class positions, 7, 27; *The Cyclone,* 3, 5–6, 16, 28–29, 30, 34; "DORIC" column, 5–6, 18, 19, 20–25, 66, *104*; early education, 57; law school, 5, 64, 111–113; major/minor, 6–7; scholastic achievement, 21, 39, 111; selection of Grinnell, 3–5; on student government, 38. See also *Malteaser*
student activism and politics: under Bowen (1955-1964), 186–190; by CBS, 205; closure of College, 200–201, 202; coed dorms, 189; curriculum reform, 202–203, 225; divestment in South Africa, 206–207, 230–234; faculty hiring, evaluation, and tenure, 203, 224; gay rights, 234, 235–236; investigations, 201–202; during JR's college days, 11, 37–38; JR's role, xix, 31–32, 188, 200–201, 230–235; under Leggett (1965-1975), 190, 200–201; multiculturalism, 204–206; in 1980's and 1990's, 230–234; occupations, 202; open meetings with trustees, 202;

Vietnam War, 55, 190; and WDTN purchase, 195
Student Council, 37
students: of color, 191, 204–206, 231–232, 233, 234, 235; debt, 217–218, 234, 235, 244, 245; graduation rates, 218, 245; international, 234; quality of, 176, 177, 178–179, 244; student government, 37–38; undergraduate research, 229. *See also* student, JR as; student activism and politics; women students
Students for a Democratic Society (SDS), 201
Students to End Apartheid, 233–234
study abroad, 185
suffragettes, 43, 45
Sullivan Principles, 231, 232, 233
Susan Thompson Buffett Foundation, 141
Swanson, Harold, 5
Swarthmore: comparison groups, 184, 244; student unrest, 187; teaching load, 225
Sweeney, James, 185
swimming, 185
symposia, 192, 210, 222

T

Tanager Guild, 36
Tanager Players, 36
Taylor, Morgan, 15–16
teacher training and

certification, 184, 228–229
television: Heritage Communications, xiv, 111, 121, 132, 133–137, 216; investment by Ruan and JR, 121, 135; WDTN purchase by Grinnell, xii, 182, 194–195, 215, 216; Younkers investment in, 66, 134–135
Temple B'nai Jeshrum (Des Moines), 51, 123
tennis, 56–57
tenure: policy, 211–212, 223–224; standards, 183
theater: Des Moines Community Playhouse, 58; investments in, 121; during JR's college years, 12, 19, 26–27; "Malteaser Follies," 26–27; Tanager Players, 36
Tiernan, Betty, 79
Tinker, John, 55
Tinker, Mary Beth, 55
Tiny-Tots, 116
Tips, 66
tornadoes, 159, 279n163
Toynbee, Arnold, 183
track and field, 15–16, 185
transfers, 176
trips: Frankel family, 53; Rosenfield family, 48, 56
trustees. *See* Board of Trustees; Board of Trustees and JR
tuition, 9, 168, 244
Turner, A. Richard (Dick), 210, 211–212

Turner, Richard (Iowa AG), 202
20 Year Club, 76

U

undergraduate research, 229
United Campaign, 75
United Church of Christ, 10, 184. *See also* Congregational Church
universities: compared to liberal arts colleges, 155; founding of first, 156
University of Iowa: athletics, 112–113; awards, 112; Bowen at, 173, 180, 189, 190; Dannie Rosenfield at, 58; faculty interaction grant, 219; JR's consideration of attending, 3; JR's philanthropy to, 112, 127; Law School, 5, 64, 111–113, 127; philanthropy by Richards, 130
University of Michigan, glee club competition, 12
US News and World Report ratings, 218, 245

V

Vassar College, 187, 244
Venture Fund, 227
Vietnam War, 55, 190
Vilsack, Tom, 144, 147

W

Walker, Waldo (Wally), xvi, 209, 210, 211, 224

Wall, Joseph, 3, 4, 170, 222
Wallace, Henry, 57
Walleser, Joseph, 18
Washington & Lee University, 244
water supply, 20
Watson Fellowships, 226
WDTN, xii, 182, 194–195, 215, 216
Weese, Ben, 209
Weitz, Fred, 118
Weitz, Rudolph (Rudy), 166, 172
Welch, Joseph Nye, 185
Welch, Murray, 172
Wellesley College, 184
Wesleyan College, 156, 184
Western of New York, 133–134
WHDH, 121
Wheat, Al, 205
White, David, 226
Wichita, KS store purchase, 67
Wilchinski, Norman, 63, 64, 65
Wilkins Department Store, 61
Will, George, 148, 149, 150
will, JR's: Grinnell, 127, 221, 238–239; Jewish community, 123; Planned Parenthood, 140; Rosenfield Campus Center, 221
Willhelm, Henry, 201
William and Mary, 156
Williams, Roger, 156
Williams College: comparison groups, 184, 244; founding, 156; "Haystack Prayer Meeting," 158
Wilson, Don, 194, 223

Wilson Chair in Enterprise and Leadership, 223
Wimer, Connie: JR's mentoring of, 130–131; on JR's philanthropy leadership, 117–118; Planned Parenthood, 140, 141, 142–143; as resource, xvi, xvii; testimonial, 248; underwriting of book, xvi
Wingate, Henry, 205
women: administration cuts, 212; mentoring by JR, 130–131. *See also* feminism; women students
Women's Self-Government Association, 38
Women's Studies, 223
women students: Cooper on, 17; in "DORIC" column, 21–23; first admitted, 159; housing, 6, 188, 201; in JR's college days, 8, 9, 10–11; League Board, 37–38; literary societies, 35–37; Mauch as first female editor, 10–11, 18; rules for, 186, 187, 201; School of Music, 8; student government, 37–38; transfers, 176
Work, James, 11, 26–27
World Food Prize, 110, 117, 122
World War I: Grinnell enrollments, 14; Rose Rosenfield, 44
World War II: GI Bill, 163–164, 166; officer training,

162, 163, 176; Ruan contracts, 114; War Bonds and Stamps, 70, 74

Y

Yale University: founding, 156; glee club competition, 12
YMCA, 75
Yoder, Sandi, xv
Younger, Paul, 180
Young Women's Resource Center, 58
Younker, Ben, 164
Younker, Herman, 61
Younker, Lipman, 60
Younker, Marcus, 60
Younker, Rachel, 164
Younker, Samuel, 60, 61
Younker family, 60
Younker Hall, 164, 205
Younkers: acquisitions and expansion, 61, 64, 66–69, 77, *99,* 119–120, 138–139; board, *96;* closing, 78–79; community service, 70, 74, 75; culture, 60, 61, 69–76, 77, 78–79; employee benefits, 71–73, *104;* employee training, 72–73; *Good Morning,* 70, 72, 73, 74, 77; history, 61, 62–64, 76–78; influence on JR, 60, 69, 75–76, 79; investment in television, 66, 134–135; media coverage, *89–92;* merger with Harris-Emery, 48, 50, 61, 63–64, 113;

Meyer's role, 48, 63; origins, 60; public offering, 67, 129; *Reporter,* 39, 65, 70–71, 72, 74, 77, *95–101;* salaries, 73; sale to Equitable of Iowa, 60, 76–77, 139; shift to Des Moines, 61; 20 Year Club, 76
Younkers, JR at: on board, 44, 48, 60, 65, 66, *90, 91, 96, 99,* 114; Chairman of Executive Committee, 65, 134; on competition with other stores, 63; as counsel for, 44, 60, 64, 65, 113–114; influence of Younkers on JR, 60, 69, 75–76, 79; investments and acqusitions, 66–69, 114, 119–120, 134–135, 138–139; and merger with Harris-Emery, 63; profit sharing and retirement programs, 71–72; retirement from, 69, *100;* sales experience, 65–66; and sale to Equitable of Iowa, 77
Younkers Tea Room, 73–74, 78, 79

Z

Zigas, Barry, 203
Zweig, Jason, 191, 213–214, 215, 221

Printed in Great Britain
by Amazon